'Peter makes you see the world, and your business in a new way. I really like what he has to say. Enjoy every minute of it.'

Mariano Dima, Senior VP, Marketing and Product Solutions, Visa Europe

'In this latest book in the Genius series, Peter again makes a host of different views accessible and actionable for all. With an eclectic mix of mini cases from business and the arts, *Creative Genius* stimulates us to think about options and opportunities in many new and different ways.'

Tim Jones, Programme Director, Future Agenda

'An excellent bringing together of our business challenges that left [us] energised and inspired.'

Peter Thomas, Marketing Director, Accenture

'Peter challenged our thinking, focused on our biggest issues, and left us inspired."

Jeff Busch, VP Strategic Communications, Meeting Professionals International (MPI)

'Thanks to Peter we now have a different view of our world. We have now learnt to see our business from the outside in, like customers do, and with many new opportunities too.'

Erdal Karamacan, CEO, Eczacibasi Group (Istanbul)

'A glimpse of an exciting new world, where people and technology come together in new ways, and where there are threats and opportunities for all of us.'

Anne Rodven, Event Director, Visit Oslo

'Peter told an incredibly provocative and compelling story of the new business world, and gave our delegates the inspiration and signposts to think and act differently.'

Steve Gilroy, CEO Vistage International (UK)

Marketing Genius by Peter Fisk

'A fantastic book, full of relevant learning. The mass market is dead. The consumer is boss. Imagination, intuition and inspiration reign. Geniuses wanted.'

Kevin Roberts, Worldwide CEO Saatchi & Saatchi and author of *Lovemarks*

Business Genius by Peter Fisk

'I loved this book, it is jam-packed with energy, ideas and inspiration ... you will find something of real value here.'

Employer Brand Forum

Customer Genius by Peter Fisk

'Wow! 50 great stories of how companies have really got to grips with customers, and 30 very practical tools for doing it yourself. Great book.'

Amazon.co.uk reviewer

creative
genius

creative genius

AN INNOVATION GUIDE
FOR BUSINESS LEADERS,
BORDER CROSSERS AND
GAME CHANGERS

peter fisk

CAPSTONE

This edition first published in 2011 by Capstone Publishing Ltd. (a Wiley Company)

© 2011 Peter Fisk

Registered office
Capstone Publishing Ltd. (A Wiley Company), The Atrium, Southern Gate, Chichester, West Sussex, PO19 8SQ, United Kingdom

For details of our global editorial offices, for customer services and for information about how to apply for permission to reuse the copyright material in this book please see our website at www.wiley.com.

Library of Congress Cataloging-in-Publication Data is available

ISBN 9781841127897 (hardback), ISBN 9781906465186 (ebk),

ISBN 9780857080233 (eSony), ISBN 9780857080165 (emobi)

A catalogue record for this book is available from the British Library.

Set in Agfa Rotis Sans Serif 10/13.5 pt by Sparks – www.sparkspublishing.com
Printed in Great Britain by TJ International Ltd, Padstow, Cornwall

Contents

The ideas factory

The design studio

The impact zone

Now forward

Future back

The wind in my hair and Nike Air on my feet
Past the roaring deer and exotic parakeets
Historic palaces and ancient oak trees
Imagining what they have seen, and what they will see
This is my time to think, to dream and reflect
We are all inspired by the world around us, by nature and people
Creative people, such as artists, musicians and architects
Inventors and designers, innovators and entrepreneurs
Stimulated by their vision and ideas, enabled by business and technology
Thinking bigger about new spaces and opportunities
Searching for the impossible then finding ways to make them possible
Listening to what people would love, not just what is marginally better
Designing the perfect solution and finding a way to make it profitable
Not just competing, but out-thinking the competition
Not just creating, but shaping the world in your own vision
Creativity is the most exciting thing that we do
Design is the most engaging
Innovation the most exhilarating
Thinking what you never thought was possible
Inspiring you to do the extraordinary
In your work and in your life

CHAPTER 1

Leonardo da Vinci

It is easy to say that a person is 'ahead of his time', but rarely has anyone been so far ahead. He could see the future – his insights suggested new possibilities, his imagination was uncluttered by today, and his inventions really did emerge from the 'future back'.

Leonardo da Vinci anticipated many of the great scientific discoveries ahead of his time, including those by Copernicus, Galileo, Newton and Darwin. He even went further than them, turning their principles into practical applications, from calculators to helicopters, hydro-dynamics to solar power.

➡ Forty years before Nicolaus Copernicus, he proclaimed '*il sole no si muove*' – 'the sun does not move', dismissing the belief that the earth sits at the centre of the universe.

➡ Two hundred years before Isaac Newton, he proposed the theory of gravity – that 'every weight tends to fall towards the centre by the shortest possible way', and that the Earth must be spherical.

➡ Four hundred years before Charles Darwin, he argued that man and monkey had the same origins, and how evolution has shaped the natural world around us.

How did he do this? The answers lie not in science or technology, but in the way in which he saw the world around him and how that made him 'rethink'. From the *Mona Lisa* to *The Last Supper*, it is the same approaches that made his paintings so remarkable, that enabled him to create, design and invent many of the aspects of life today.

What was it that inspired, shaped and sustained his creative genius? What were his talents and traits that we could seek to recreate in our own quest for creativity and innovation? Psychologist, and professional juggler Michael Gelb proposed seven components to da Vinci's distinctive approach. He labelled them *curiositá*, *sensazione*, *arte e scienza*, *connessione*, *sfumato*, *dimostrazione* and *corporalitá*. Whilst there is nothing futuristic in these attributes themselves, they did enable him to see things differently and, as a result, think different things.

So how can we apply these ideas to business today, and specifically to the challenge of more effective innovation, innovation from the 'future back'?

1   **Relentless curiosity** ... an insatiable hunger to learn, to search for better answers and to articulate his ideas in pictures, and propose new possibilities.

2   **Seeing more** ... he observed things differently, using all his senses to appreciate richer detail, to align perspective and perception, and thereby to understand his subject better.

3   **Thinking bigger** ... appreciating art and science, logic and imagination, he was able to think more broadly, embracing rigorous analysis whilst also trusting his intuition.

4   **Making connections** ... to connect the unconnected, to embrace the fusion and inter-section between the natural and physical world, the tiniest seeds to the stars above.

5   **Embracing paradox** ... thriving on ambiguity and uncertainty, creating mystery and depth, be it the contrast in his sketches or asking questions without obvious answers.

6   **Courageous action** ... always seeking to prove his hypotheses, to experiment and test, to make his ideas tangible, and to do what nobody had done before.

7   **Enlightened mind** ... constantly renewing mental and physical fitness, exploring new worlds to spark new ideas, not being a slave to work but living a full life.

Leonardo had an insatiable curiosity and an imagination unconditioned by his surroundings. This combination of catalyst and creativity enabled him to make some of the greatest technological advances of the modern world.

Beyond his art, Leonardo is admired for his technological ingenuity. As a scientist, he contributed much to the evolution of knowledge – particularly in the fields of anatomy, optics, mechanical engineering and hydrodynamics. He developed highly original concepts, captured in immaculately detailed designs, for everything from a helicopter, a tank, a calculator and a double-hulled catamaran, to a basic theory of plate tectonics.

Da Vinci is still thought of by most people as primarily an artist, but his world-changing approach to realistic painting was only possible due to his fascination with science.

He took this fascination with understanding and recording the world around him to extreme lengths, dissecting many bodies and drawing them in great detail. He saw the body as a machine, a complex mechanism that could eventually be understood. He was one of the first, for example, to identify the pumping action of the heart.

He even replaced muscles with strings to experiment and see how they worked with the levers of the bones. His understanding of anatomy and his experimental approach opened the way for others to follow in later centuries.

The Renaissance, and in particular Florence, is famed for its unusual concentration of great men at the time, although they rarely worked together. Leonardo was 23 when Michelangelo was born and 31 when Raphael was born.

Unique to the period was the encouragement by patrons and thinkers of a 'cross-over' between the arts and sciences (or social philosophies as they were regarded at the time), which challenged many of the conventions around, and found newness in their intersection rather than isolated extremes. This became known as the 'Medici Effect', enabled by the gathering of diverse talents encouraged by rich benefactors, such as the Medici family. Leonardo was

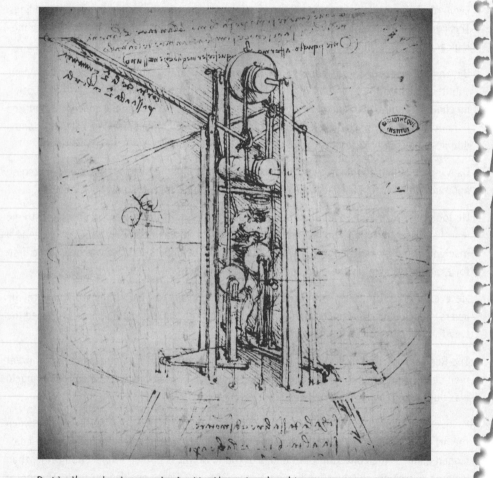

Da Vinci's mechanics were inspired by the natural world

a master of cross-over. He combined ideas from animal and plant studies with psychology, fashion, anatomy and architecture. From this he formed his understanding of mechanics, and everything from hydraulic pumps to new musical instruments emerged. He used analogy – for example, he wrote short fables like Aesop, stories that seemed to be to entertain children but were in fact to communicate to adults the danger of greed and so on.

Few of his design concepts were ever constructed. Not because they weren't practical; more often because the technologies and resources to create them were not available at the time. However, some of his smaller inventions, such as an automated bobbin winder and a machine for testing the strength of wire, became reality.

In 1502, for example, Leonardo produced a drawing of a single-span 240-metre bridge as part of a civil engineering project for Ottoman Sultan Beyazid II of Istanbul. The bridge was intended to span an inlet at the mouth of the Bosphorus. Beyazid did not pursue the project because he believed that such a construction was impossible; however, Leonardo's vision was resurrected in 2006 when the Turkish government decided to construct Leonardo's bridge to span the Golden Horn.

So what can we learn from Leonardo da Vinci? How can his life and work inspire us to be more creative, enlightened, inspired by our surroundings, and able to innovate from the future back?

Steve Jobs has many great attributes, but he too is not perfect. Maybe surprisingly, much of advanced technology is Greek to him. His skill is to rise above this, to understand people, the simplicity of user-centric design in all its facets, and the power of communication. Maybe we can learn something from this in today's world – where words and numbers dominate our communication and restrict our imagination. Maybe P&G have the right idea when they stipulate that any new proposal, innovation or investment should be communicated in a one-page poster rather than in lengthy reports or slideshows.

Certainly the ideas of looking further into the future and deeper into the consumer's world are only beginning to matter in business today. Techniques such as scenario planning on consumer immersion are still rare. Going beyond the assumptions and research statistics to live with consumers, to understand how products and services are used, enable people to do more, enrich their lives – by seeing the challenge and opportunity from their perspective.

We now examine Leonardo's seven talents in a little more detail, looking at what they mean for creativity and innovation today, and how you can embrace them in pursuit of your own creative genius.

Talent 1: Relentless curiosity

'*Curiosità*' is translated from Italian as an insatiably curious approach to life and unrelenting quest for continuous learning. It is the ability to constantly question yourself and others; the relentless pursuit of knowledge and truth, learning to ask better questions; the ability to solve the most challenging problems by keeping an open mind.

Leonardo believed that man is not divorced from nature, or any object from its surroundings. And that observation should be accompanied by reason and application. He saw this as a creative challenge. As Vasari put it, 'he taught us that men of genius sometimes accomplish most when they work least, for they are thinking out inventions and forming in their minds the perfect ideas which they subsequently express and reproduce with their hands'.

Leonardo was intensely curious about everything he encountered. His incomplete notebooks are full of spontaneous, random drawings but few words, demonstrating an agile mind: observing, thinking, imagining – capturing new insights or fragments of invention, recognizing that future possibilities are unlocked by a better understanding of current phenomena, and then searching for more.

How does relentless curiosity drive creativity?

Our world is more uncertain than ever. Change is relentless, technologies emerge at break-neck speed, and markets and behaviours are incredibly complex. Neuro-imaging can give us new insights into the mind and space travel is unearthing life beyond this planet. Seeking to understand this world – at least partly – offers you the best clues to making a bigger difference in it.

Thinking from the future back helps you to challenge the conventions of today. Asking why is always a better starting point that asking how; understanding the context is a more useful place to understand a problem that the symptoms themselves; and developing a better product starts by understanding what people seek to do with it, rather than what it actually is.

Steve Jobs, a little like Leonardo da Vinci, has many talents. But like Leonardo's linguistic weaknesses, Jobs readily admits that there are many who understand technology better than him. Yet he also sees this as a virtue, as it means he is not inhibited like others. Instead he takes a human perspective, challenging every aspect of design, usability and communication.

Meet any other entrepreneur – such as Richard Branson, for example – and they are intensely curious about you and your thoughts, about why things are as they are, and how they could be different. In Branson's pocket there is always a small notebook full of scribbled notes, untidy pictures, questions and new ideas. Every situation, every person, every hour, he adds more to his thinking.

How can you be relentlessly curious?

It is easy to be so focused, that there feels like no time or space in which to think. Yet thinking is perhaps your most valuable use of time. The motivation to think does not come from others, but inside. It comes from being curious.

Take a notebook everywhere you go – small and without lines, so that it is more portable and less restrained. Capture ideas and insights, and spend a few minutes every day reflecting on discussions and experiences. Then you can occasionally sit back and review what you have created. Look for patterns both obvious and not, and seek symmetry where there is currently none.

Sometimes it is easier to focus on one theme at a time, or to even force yourself to generate as many ideas as possible around that theme. This is sometimes referred to as 'brainwriting' – a personal brainstorm, unlocking your stream of consciousness. A few minutes of thinking time is the best possible starting point to being a creative person.

➡ Time and space (Chapter 2) explores the places where no business has gone before.

➡ Shigeru Miyamoto (Chapter 3) applies his curiosity to transform Nintendo's games.

➡ World changing (Chapter 4) responds to the shifting power in the world and the implications for innovation.

➡ Future back (Chapter 6) explains how to stretch your people to be more curious.

➡ James Dyson (Chapter 9) describes how running up sand dunes led to vacuum cleaners.

➡ Philippe Starck (Chapter 11) inspires us to stay crazy through creativity and design.

Talent 2: Seeing more

'*Sensazione*' is the continual refinement of the senses, especially sight, as the means to enliven experience. Of all these, da Vinci was most focused on sight, making '*saper vedere*' – knowing how to see – the foundation of all his work.

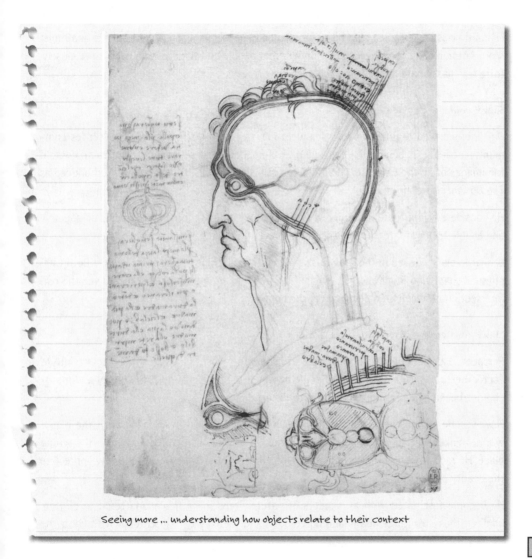

Seeing more ... understanding how objects relate to their context

Leonardo was not satisfied with his ability to depict physicality, and sought out the anatomist Marc Antonio della Torre to help him understand people and their motion even more closely. Torre was passionate about using the eyes in new ways.

Sight and perception

Da Vinci believed that the five senses were connected to a single point: the 'senses communis', located just behind the eye. 'Who would believe that so small a space could contain the images of all the universe?' he pondered in his notebooks, translated and reproduced as *The Da Vinci Notebooks*.

He considered sight to be the superior sense because it gives more context, adds perspective and enables scientific reasoning, and is therefore the foundation of creative talents.

Leonardo also believed in the *idolum*, the power that all things possess to give off both their physical shape and inner energy, and that only by looking more closely can you see the real intersection between an object and its surroundings.

Light and perspective

Perspective became a defining principle of Leonardo's work, showing how objects relate to each other, and to the distance and angle at which they are observed. Geometry and mathematics became increasingly important to his art.

However, he did not believe art was a 'desk job'. He believed in mingling with the bigger world, thinking big before small, believing that otherwise his detail could be in the wrong place. He recommended that artists walk alone in the countryside to more keenly appreciate the beauty of nature.

He became fascinated with all aspects of nature. Trees in particular mattered to him: he admired their structures and changing colours, and the way they interacted with light. The shadow of trees, he said, is as much about the light patches as the darker patches, and their vibrancy and transparency.

How does seeing more drive creativity?

We dive into problems and opportunities with little thought for either their context or indeed whether we are focused on the right areas. We are all too keen to understand people today, and maybe in the past, but less interested in things that they do not yet say they need, or for which words have not been created. We are comfortable seeking to make sense of our own world, but we lose confidence as soon as we enter a new space.

Opening up before closing down is key to innovation: exploring possible markets, existing or emerged; understanding possible future scenarios, rather than assuming one; considering non-customers as well as customers, because there must be reasons why they are not customers; and considering more ideas, options and potential solutions before making choices.

By considering different viewpoints, we can see an opportunity from different perspectives – as a customer, competitor, technologist, futurist, artist and more. By spending more time with customers, we can learn far more about their motivations and aspirations rather than just their needs and wants. By giving ourselves time to think big, we are more likely to find the best opportunities, rather than just better ones – to do the right thing rather than just do things right.

Thinking from the future back is perhaps the most useful of all perspectives, because it is without restraint, without prejudice, but with infinite possibility.

How can you see more?

Learn how to draw. Drawing unlocks your creative spirit like no other: it allows you to express ideas without the necessity of established words and meanings, to develop the ideas as you draw, to connect ideas that are usually addressed individually, to reflect this in a unique and personal manner, and to engage people more emotionally.

Above all, learn to draw with a stream of consciousness – with your 'right brain' rather than your 'left brain'. Whilst the brain is more complex, in simple terms, the right side is more intuitive, spontaneous and holistic, allowing us to make connections and see the bigger picture. However, many of us are slaves to the left side (numbers, logic, structure and focus), which is important but can often limit creative thinking in the initial stages. 'Creativity' emerges from the connection of both.

As you draw, use all your senses. Listen to sounds around you, articulate the most important ideas prominently and then connect supporting ideas around them. Think about the touch and smell, as well as sound and vision, describe them and how they make you feel. Remember sometimes that less is more, simplicity as well as detail. And above all, don't feel embarrassed by your drawing skills!

➡ Seeing things differently (Chapter 12) encourages us to explore different worldviews.

➡ Deep diving (Chapter 15) immerses you in the intuitive world of customer aspirations.

➡ Paul Smith (Chapter 17) reflects on quirkiness and how to embrace parallels and extremes.

➡ Co-creation (Chapter 23) adds new ideas to business that you might never have thought of.

➡ John Maeda (Chapter 27) uses graphic design to find simplicity in our complex world.

➡ Cai Guo-Qiang (Chapter 45) encourages artistic experimentation to find genuine newness.

Talent 3: Thinking bigger

Da Vinci was able to think beyond his peers because he combined opposites and adjacent fields – art and science, man and machines, logic and imagination. This requires new ways of thinking – the ability to synthesize information in new ways, work in parallel at different levels and even hold two opposing views at the same time.

Leonardo was fascinated by the proportions of the human body. The Roman architect Vitruvius had previously related these to fundamental geometric principles, but Leonardo went much further, defining his symbolic drawing of the 'Vitruvian Man'.

> '... Four fingers make one palm; four palms make one foot; six palms make one cubit; four cubits make a man's height; and also one pace; and twenty-four palms make a man ...'

He was obsessed with finding harmony, symmetry and balance: 'the span of a man's outstretched arms is equal to his height' and 'every man at three years is half the full height he will grow to at last'.

In mathematics, and in the arts too, two quantities (a and b) are in a 'golden ratio' if the ratio between their combined value (a + b) to the larger value (a) is the same as the ratio between the larger value (a) and the smaller value (b). The ratio is a mathematical constant, approximately 1.6180339887. Behind many of Leonardo's greatest works lies this almost spiritual geometry.

His intellectual 'border crossing' was also evident in his mechanical breakthroughs. He explored the human body with meticulous dissections, learning from every muscle as if a masterpiece of mechanical engineering that could be applied on much larger scale in the physical world, from levers and pulley systems to visions of automation and flight.

Thinking bigger ... Vitruvian Man and the Golden Ratio

How does thinking bigger drive creativity?

Reductionism, incrementalism and efficiency: the enemies of effective innovation in business today. With our heads in our spreadsheets, we focus on the minute details. We seek to improve sales, reduce costs or enhance performance by small percentages. We seek to optimize the things we currently do rather than do things differently, and we stick with the ideas we can quantify rather than those that are more difficult. Thinking bigger is about understanding people outside their boxes, our home market as the globe not our locality, and opportunities beyond the three-year plan. It is about understanding a person's surroundings, and then the person; applications before products; attitudes before behaviours. And it is about having the imagination to stretch beyond what is known, comfortable or predictable.

Thinking from the future back is a better starting point, because everything is possible.

How can you think bigger?

The answer lies in this book. To stretch your imagination beyond reality to possibility, and then work backwards to understand how you could do more. To stretch not only in time, in terms of years ahead, but also in space, in terms of adjacent markets. Once you have stretched you can then connect it back to today – future back, now forward – to target an emerging market or leapfrog a convention.

Package your bigger thinking in more acceptable ways for people, for example by saying 'let me propose a hypothesis' rather than being dismissed for crazy, impractical ideas. Hypothesis-thinking is far-stretching but also credible – scientific, if you like – and gives you the opportunity to prove or disprove it, and at least explore it further.

Hold back on the spreadsheets. Use your imagination and intuition to reach new domains before seeking to analyse them in detail, rather than diving into the wrong ocean. Equally, once you have settled on a thinking space, evaluate it for the best opportunity areas – the best potential customers or products, for example – and then focus your creativity on what matters most.

➡ Virgin Galactic (Chapter 2) tells us how a dream of space became reality in a few years.

➡ Tim Berners-Lee (Chapter 12) thought bigger to reconnect the world through his web.

➡ Future scenarios (Chapter 14) develops alternative futures to help make better decisions.

➡ Context reframing (Chapter 22) helps us to redefine situations in more powerful ways.

➡ Market shaping (Chapter 36) recognizes innovations as just the starting point for change.

➡ Zaha Hadid (Chapter 36) never stopped fighting to make her big ideas come true.

Talent 4: Making connections

Da Vinci had a deep appreciation of the interconnectedness of all things. This helped him to find new connections and combinations, and to open up whole new fields of science and philosophy.

> 'Whatever exists in the universe, in essence, in appearance, in the imagination, the painter has first in his mind and then in his hand; and these are of such excellence that they present a proportioned and harmonious view of the whole, that can be seen simultaneously, at one glance ...'

The Medici effect

Leonardo believed that an artist should not just copy nature; he should understand it, saying that a creative expression is only achieved by a total immersion in a task, finding harmony with the natural world in order to see its detail.

Not only did he revolutionize the use of perspective in art with the mathematical application of proportions, he also introduced a systematic approach to 'immersing' himself in the world of his subject. In this way he understood how life interacts with what surrounds it, and how it succeeds better when it is in harmony. Leonardo believed that an artist's role was to hold a mirror up to nature.

'He should act as a mirror which transmutes itself into as many colours as are those of the objects that are placed before it ... Above all he should keep his mind as clear as the surface of a mirror.'

However, as a scientist, he also believed in questioning what appeared in his mirror, arguing that better understanding enables better judgement, and better art.

Leonardo only believed this was possible by staying in touch with real people – walking the streets, talking to people, observing their behaviour.

'You should go about and often as you go for walks observe ... the actions of the men themselves and of the bystanders.'

But he also said that observation was not enough, that understanding why people behave is more significant – how they are influenced by others and their surroundings:

'... Consider the circumstances and behaviour of men as they talk and quarrel, or laugh or come to blows with one another.'

Art and science

Most impressive of all was da Vinci's convergence of art and science. His observations and drawings were ultimately the enablers of phenomenal scientific breakthroughs and innovations. But it was the purity of art rather than the limitations of academia that enabled him to achieve that. He demonstrated how to lift and draw great weights by means of levers, hoists and winches, or ways to pump water from great depths. He rejected conventional wisdom and accepted truths, preferring instead to trust his own eyes and interpretation.

How do connections drive creativity?

The best ideas are often a combination of smaller ideas, and indeed the best solutions for customers are usually a combination of various products and services. Therefore, seeking to solve the problem rather than creating a product is a far more connected approach to innovation.

Working with a wider range of partners enables you to access ideas, capabilities and customers that you would never have been able to alone – through open innovation, joint ventures or affinity brands. Rather than being restrained by specific capabilities, retain more flexibility and reduce risk in an ever-changing world. These connections extend to your customers too, collaborating – or 'co-creating' with them in new ways to develop ideas, produce and evaluate them, and even sell them to others.

Thinking from the future back gives us a bigger picture where we can see patterns and potential connections that are perhaps invisible day to day. Consider parallel sectors that have similar challenges or different worlds altogether. Architects can learn from nature; banking can learn from retailing; public sector can learn from private sector, developed nations can learn from developing nations.

How can you make connections?

Take two different ideas and see how they can produce better ideas. If you want to think how social networks can work for you, then fuse ideas such as Facebook with something completely random, like a birthday cake. Think about the attributes of each – people, friends, profiles, photos, games, candles, icing, flavours, party, annual – and then connect some of them, such as real parties for online friends or a featured profile if it's your birthday.

Talk to a person with similar challenges to you in a completely different market. If you are a bank trying to attract young people, talk to Apple or H&M. If you want to give your shoes more marketing buzz, see what you can learn from Disney or Bloomsbury (the publisher of Harry Potter books). If you want to understand the likely impacts of deregulation, track what happened in industries where similar events have already taken place.

If all else fails, try something completely different. Read a book about something you know nothing about. Watch a different television channel. Go for a walk in the woods, or browse in a shop you've never been in before. Look for ideas and connections to whatever you are working on.

⇒ Samsung (Chapter 8) reinvented itself through a design language based on yin and yang.

⇒ Extremes and parallels (Chapter 17) drive radical ideas through unusual connections.

⇒ Concept fusions (Chapter 26) brings the best ideas together to create better solutions.

⇒ Going further (Chapter 38) uses licensing to replicate ideas in adjacent markets.

⇒ Lego (Chapter 42) opened its research labs to the kids who can really play.

⇒ IBM (Chapter 47) uses 'InnovationJams' to bring people and partners together.

Embracing paradox ... light and dark, shadow and sharpness

Talent 5: Embracing paradox

'*Sfumato*' in Italian suggests a willingness to embrace ambiguity, paradox and uncertainty. This gave da Vinci's work a great sense of mystery or even uncertainty in the mind of others.

Intrigued by light, he saw it as the physical element that stimulated the eye, but also figuratively as what stimulated the mind:

> 'Light is the chaser away of darkness. Look at light and consider its beauty. Blink your eye and look at it again; what you see was not there at first, and what was there is no more.'

As an artist he considered how to interpret where inner and outer light meet, which gave contrast to his paintings, but also depth to their meaning. His paintings demonstrate infinite graduations between dark and light. He understood the power of darkness as well as light, perfecting the techniques of 'chiaroscuro'.

How colours mix and contrast, how colours split and give more meaning became his new obsession – he declared that 'where there is most light the true character of a colour in light will be seen'.

The Laughing One

Sitting in the Louvre is perhaps his most famous creation, the *Mona Lisa*.

The painting – also known as '*La Gioconda*', or 'The Laughing One' – is most famous for the mysterious quality of the subject, the elusive smile on the woman's face, brought about perhaps by the fact that the artist has subtly shadowed the corners of the mouth and eyes.

Faces said everything to Leonardo. Not only anatomically, but in the way they reflected thinking, emotions, relationships and surroundings. He conveyed his beliefs in some of the greatest masterpieces. Of the portrait, Vasari said 'The eyes had their natural lustre and moistness. The mouth joined to the flesh tints of the face by the red of the lips, appeared to be living flesh rather than paint. On looking closely at the pit of her throat one could swear that the pulses are beating.'

The shadowy quality for which the work is renowned became known as 'sfumato', or 'Leonardo's smoke'. Other characteristics found in this work are the unadorned dress, the dramatic landscape background in which the world seems to be in a state of flux and the subdued colouring.

How does paradox drive creativity?

Paradox is the 'big daddy' of innovation. Finding ways in which to resolve a fundamental contradiction in people's lives, where they want two opposite things but have to choose one, can be the catalyst for significant breakthroughs. How can you resolve their dilemmas?

Ambiguities lie all around us. Brands are often forced to compromise as they try to meet the needs of different audiences, creating average solutions or a whole range of features that many people don't need or want. The small things, like the shading in Leonardo's drawings, can make a big difference – particularly to the aesthetic qualities and the emotional engagement of customers.

Thinking from the future back allows us to address uncertainties by understanding how to reduce risk and concern. It helps us to see how small frustrations or imperfections can have big consequences in the longer term. It allows us to break free of the constraints that cause many paradoxes and create solutions, which we can then set about finding a way to make happen today.

How can you embrace paradox?

Seek out ambiguity in everything you explore – in the lives of customers, in product composition, in channels to market, in ways of making money and more. Look to the margins not the mainstream for ways in which people have adapted standard products and services to their own needs: the person who ties a ribbon around the suitcase because they all look the same, or deliberately makes their designer clothes look worn and dishevelled because it looks cooler than if they were new.

When listening to or researching customers, don't ask them what's good or what they want; focus instead on what's not so good, or frustrating, and understand why. Probe their answers more deeply until you find some fundamental contradiction in their needs or in the solutions available to them. Understand how you could make it better.

Explore possibilities by asking questions to which there is no obvious answer (sometimes known as the 'Socratic method'). Of course, this could just seem like you are being difficult, so it is also worth adding that you understand that there is no obvious answer, but that it is still worth asking the question.

➡ Aravind Eye Care (Chapter 4) transforms sight in India with a non-profit healthcare model.

➡ Creativity (Chapter 7) uses the Jester to challenge your thinking and open your mind.

➡ Patterns and paradoxes (Chapter 13) explores the world of paradoxes and possibilities.

➡ Rule breakers (Chapter 18) challenges you to disrupt normality and embrace discontinuity.

➡ Alessi (Chapter 29) reveals his secret formula for connecting function and form.

➡ Tesla (Chapter 34) demonstrates that fast sports cars can also be environmentally friendly.

Talent 6: Courageous action

Da Vinci was not just a smart thinker; he had a bias to making things happen. Having an idea is one thing but proving it is another: scientific method is all about experimentation and continually testing to prove that the proposal is valid – or to learn through mistakes how to create a better solution.

Mathematics was central to Leonardo's thinking. While much of his interpretation was intuitive, he saw analysis as supporting hypothesis, needing to make a leap of faith before proving it. He supported his proofs with repeated experimentation and only after such rigour did he trust his conclusions. He also found that new ideas often arose through deeper analysis and testing, and often took him closer to the origins of phenomena.

He brought all this together in his scientific four steps method:

1   **Observing:** Trusting your eye and other senses to understand the subject, its contextual surroundings and the influence they have.

2   **Interpreting:** Making sense of these observations and from them hypothesizing reason, which can be postulated as scientific laws.

3   **Demonstrating:** Showing how factors such as mathematical proportion can be found in many different situations, and its implications.

4   **Articulating:** Testing the logic through repeated experimentation and visualizing the logic in pictures, diagrams, words or numbers.

Creative engineers

Leonardo designed incredibly sophisticated machines beyond anything that had been articulated before. However, his focus was not on the invention, but on the mechanical engineering that solved the problems or enabled new possibilities. He was less interested in devices, more in the processes behind them, and their applications that made people's lives better.

His creative engineering created a new world of weights and forces, levers and pulleys, cogs and wheels. From this he created everything from a loom to spin wool to clocks that kept time. His understanding of propulsion led to the first designs for a bicycle; his insight into water displacement allowed him to imagine what a submarine could do.

Fly like a bird

His visions of flight were his most ambitious, fundamentally challenging what people at the time dreamed was possible. Examining motion through air, Leonardo studied the flight of birds to understand how their delicate structures were able to resist the force of gravity. He marvelled at the natural technology of wings and considered how he could replicate it:

> 'The wing of a bird is always concave in its lower part extending from the elbow to the shoulder, and the rest is convex. In the concave part of the wing the air is whirled round, and the convex is pressed and condensed'.

He sought to understand not only the movement of objects in flight, but the movement of air as it passed by the object. By addressing the problem in reverse, he explored how air could be channelled to keep much heavier objects in flight – and ultimately to create flying machines.

How does courage drive creativity?

Thinking from the future back requires courage. A more conventional approach would be customer-centric, where the customer (or more often the customer research) says that something is wanted so therefore must be the right solution. Too much innovation is still based on the current articulated needs and paradigms of customers. But breakthrough requires stretch and challenge, perhaps collaboratively with customers, taking you beyond the safety zone of quantitative research, fusing insight, imagination and inspired implementation.

It is one thing to sit around having good ideas and another to make them happen. Test new ideas with experiments and prototypes, either physical builds or computer-generated graphics. Use this testing approach to learn and improve the designs, build commitment from stakeholders, and engage customers and partners.

Few of us are confident in our drawing capabilities, less still in our model-making skills. But we can all be tremendously inventive when we try. Draw pictures, cartoons or diagrams of your ideas, rip out pictures and slogans from magazines, and build collages to give a sense of the look and feel of a new idea. They might look ridiculous, but they help you to then describe your new possibility far better than words.

How can you act courageously?

Test and challenge all of your assumptions. Apply it to real situations and consider how it would work, if it's a product, when and where would people buy it from, who the competition would be, and what price it could demand. Ask customers, colleagues and partners, friends and relatives: they don't need to be an expert to have a view – it is better if they bring different perspectives.

Make things happen. Draw your pictures, stick them on the wall. If you are working as a team, consider recruiting an artist or cartoonist who can capture all the best ideas as spoken or developed, and create a visual record of the evolving ideas. Make models – even the most amateur combination of cereal boxes and toilet rolls is good. Engage people with it – 'imagine this is a 60-centimetre LCD screen, and this is a body sensor', or whatever.

Learn from failures (yours and others') and find ways to make it better. Persevere, keep trying, each time getting a little closer to your dream, and to a practical solution. Enjoy the journey, not just the result. If the idea is good enough, the reality will be worth the effort.

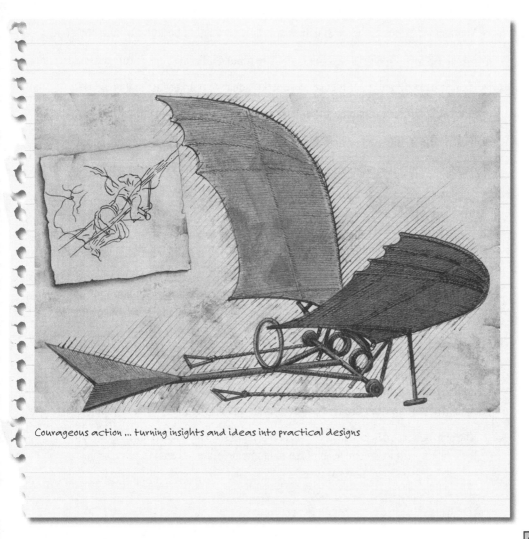

Courageous action ... turning insights and ideas into practical designs

➡ Muhammad Yunus (Chapter 6) is transforming third world business with micro-credits.

➡ Honda ASIMO (Chapter 13) is the cute little robot that makes the future more possible.

➡ Launch pads (Chapter 31) focuses on getting ideas to market fast and effectively.

➡ Innovation process (Chapter 44) defines the disciplines of new product development.

➡ Reid Hoffman (Chapter 46) is the networking and investment star of the digital world.

➡ Game changing (Chapter 49) keeps us thinking bigger, about creating a better world.

Talent 7: Enlightened mind

A healthy body creates a healthy mind. More than artist or scientist, da Vinci was a thinker, a philosopher. He reflected on life and its meaning, problems and possibilities.

And he was more still. As a court entertainer, he designed sets and costumes, often loaded with symbols and significance. Sometimes this symbolism reflected his patronage, but it was also just another aspect of his curiosity.

Leonardo became a great storyteller, partly in his role as entertainer, but more importantly as a way to communicate and spread his ideas. His stories were thoughtful and amusing, and his company was sought by royalty and nobility across Europe. One of his most famous, or lasting, is 'The Ant and the Grain of Millet', simple yet provocative. It made people think.

'The ant found a grain of millet. The seed, feeling itself caught, cried out "If you do me the kindness to allow me to accomplish my function of reproduction, I will give you a hundred such as I am." And so it was.'

Enlightened mind ... from art to aeronautics, imagination without limits

Leonardo pushed the boundary of knowledge, exploring things that did not become accepted and physical until hundreds of years later. His notebooks were not published until four centuries after his death, and in them people were amazed to find that what they had thought was the latest discovery had been imagined many years before.

Yet his contemporaries also realized that they lived alongside a supremely gifted man – a genius – a man who could see things differently, and think different things.

A man who redefined his world from the future back.

How does enlightenment drive creativity?

It sounds almost spiritual, and certainly requires spirit … the personal energy to stretch yourself, to look wider and deeper, to listen harder and interpret better, to think what has never been thought and to connect the unconnected, and to turn ideas into practical solutions for implementation.

Thinking from the future back is exhausting but exhilarating. Like a racing driver or tennis player, it doesn't look too physically demanding, but it requires immense mental presence. There is no magic formula, no definitive process, just a number of talents that you can embrace. The rest is up to you, to embrace curiosity and perspective, and all the other factors. Yet if there is one essential ingredient, then it is an enlightened mind that has the fitness and agility to think beyond the norm.

The agility comes from mental fitness and, like physical fitness, this requires training. It demands regular stimulus in many different ways – artistic and scientific, business and personal, analytical and creative, the big picture and the detail.

How can you enlighten your mind?

Develop your aerobic conditioning. Build body awareness, spiritually and physically – yoga and dance, juggling and fitness. Morning runs, lunchtime swims or an evening at the gym. Do it regularly – not as a lung-bursting, muscle-burning workout, but a sustained effort that can be repeated often, and from which you feel better than when you started.

Physical fitness heightens your mental agility, ready for your mind to be fuelled with new and interesting stimuli. You can achieve much of this in the way you live, your interests, the magazines you read, the people you meet, in the workplace and even the food you eat.

Break your conventions. Encourage your ambidexterity, using your non-dominant hand at least once every day. With colleagues and teams, shake things up a little – throwing in some random ideas, changing the subject regularly, work on multiple projects at the same time and make unusual but interesting connections.

It can be a little disorientating at first, but it breaks you and them out of your conventions, and eventually becomes fun and inspiring.

➡ Creative genius (Chapter 10) defines the nature of 'genius' in today's business world.

➡ Steve Jobs (Chapter 10) is the 'reality distortion field' that we all want to learn from.

➡ Dave Stewart (Chapter 35) transforms himself from rock star to ideas man at Nokia.

➡ Creative people (Chapter 45) explores the attributes that drive your own creativity.

➡ Niklas Zennström (Chapter 49) stays on the edge, always looking for the next big thing.

➡ Now forward (Chapter 50) inspires you to stay crazy in practical and profitable ways.

Future back

Leonardo da Vinci created a future way beyond most people's imagination, in which so much innovation and so many people have been inspired.

He imagined and shaped the future like nobody else. His peers were not just his contemporaries, and his context was not just the world as it is. He looked beyond the science and conventions of the time, to understand people and nature like never before. He rewrote the rules of science and technology, many of which we still use today.

His ideas were centuries ahead of his time, his insights had a depth not before encountered, and his results were extraordinary.

CHAPTER 2

Time and space ... exploring the future world

'Now here, you see, it takes all the running you can do, to keep in the same place. If you want to get somewhere else, you must run at least twice as fast as that.'

Lewis Carroll

Imagine that you are a time traveller. Explore the world centuries ahead, meeting your future generations and seeing what has become of the world we live in. Go backwards into history to stand alongside the great figures, or maybe even do something to change history and our world today.

For most of us this is pure fantasy – we are satisfied to live in the world we do. Yet predicting the future has never been easy. In a time of accelerating change and unpredictable turbulence it is even harder. The future is no longer an extrapolation of today; visible insights and trends are rarely the source of the best ideas or breakthrough innovations. They help but we need to do more, to use our imagination too.

As David Pescovitz, research director of the Institute for the Future in Palo Alto, reflected in a recent interview with *The Times*, 'things are more volatile than they have ever been, and we are barely at the beginning. The World Wide Web emerged in 1993, which wasn't really that long ago. It's an incredibly transformative time.'

How will your world change in the next ten years? Where will the best opportunities emerge? Will people still want what you do today? What will most influence them?

We struggle to keep pace with today, let alone take time to look ahead. If we do, we have a tendency to dismiss it as uncertain. We prefer to exploit the opportunities closest to us. But without a view of where we are going, we are unlikely to move forwards; we fail to 'future-proof' our investments and innovations, and we create more rather than less risk in our businesses.

Nobody wants to always be a step behind – never shaping your world, always being shaped by others.

Future possibilities

Ever since Jules Verne and H.G. Wells, scientists, philosophers, writers and artists have tried to imagine the world of the future. The optimists believe that progress, largely driven by scientific research, will conquer problems and uncertainty, and continue to make our lives better. The pessimists believe that problems are intrinsic and inevitable – a little like Frankenstein's monster eventually coming back to destroy its creator – and that mankind only has itself to blame for an imperfect world.

The early twentieth century saw the rapid emergence of cars, trains and planes. Fuelled by this growth, the 1950s vision of the future was shown in *The Jetsons*. The cartoon pictures a traditional family living in a hi-tech flat, high up in a towering skyscraper. Dad goes to work in his personal space vehicle. He calls Mum from the office on the videophone to tell her when he will be back. She is at home with the children, helped by a semi-human robot who is also the cook, cleaner and babysitter. The children play with futuristic toys, including a robot dog and an incredibly-fast spinning top. Summer holidays are a trip to the Moon.

So we could assume that everything will just become bigger, faster, more powerful and more efficient, while culture and society remain basically the same. A century later, however, we have not found ourselves living the life of *The Jetsons*. We still drive cars and fly planes, although with a little less amazement and more concern about their impact. Few of us have progressed to personal planes. Robots are still largely the stuff of science fiction and despite having taken our first steps on it, the Moon still seems distant and surreal.

Some things have changed. We don't need robots to do the washing, because we developed more intelligent washing machines. We have found ways to work more remotely, rather than just having gadgets to take to work. As many women work as men, and the social dynamics of family and community have changed too.

So innovation is not just about a technology timeline, or mimicking existing behaviours in faster or more efficient ways. Cultural attitudes, behaviours, needs and expectations change more. The context for innovation is perhaps more important than the innovation.

Time matters, but space matters more.

Spacetime

Time is easy to measure; space is more difficult. It has many different formats, and multiple dimensions. We might interpret space in terms of geography and witness the rapid globalization of our culture and markets. In life, we might have changing lifestyles, interacting with different people with evolving priorities. In business, companies and markets evolve over time. The opportunities of evolving and emerging spaces are much more interesting than the future in itself.

In physics, 'spacetime' is about considering space and time in the same context, or mathematically in a single continuum. Spacetime is usually interpreted with space being three-dimensional and time playing the role of a non-spatial fourth dimension. By connecting time and space, physicists have significantly simplified a large number of theories, be they super-galactic or sub-atomic.

In classical mechanics, time is treated as a constant, independent of the state of motion of an observer. However, Einstein taught us that life is not so simple and all perceptions are relative. Time cannot be separated from the three dimensions of space because the rate at which time passes depends on an object's velocity relative to the speed of light and also on the strength of intense gravitational fields, which can slow the passage of time.

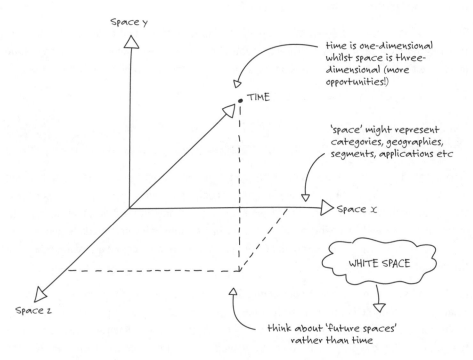

Opportunities emerge in space not just in time ... finding the best 'whitespaces' from the 'future back'

In *Doctor Who*, The Doctor describes himself as 'the last time lord'. Maybe because he understood that time was not enough, and instead transports himself across centuries and parallel worlds in his TARDIS, which stands for 'time and relative dimensions in space'.

The point is not to baffle you with science, or fiction. The point is that timelines are not enough.

We cannot simply understand the future based on an extrapolation from today. We need to open our eyes to a bigger, complex and changing world where the spaces we do business – the 'marketspaces' – are likely to evolve the most. The Institute for the Future no longer focuses on timelines or trends; instead, it looks for 'blobs' of interesting areas where newness is emerging. The sources of new ideas and opportunities are less about the future itself but instead about these blobs – or, more eloquently, the 'whitespaces' that are likely to emerge in that time.

Whitespace

Insight is much more than understanding what people currently want. Markets are much larger than their existing limits and new opportunities emerge in many different ways. Instead of focusing too much creative energy on the existing definitions of our world (the 'greyspace'), we should invest more in finding and exploiting the emergent areas (the 'whitespace') – the differences between the two are shown in the following table.

Greyspace	Whitespace
Focusing on markets that are defined by current products and competitors	Focusing on markets as defined by our imagination, by focusing on solving people's problems, and redefining the context
Addressing the articulated needs and wants of existing customers	Addressing the motivations and aspirations, and the articulated and unarticulated needs, of customers and non-customers
Guided by customer research that is limited by current paradigms and data that reflects averages	Guided by 'insights', more stretching and deeper, by bringing together many sources of knowledge to find new and significant opportunities
Seeking to implement one idea from a quick brainstorm; tactical and cosmetic	Seeking to create more disruptive change, through breakthrough concepts that connect many ideas to form better solutions
Innovating around the 'what', creating an innovative product or technology	Innovating the 'why, what and how', creating an innovative solution or experience, or an entirely new business

Predicting the future is easy and largely irrelevant, because it could take an infinite number of forms. Creating it is much more important: why should we stand back and let others shape it for us, and live by their visions?

Virgin Galactic ... spaceships and stardust

'To be able to float around in Zero-G, I just wish everybody could experience this. The view is so hard to describe, it's moving, it's emotional,' reflected John Glenn on returning to Earth.

Glenn, and many of his fellow astronauts over the last 45 years, have struggled to convey the enormity of what they have experienced and how their perceptions of our world have fundamentally changed. Now Virgin Galactic seeks to extend that privilege.

On 4 October 2004, Burt Rutan's *SpaceShipOne* rocketed into history, achieving what only three of the world's most powerful nations had managed to achieve before him and claiming the $10 million Ansari X Prize. Soon he will launch the world's first commercial space business, although over the longer term he sees Virgin also replacing intercontinental travel on Earth – using space hops to reduce long-haul flights from hours to minutes.

Indeed, nothing excites Virgin's founder Richard Branson more than his ground-breaking venture into 'space tourism'. Sitting interviewing him, he talked about his life and his business experiences – a familiar story to many of us. But when I mentioned space, his eyes lit up as he recalled his schoolboy excitement of watching the first moon landing at home on a black and white television in 1969. He was spellbound, he said. From that moment, he promised himself that one day he would follow those astronauts into space.

Making the impossible possible

Branson described the challenge in defining what at the time seemed impossible, and then finding a way to make it happen: 'Space travel is absolutely, unbelievably exciting. For a British company to be preparing to be the first to take fare-paying customers into space is phenomenal. Having registered the name Virgin Galactic, we spent a decade looking for potential engineers to build a reusable spaceship.'

'We explored mad, zany ideas, and then found Burt Rutan who's the absolute genius in this area. He'd come up with the idea of turning the spaceship into a massive shuttle-cock, to slow the vehicle on its dangerous re-entry phase. The whole project is almost carbon-neutral. Each space flight will generate fewer emissions than a flight to New York, whereas NASA uses the power of New York City to send up the Space Shuttle.'

Back in 1996, the Ansari Foundation launched its X Prize to be awarded for the first non-governmental space flight. Initially supported by Microsoft co-founder, Paul Allen, *Space-ShipOne* was developed by Burt Rutan, and a month after Branson got involved the space-craft flew to an altitude of 112 kilometres and claimed the prize.

Further developments led to *SpaceShipTwo* (subsequently renamed *VSS Enterprise* after his love of *Star Trek*), which is twice as large and built of an incredibly light but strong composite material. This, combined with the innovative horizontal launch concept from its mother-ship, would deliver a launch process of relatively low cost and significantly less noise and carbon pollution. Inside, a fully pressurized cabin with floor-to-ceiling windows would create a unique experience for the six passengers and two pilots.

Better than climbing Everest

Launching initially from Spaceport America in New Mexico, Virgin's astronauts will need to pay around $200,000 and undergo three days of preparation. There is a medical check before travel, although no upper age limit – Branson's father Ted is particularly excited about being on the maiden commercial flight, despite being well into his eighties.

The venture's leader, Will Whitehorn, argues that the price is equivalent to the cost of climbing Mount Everest, which hundreds of people now do every year, an 'almost as exciting' experience. More strikingly, he compares it to the alternative way to travel in space, costing around $20 million and two years of training with the Russian space agency. He sees Virgin's prices falling by around 50% once the business is fully operational.

Around 300 individuals had already signed up for space travel, even before the official launch. They include designer Philippe Starck, scientist Stephen Hawking and James Lovelock, one of Branson's heroes and inventor of the Gaia concept that the Earth functions as a single connected organism. They will experience six minutes of weightlessness during what will be a two-hour end-to-end flight, and just to add to the drama of the first voyage, Duran Duran will play live in-flight too.

> 'It's incredible to think only 450 people have ever been into space; that's including all the Russians, all the Chinese and all the Americans put together,' said Branson. 'We should be able to take maybe 1000 people, or should I say astronauts, in the 12 months once we start.'

CHAPTER 3

Creative minds ... new thinking for the new world

'When it comes to the future, there are three kinds of people: those who let it happen, those who make it happen, and those who wonder what happened.'

John Richardson, pioneer of future modelling

We live in a creative world, an ideas economy.

This is a world where people engage more emotionally, intuition beats logic, imagination fuels insight, pictures say more than words, form matters as much as function, ideas are the most valuable assets, and creativity the most precious talent.

In business, we slowly realize that analytical spreadsheets, focus and efficiency are unlikely to uncover the best opportunities, or win us competitive advantage. Despite the many hours with heads down in our Excel spreadsheets, we realize that ideas and imagination can deliver more success.

Scientists exploring new super-string theories, engineers working with nanotechnologies, designers working with 3D graphics, teachers seeking to educate digital native kids, artists in ambient media, retailers delivering experiential theatre, social networkers, bloggers, tweeters ... Richard Florida calls them the 'creative class': people who are defined by their ideas, are largely dependent on creativity to create value and inspire others to create too. In developed markets they now account for around 30% of the workforce. Florida estimates that in the US alone, there are around 40 million creative professionals.

Every profession is becoming more creative: healthcare is more about people and wellness, accountants develop all sorts of elaborate schemes to improve the bottom line, lawyers seek to find ever more imaginative ways to defend their clients, and even politicians need to work harder than ever to engage their audiences. By 2020, around 50% of all workers will be creative professionals of one sort or another. They bring together information and experience, insight and imagination to solve problems in better ways, and to customize solutions.

But creative people are different. They reject sameness and structure. No longer are they prepared to work 9 to 5, sometimes coming in earlier and/or leaving later, but otherwise wanting to be more flexible with their time, which becomes their most precious commodity. They throw off their white shirts and ties, they express themselves as individuals, they give much more, and expect much more in return.

The secret of high performance and satisfaction – at home, school or work – is the deeply human need to direct our own lives, to learn and create new things, and to do more for our world. Dan Pink, author of *Free Agent Nation*, argues that we increasingly want to work for ourselves rather than others, and that autonomy, mastery and purpose will be our new guiding forces.

As we approach the future, we need to rethink what skills and knowledge are needed. Schools today should be preparing children for very different careers from their parents. These will typically be more creative roles, combining the potential of new technologies and human performance, supporting the innovative practices, and adding value to society in new ways. Imagine these professions of the future:

➡ **Memory guards** – neurosecurity experts responsible for the protection of our best ideas.

➡ **Personal branders** – managing our identities and reputations, the future stylists and publicists.

➡ **Social network counsellors** – helping you through the trauma of multiple online relationships.

➡ **Time-traders** – banks that deposit, and trade time as a valuable asset, rather than money.

➡ **Avatar managers** – personal knowledge assistants replacing teachers and advisors.

➡ **Weather controllers** – firing rockets with silver iodide into the air to provoke rainfall.

➡ **Ethics advisors** – helping you to make the right choices in a complex and confusing world.

Shigeru Miyamoto ... the ultimate game designer

When the great Walt Disney died in 1966, Shigeru Miyamoto was a 14-year-old aspiring cartoonist who adored the classic Disney characters. And when he wasn't drawing, he made his own toys.

Shigeru Miyamoto is now the world's most famous and influential videogame designer – the creator of legendary games such as *Donkey Kong* and *Super Mario Bros.* and more recently, the Nintendo Wii. Yet he is still a hands-on artist, working with colleagues, sharing ideas and passions, smiling and having fun, virtually unknown outside of his design studio, but the hero of game-players around the world.

As the creative mastermind at Nintendo for almost three decades, Miyamoto has seen a transformation in mass entertainment – riding the waves of digital technology progress – from the early personal computers to sophisticated wirelessly networked devices. His products are at the top of most children's gift lists, and many parents' too.

Compelling, irresistible, relentless – his games have led to phenomenal financial success too, unparalleled except perhaps for Disney. He has transformed the gaming industry as well as aspects of modern culture, and is personally responsible for the consumption of more billions of hours of human time than anyone else alive.

Miyamoto joined Nintendo in the late 1970s and rose quickly through the company, first standing out in the early 1980s when his *Super Mario Bros.* games helped save the industry after the collapse of Atari, maker of the first broadly popular home console. Nintendo's NES game console, released in 1985, became the best-selling game machine of its era. Since then Miyamoto, supported by his 400-strong team, has given the world at least 70 games, including recent hits such as *Mario Kart Wii, Super Smash Bros., Brawl, Super Mario Galaxy* and *The Legend of Zelda: Twilight Princess.*

His designs are meticulously detailed, engaging and compulsive. This is because of much more than the impressive graphics: it's the way his characters move and stories unfold, the incredible environments in which they find themselves, and the endless goals set for them. Who would have expected a generation to become addicted to a strange, frantic plumber in blue overalls? And beneath this is a rigorous system design that enables more.

Life in Kyoto

If Miyamoto had grown up in a different world – San Francisco rather than Kyoto, perhaps – then he would be a celebrity on par with Jobs and Spielberg. He would have set up his own studio, probably licensing his games to the leading brands – a celebrity everywhere he went and worth billions.

Instead, despite being a cult figure at Nintendo HQ, he almost comes across as just another worker, rushing home to his wife and two school-age children at the end of the day. Maybe this normality is a big part of his (and Nintendo's) success. Focusing on the games, creating new ones, and making the others better, is the obsession, not money or fame. His ideas are well established, and protected, and he attracts the best talent to work alongside him. 'What's important is that the people that I work with are also recognized and that it's the Nintendo brand that goes forward and continues to become strong and popular,' he said in an interview with *The New York Times*, when comparing Walt Disney's role with his own. He has the trust and admiration of senior management, meaning that creativity and the creative process can flow without interruption or compromise.

Mario, the moustached Italian plumber he created almost 30 years ago, has become the planet's most recognized fictional character, rivalled only by Mickey Mouse. His games have together sold more than 350 million copies, and Miyamoto – despite his anonymity – was voted the most influential person on the planet by *Time* magazine.

Wii and Mii

More than games, his influence is through the Wii, an innovation that has largely reinvented an industry. The idea was revolutionary in its simplicity: rather than create a new generation of games for existing players, Nintendo wanted to reach out to new audiences – and developed the Wii as an easy-to-use, inexpensive diversion for families, to women, to parents and even grandparents.

Largely thanks to Miyamoto, digital games have become Japan's most successful cultural export, and Nintendo has become one of the most valuable companies in Japan. It is often said that without Shigeru Miyamoto, Nintendo would still be making playing cards, the original focus of the games maker when it began in 1889. Indeed he has been such a driving force to the industry that there might not even be videogames today without him.

His inspiration has shifted over time – from the desire to dream up new worlds and characters, to a realization that his own personal experiences can be just as significant inspirations.

Nintendogs was inspired by his Shetland sheepdog at home; then there is his love of rock music (particularly the Beatles) and his love of playing the piano and banjo, from which emerged *Guitar Hero* and *Rock Band*.

As consumers want to become a part of their entertainment, and shape it, Miyamoto is creating a new star in his fantastical stable of characters: you, or rather Mii, the avatar that Wii users create of themselves. In the interview with *The New York Times* he reflected that Miis were 'the most recent character creation'. Each Mii is unique and much more relevant to the player, who is now part of the game rather than just playing it.

Shigeru Miyamoto: the Walt Disney of the digital generation.

CHAPTER 4

World changing ... seismic shifts that are transforming markets

'All is flux,nothing stays still. Nothing endures but change.'

Herculitus in 480BC

Look East not West.

If you're looking for the hottest fashions go to Shanghai. If you want the best website designers, try Mumbai and Johannesberg. For game designers, Tokyo is still the place. If you're seeking funding for your new business, Shenzhen is where the venture capitalists hang out. If you want high quality production try Taiwan, or the Philippines for clothing. Education and knowledge is centred on Singapore, and for making it all happen, Hong Kong.

The rampant spread of economic crisis in 2008–9 demonstrated the way in which the world has become interdependent, the foolish practices of undisciplined moneylenders in California having an almost cataclysmic impact on the fortunes of businesses in London or Lagos, and the lifestyles and ambitions of people in Moscow and Mumbai.

And whilst people focused on the problem, the turbulence that it caused and how they could get back to how they were, they didn't realize that the world was fundamentally changing.

They missed the real cause of the disruption – a fundamental shift in wealth and power. We felt that impact on stock markets and in our pockets, and the economic crisis acted as a 'tipping point' for seismic change.

Fuelled by changing attitudes, networked technologies and emerging industries, the change is not always visible in our daily lives. But look more closely and it is all around us:

➡ the simple, colourful styling of the Flamenco or pop-art influencing the designs in H&M;

➡ the organic cheese from the local, trusted dairy rather than the big-branded multinational;

➡ speciality Jones Soda drinks that are not for everybody, but loved by some; and

➡ Threadless T-shirts designed and voted for by you.

The brands that realize it's better to be distinctive for some, rather than average for many. People are less interested in that old cliché 'value for money'. They want a piece of the action.

We need to reset our prejudices and expectations, recreate our businesses based around the new value drivers, and refocus our brands, innovation and marketing on the new opportunities.

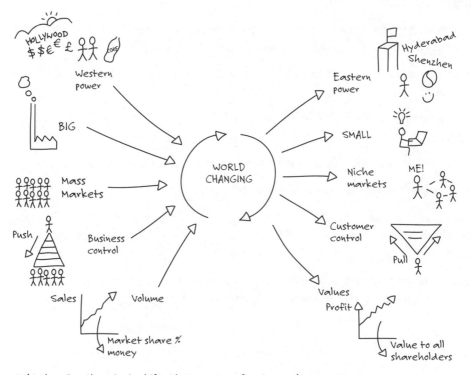

World changing: the seismic shifts that are transforming markets and business

West to East

Asia is no longer the shop floor of the Western consumer, power and ideas have swapped sides and the roles are being rapidly reversed. Companies such as Infosys and Reliance are driving the business agenda, whilst culturally we immerse ourselves in Japanese gaming or Indian meditation. The new Asian currency unit, the ACU, will accelerate the trend, becoming a third global reserve currency and a strong rival to the dollar and euro.

→ **The economic growth of China and India far outstrips Europe and North America, so where would you invest your money?** Shenzen is the new Wall Street.

→ **The hottest start-ups, the most sustainable businesses, the best creative talent?** No longer in California or Scandinavia; try Shanghai or Hyderabad.

→ **The most likely business to acquire you, and your most dangerous competitor?** No longer the Americans or Germans; look out for Hon Hai and Haier.

→ **The most advanced laptops and televisions?** They will be from South Korea not California, made cheaper and better by Lenova, not IBM.

→ **Eastern or Western Europe?** Communism is largely forgotten, replaced by a young, entrepreneurial and sophisticated workforce.

Of course, it is not so simple. North to South is a longer-term trend, the fast-growing Brazil being followed by its South American neighbours, and eventually Africa. But it's also about the connection points, partnerships and combinations. Istanbul is the new centre of the world, and the Chinese are now the largest investors in Silicon Valley.

Big to small

The status symbols of the new decade are not the big cars, swanky offices and excess of before. A new altruism has emerged. The BMW Mini is far cooler than the latest Mercedes Benz or 4 x 4. Home-based offices or hot-desks are the cool workplaces.

→ **What kind of brands do people trust most?** Smaller, more human brands, local not global, rather than big faceless corporations.

→ **Where do the best ideas emerge?** Not in one of the big corporate R&D labs, or in the largest corporations, but through entrepreneurs, often with a social purpose.

→ **Which companies can adapt fastest in a changing world?** As Darwin reminded us, it is not the biggest or most intelligent, but those who evolve who survive.

→ **What kind of company are you more likely to partner with, or seek out for specialist help?** Small companies who will be fair partners rather than monoliths who like to dominate.

→ **Which is a more enjoyable and flexible place to work?** Small companies where you can learn faster with more responsibility, not big organizational bureaucracies that make you conform.

New ideas 'trickle up' rather than impose themselves. Markets are now 'long tails' of niche customers and specialist businesses. Alibaba, a worthy rival to eBay and a platform for a million small Chinese businesses, enables small companies to have a big impact.

Mass to niche

At one time Starbucks was on course to take over the world, opening three new stores every week on yet another street corner of a global city. And then, as with McDonald's before, came the backlash. Whilst the coffee was fairtrade and organic, and the service came with a smile, people just didn't want to be the same.

→ **Unfocused to focused:** No longer do we create multi-sector conglomerates with unrelated businesses, instead seeking coherence and synergy by focusing on particular markets.

→ **Many to few:** Instead of reaching out to as many people as possible, we want the best potential customers.

→ **Average to individual:** 'One size fits all' is no longer tolerated. Selling average products to average customers doesn't work. Customization is the new norm.

→ **Irrelevant or relevant:** People connect with companies that reflect their own values and aspirations.

→ **Same or special:** Being famous for something. When physical boundaries disappear, what are you going to do uniquely in the world, and who are you going to be special for?

Markets are huge collections of niches, either within them, or working across them – a particular kind of product, or a particular attitude that can work across product categories. The challenge is to choose the niche(s) that you want to focus on, firstly from a customer perspective and then in terms of meeting their needs in the most relevant, tailored ways.

Business to customer

Vodafone recently changed its tagline from the 'power of now' to the 'power of you'. Technology and global markets have created a transparency that puts the customer in control. They can choose to buy from suppliers anywhere, prices can no longer be concealed, and customization is expected.

→ **Product to customer:** From Philips to P&G, organizations are reshaping around customers rather than categories, enabling more focus, relevance and integrated solutions.

→ **Standard to personal:** From Build a Bear Workshop to Nike ID, customers have become used to designing, or at least cosmetically modifying, their products and services.

→ **To you or to them:** No longer can you open a store on the High Street and expect people to come to you during working hours. M&S Food went to rail stations and road junctions instead.

→ **To them to with them:** Instead of 'value for money', customers want a piece of the action. Giff Gaff reduces your phone bills the more you contribute ideas or refer others.

→ **With them or between them:** Customers rarely want relationships with brands, but they do want to be connected with communities of like-minded customers.

In markets of surplus supply, rather than surplus demand, customers call the shots. Business needs to learn to do business when, where and how the customer wants, rather than what is commercially most convenient and efficient for the business. Instead of seeking to impose relationships, companies should become facilitators of customer-based networks, enabling and supporting them to do what they do.

Volume to value

Corporate egos obsessed with size and market share have come unstuck as markets have changed, costs risen or sales fallen. The objective of business is not to sell as much as possible, particularly when revenues don't lead to profits. Market share was the goal when economies of scale were derived from covering manufacturing costs. That is rarely the business model any more.

➡ **Volume to profit:** Economic value creation is driven by profit growth, not scale. The largest companies are not the most successful – look at the decline of Ford and GM.

➡ **Market share to customer share:** Some customers will never be profitable, but you want as much as you can from the ones who will be.

➡ **Cost to perceived value:** Companies should spend more time improving their perceived value, by reframing context and adding value rather than falling into downward discount spirals.

➡ **Scale to focus:** If scale and share are no longer priorities, then portfolio management is – getting the best mix of markets, segments, channels, products and customers.

➡ **Biggest or best:** So what is market leadership? Instead of being big ... be the thought leader, the customer champion, the innovator, the market shaper and the best.

Value creation is not about being a slave to financial numbers, or even to the shareholders. Profits created this year, and the stream of profits likely in future years through the right choices and innovations, can be invested in all stakeholders – to fund more strategic and significant innovations, to attract the best talent, to support communities and environments in mutually relevant ways, and to ensure that investors realize a more sustained return on their investments.

Aravind Eye Care ... bringing a new vision to India

Madurai is best known for its spectacular Hindu temples, but in recent years, it has been attracting thousands of new visitors. In Madurai, they have heard, there is one of the finest eye hospitals in the world.

Over the last three decades, Aravind Eye Care has been on a mission to cure blindness in India. The centre has developed a wide range of affordable solutions, from low-priced intraocular lenses to rapid cataract surgery that allows high volume at lower cost.

Aravind Eye Care was founded in 1976 by Dr Govindappa Venkataswamy. Given the magnitude of blindness and the challenges in the country, the Indian government could not address the problem alone. At that time there were perhaps no more than eight ophthalmologists across the country. Realizing this predicament, Dr Venkataswamy wanted to establish an alternative healthcare model that would supplement the efforts of state hospitals and also be self-supporting.

The network of not-for-profit hospitals and 'vision centres' carry out more than 300,000 eye surgeries each year, 70% of them at no fee. This is only possible through an innovative care model that ensures speed and efficiency. Operations continue 24 hours, broadband connections are used to on-call doctors in city hospitals for instant diagnosis, and nurses handle most of the non-essential activities rather than them taking up the time of doctors. This model allows the company to give away free surgeries to the poor while still earning a profit. More than 1500 eye care 'camps' in rural areas screen thousands more patients weekly.

Today, Aravind is more than an eye hospital. It is a social organization committed to eliminating needless blindness through comprehensive eye care services. It supports a training centre for ophthalmic professionals all around the world, an institute for research that contributes to the development of new eye care techniques, and even a large guest house to accommodate all its visitors. Aravind also runs Aurolab, which manufactures a wide range of around 700,000 pairs of affordable lenses every year, a quarter of which are used by Aravind and the others exported to other developing markets.

Over 30 years, Aravind has treated over 2.4 million poor Indians. In 2008, he won the prestigious Gates Award for Global Health.

CHAPTER 5

Whitespaces ... women, water and 50 billion devices

'He who does not expect will not find out the unexpected, for it is trackless and unexplored.'

Heraclitus

Are you interested in the future of your market? Where your future customers will come from? What kind of business will you be in 20 years' time? Are you out-thinking your existing and future competition?

Five factors that will define an ever more dramatic future are:

➡ **Speed** – the rate of change, driven by technology and expectation.

➡ **Complexity** – an avalanche of seemingly unrelated forces as they collide.

➡ **Risk** – from crime and terror to economic and environmental.

➡ **Change** – learning to adapt to ever more turbulence inside and out.

➡ **Surprise** – more frequent, more dramatic, life is ever less predictable.

So what are the big opportunities that will emerge out of these seismic shifts in our world? How can we adapt our existing businesses or break out into completely new domains in order to exploit these opportunities?

There are many excellent sources of trends and patterns. For example, specialist organizations such as Trendwatching, where founder Reinier Evers has a network of 5000 volunteer trendspotters all around the world, crunch it all together and articulate the emergent zeitgeist through evocative language – nowism, foreverism, (f)luxury, infolust, maturialism, sellsumers, generation g(enerosity), perkonomics, ecoiconic, crowdclout, trysumers ...

Behind the names are tales of new business ideas or social behaviours that we can observe on the fringes of our daily lives. Springwise is an excellent place to explain the margins of your particular business, as are sites such as Coolhunter and Trendhunter. For more colour and interpretation, keep updated with some of the most observant, and throughtful, bloggers around. Richard Watson from Now and Next, and Ross Dawson at Future Exploration Network, are two of the best.

Trends are observed behaviours, patterns in the zeitgeist that rise above fashions and fads. 'Future spaces' are the new marketspaces that emerge because of the trends, where new needs and desires are established, with creative and practical ways to exploit them commercially.

Whitespace 1: Women and boomers

Women now control around $20 trillion in annual consumer spending, anticipated by Harvard Business School to increase to near $28 trillion by 2015. Their $13 trillion in annual earnings could reach $18 trillion in the same period, giving them enormous spending power and influence beyond.

Women represent a growth market bigger than China and India combined: between 2009 and 2014 China's GDP is likely to grow by $2.2 trillion, whilst India less so, by around $0.6 trillion. Women represent 51% of the population, but influence closer to 80% of consumer purchase decisions and therefore around 67% of global GDP.

It would be foolish to ignore or underestimate the female consumer. Yet many companies still do, like Dell's pink-coloured Della website, which emphasized colours and style, and the computer's ability to find recipes and count calories. It caused uproar amongst female audiences for its 'slick and condescending' style. Within weeks it was gone.

Similarly, older people will have enormous influence on our futures. People are living longer, and more people are getting older. The median age across the world was 23.9 years old in 1950, rising to 26.8 in 2000, and predicted to shoot up to 37.8 by 2050. In more developed countries, people are even older, from 29.0 in 1950 to 37.3 in 2000, and rising to 45.5 by 2050.

Asia and Europe have the most ageing populations. Japan has one of the world's fastest-ageing populations – something to do with the diet and lifestyle, perhaps – and by 2025 will have twice as many people over 65 as under 20. In China, more than 150 million people are aged over 60. That represents 10% of the entire population and is predicted to increase to 30% by 2050.

Older people tend to have more savings than younger people, but spend less on consumer goods. They have more time than younger people, with grown-up families and retired from full-time jobs, they want to travel the world, having missed out on gap years when they were younger.

The new over-60s don't sit at home with their cardigans and walking sticks. They are the baby boomers, the kids of the 1960s, they wear jeans and listen to rock music. A few of them are fuelled with Viagra, but most of them with unfulfilled ambition – they still have much to achieve, and to give.

Whilst the growth of female consumers is good news for fashion and cosmetics, the impact of an ageing population will be most significant on healthcare and, to a lesser extent, travel. The big opportunity is to realign businesses that had previously not addressed female audiences in more relevant and engaging ways.

Whitespace 2: Cities and communities

Less than a century ago, only 5% of the world's population lived in a city. By 2010, that figure had grown to well over 50%. In the last two decades the urban population of the developing world has grown by an average of 3 million people per week. By 2050, it will have reached 70%, representing 6.4 billion people.

Most of this growth will be in developing markets, with the Asian megacities hosting 63% of the world's urban population (or 3.3 billion people) by 2050. I witness this every time I go to a city such as Istanbul. Each time I visit, sometimes only weeks after the last trip, a new tower block has been added to the skyline, or an outer-city forest has been transformed into another housing complex or shopping mall.

In cities of the developed countries, urbanization was driven by a concentration of human activities and settlements from the countryside or from other countries. This led to impoverished city centres. In more recent times, inner city redevelopment schemes have reversed this effect. Look at Docklands in London, or the renovation of industrial slums in Bilbao. In developing countries, huge sprawling 'shanty towns' grew up on the edges of cities.

As cities lost their soul, people built stronger affinities to local communities with their own centres – towns within London, villages within Manhattan – and local government. Immigrants clustered together, giving different areas distinctive cultures, and cities became a mosaic of wealth and poverty, languages and ethnicity. This has an effect on rural areas too, draining talent and local economies. Governments concentrate resources on these urban majorities, often meaning that rural communities get less.

Yet there is also a backlash against this concentration as people start to appreciate the value of their environments. Rural areas become niche and farm shops go premium, serving the Range Rover set rather than their own farm communities. Despite this, people increasingly value communities, localness and the people around them.

The big opportunity is to do more for urban communities, enabling them to be small and local whilst still part of a bigger place.

Whitespace 3: Individuality and identity

People want to express their individuality in what they buy and in what they do and say. Indeed, they want to express themselves in ways never before possible – telling the world about every movement through Twitter or capturing every special moment in photos uploaded to Flickr. Self-publishing is easy: 50 million blogs are being published and updated every day. And as people want to be more different, identity becomes more precious.

This leads to a paradox. On the one hand they want to tell the world everything about themselves, but on the other hand they protect their identity and their privacy like never before. Footballers, musicians, movie stars and others use their images to influence our lives, yet they are the first to call in lawyers if we seek more than they want to give, to learn the wrong things about them.

Customization is the new norm, recognized as worthy of a premium. Personal service, personal shoppers, personal bankers, personal advice – we want it all tailored just to us. These are traits of the 'experience economy', where standard products and services are the commodities from which to add value. At the same time, identify theft and identity protection have both become big businesses, as will identity management in the future.

The big opportunity is to enable people to express their individuality, achieve customization and build their identities in positive as well as profitable ways.

Whitespace 4: Carbon and water

The issues of climate change are complex and how to resolve them even harder – for example, how to support emerging nations in their pursuit of growth whilst trying to do it in a cleaner way. Around 47 billion tonnes of CO_2 are emitted annually into the atmosphere worldwide. This figure is due to grow to 54 billion tonnes by 2020, but has to be cut to at least 44 billion by then to avert irreversible and dramatic shifts in our climate.

Whilst business and politicians focus on carbon reduction, other factors matter just as much. Reducing biodiversity is a huge invisible trend, as our marine life is destroyed by our pollution and greed. The scarcity of fresh drinking water, as well as the rising sea levels, will emerge as even bigger challenges. Today 6.5 billion people share the same volume of water that 1.6 billion did a hundred years ago. By 2050 that figure will be 9 billion. Every year we destroy 44 million acres of forest, creating an increasing imbalance in the way nature produces and absorbs carbon dioxide. We emit 8 billion tonnes of carbon into our atmosphere, only 3 billion tonnes of which can be reabsorbed. We use 160 billion tons more water each year than is being replenished by rain – enough to require a 450,000 km convoy of trucks.

As a result of this damage, 200 million people will become refugees due to flooding and drought if the climate warms by 2–3°C by 2050. Or financially, insurance claims will increase by $320 billion due to storms and floods if carbon emissions continue to rise at present rates, making insurance premiums too expensive for most individuals or companies. The deforestation will reduce crop yields across Africa by 33%, adding to the hunger. And a five-metre rise in sea levels, caused by melting polar ice caps, will wipe out many coastal areas, with consequences including a predicted 11% decline in China's GDP. A billion people survive on less than $1 a day, 3 billion on less than $2 a day. Three billion people have no access to clean water, 800 million are hungry, and 10 million children die before they are five. Yet the people at the 'bottom of the pyramid' seek better lives and demand more. Together, they represent an estimated $5 trillion market.

'Green' is the new status symbol, although it is often overused by companies jumping on the bandwagon and as a result can also feel fatigued. In the sense of being responsible, caring about social and environmental issues, 'green' is here to stay and perhaps the biggest stimulus for innovation.

Green products and lifestyles are definitely no longer for tree huggers, nor is green a compromise for performance. Tesla is able to create an electric car with superior acceleration, speed and longevity than many of its more famous competitors. Noir has launched luxury eco-fashion products, including organically certified African cotton products, and Linda Loudermilk's Couture line includes glamorous and sophisticated pieces made from bamboo and soya. This new luxury eco-fashion is increasing in scale, and celebrities are also jumping on the environmental bandwagon. Lindsay Lohan is wearing second-hand clothing for environmental reasons, and Leonardo DiCaprio co-produced, wrote and narrated the documentary *The 11th Hour* to 'raise awareness about global warming and the problems we face in promoting a sustainable environmental future for our planet'.

The big opportunity is to embrace sustainability as the basis for innovation, finding ways that your services can do more good for people and the planet, and increase profits too.

Whitespace 5: Networks and Web 3.0

It is said that everyone on the planet is separated by six other people. This is the power of networks. YouTube, Facebook, Wikipedia – often described as second generation websites, or Web 2.0 – enable collaboration between users, and where content is largely generated by and shared by users.

They represent online communities that some regard as social networks, but also form the basis of collaborative sourcing, production, communication and distribution. Millions of people worldwide can participate in this economy like never before: selling antiques through eBay, uploading home-made documentaries to Current TV, remixing their favourite music for iTunes, designing new software, editing school homework, inventing new cosmetics, finding cures for diseases or sequencing the human genome.

And of course networks can be physical too, like FedEx's ability to deliver a parcel from any point to any other on Earth within 24 hours, or Star Alliance's integration of airline route networks to make travel easier and cheaper. Best of all is when physical and virtual networks converge to provide the best of both worlds – digital reach combined with human experience – like the best retail propositions today, or when buying a new car or home.

However it is the emergence and evolution of digital networks that currently offer the most innovative opportunities to reach new markets and add value in new ways.

The value of these networks lies in the content that is developed through their connections.

The scale is awesome. Just in 2007, a staggering 7 billion user-generated videos were streamed each month; 120,000 new blogs were created every day adding to more than 70 million worldwide; in the US 30% of all web users access YouTube, iTunes and Wikipedia each month. Meanwhile, Google paid $900 million to provide advertising on MySpace, but also got sued $1 billion by Viacom for alleged copyright infringement on its $1.65 billion acquisition, YouTube. In July 2009, Mark Zuckerberg, founder of the world's largest social networking site, wrote on his blog:

'As of today, 250 million people are using Facebook to stay updated on what's happening around them and share with the people in their lives. The rapid pace of our growth is humbling and exciting for us, and it affirms that people everywhere are realizing the power of staying connected to everything they care about.'

However connections and content are just beginnings. Web 2.0 does more for people, particularly through user-generated content, and it has value beyond its participants. Customers are only too willing to contribute content – words, pictures, and especially videos – to something that is of particular interest to them, sharing their passion with other people like them. Yet there is a vision of the power of networks that goes far beyond this too and has real intelligence and ability, where participants immerse themselves more deeply, and the web does more itself. This is labelled Web 3.0, or as Tim Berners-Lee called it when envisaging the potential of the World Wide Web which he created, the 'semantic web' – the thinking web, the ideas web. In his book *Weaving the Web*, Berners-Lee wrote:

'I have a dream for the Web in which computers become capable of analysing all the data on the Web – the content, links and transactions between people and computers. A *semantic web*, which should make this possible, has yet to emerge, but when it does, the day-to-day mechanisms of trade, bureaucracy and our daily lives will be handled by machines talking to machines'.

The big opportunity is to embrace networks in your operations and markets, not just as social meeting points, but in ways that enable you and your customers to do more exponentially.

Whitespace 6: GRIN and 50 billion devices

GRIN technologies are the uber-technological drivers of our age – genetics, robotics, information and nanotechnologies – that together are predicted to generate more than 50 billion futuristic devices that can solve problems from climate change to space travel to aging.

Genetic science decodes our bodies, leading to DNA scanning, and a whole new approach to well-being and medicine. It has the potential to alter the genes of human embryos and to prevent diseases, maximize the functioning of organs and muscles, and perhaps even increase intelligence. Alongside these changes come huge ethical dilemmas, as evidenced by the debate over stem cell research. The movie *Gattaca* provides an in-depth look at what could happen in the future if some people are genetically superior and the rest are discriminated against.

Robots are in heavy use already, but will rapidly become cheap and advanced enough to be practical in many day-to-day as well as scientific and industrial applications. Intricate robotics are already used in modern surgery, but they could eventually replace surgeons. Advancing computing power and new programming seek to boost the skill level and accuracy of robots to eventually be better than humans because of their precision and consistency.

Nanotechnology refers to the practical application of atomic and sub-atomic particles – cleaning fabrics with threads a thousand times thinner than a human hair, and associated improvement in effectiveness, for example, or miniature machines that can move along blood vessels to perform heart operations – and much more – without invasive surgery. For the pharma industry, it represents a step change in the science and production of drugs, and for engineers it means applying big world knowledge to an invisible world.

The smaller size, increased efficiency, and exponentially advancing computing power suggests an infinite evolution of devices, and a challenge to the human brain. As computing power challenges our intelligence, our own brains need to refocus on more creative and emotional purposes, the source of change and satisfaction,

The big opportunity is to consider the relevance of technology to solve your customer's problems, finding practical applications to the new materials and intelligence now possible.

Whitespace 7: Authenticity, meaning and happiness

In the midst of technological breakthrough and environmental breakdown, people are more emotional, expectant and demanding than ever.

Authenticity matters because technologies have greatly increased the scope of the inauthentic. Authenticity drives trust. People's trust in brands is in steep decline, diminished by insincere marketing and superficiality. It has been further hurt by the boardroom scandals and executive greed that hog the business headlines. Faced with infinite choice from around the world, we struggle to choose which brand to trust amongst all the competing, similar claims. Reality TV, the pseudo-science of advertising and the growth of word of mouth have redefined our sense of reality, making us question everything. Consumers are bombarded with telemarketing and direct mail that is interruptive and crude, annoying rather than engaging us. Networks enable consumers to pass on this frustration, and that fragile asset called reputation is quickly shattered.

Meaning is achieved by having a greater purpose, a product that has reason beyond its basic functionality, a business that seeks more than just making money. Meaning drives engagement.

A business should have a higher purpose beyond the pursuit of profit, or even being the best at what it does. The challenge is to define purpose in terms of customers, or even society at large. How does this business make life better, for the customer, and for society? What would we miss if the business no longer existed? This purpose becomes a belief system. For customers, it is a deeper, richer reason for choosing the brand, particularly if the purpose is directly relevant to them. Shared values are important too, although they emerge through attitudes and behaviours rather than a list of well-worn adjectives trotted out by most companies.

Happiness is achieved by touching people's emotion more personally, enhancing their lives in a way that goes beyond just living. Happiness drives desire. It is rare to make someone smile in markets crowded with sameness, with products and services that are largely enabled by technology – targeted at the (non-existent) average person – and in life that is so focused on quantified achievements in minimum time. On the new search for happiness in business, *Forbes* magazine reflected that 'happy people do better than unhappy people in most realms of life; they have better social relationships, do more volunteer work, have better health and make more money. So money may not make you happier, but being happy may make you more money.'

The big opportunity is to achieve all three: authenticity that achieves trust, meaning that engages people more deeply and happiness that drives unconditional desire.

Pixar ... from Snow White to The Incredibles

Since the release of *Snow White and the Seven Dwarfs* by Walt Disney in 1937, animated films have become one of the most universally enjoyed forms of entertainment.

Disney has a long history of developing, producing and distributing films such as *Beauty and the Beast, Aladdin* and *The Lion King*. The stories and characters of these popular animated feature films have become part of our modern mythology, enjoyed by generation after generation. Traditionally, these popular animated feature films have been created using the time-consuming and labour-intensive process of two-dimensional, hand-drawn cel animation.

Pixar Animation Studios became the birthplace of a new generation of animated feature films, combining proprietary technology and great storytelling to develop heartwarming stories that are brought to life through the latest computer animation techniques. In 1986 Pixar was acquired by Steve Jobs, shortly after he had parted company with Apple. As the new CEO, he added capital, focus and vision to the business.

From machines to movies

Initially, Pixar specialized in hardware: its Pixar Image Computer was primarily sold to government agencies and the medical community. One of the leading buyers of Pixar Image Computers was Disney Studios, which was using it in a secret project to migrate the laborious 'ink and paint' part of the animation process to a more automated and efficient method. The system never sold well. In a bid to drive sales, Pixar turned to John Lasseter who had been making mini-animations to demonstrate the system's capabilities, to make more of his production skills. For some time, Pixar survived on the income from Lasseter's team making computer-animated commercials.

In 1991, after a significant restructuring, Pixar agreed a $26 million deal with Disney to produce three computer-animated feature films, the first of which was *Toy Story*. The film received tremendous critical acclaim and became the highest grossing film of 1995, generating $362 million in worldwide box office receipts. *Toy Story*'s director, Lasseter, received a Special Achievement Academy Award.

Lasseter built a creative team of highly skilled animators, a story department and an art department. To attract and retain quality animators, those with superior acting ability and who could bring characters and inanimate objects to life, the company founded Pixar University, which conducts three-month long courses for new and existing animators. Pixar also has a complete production team that gives the company the capability to control all elements of production of its films. Blockbuster animated movies quickly followed: *A Bug's Life*, *Toy Story 2*, *Monsters, Inc.*, *Finding Nemo*, *The Incredibles*, *Cars*, *Ratatouille*, *Wall-E*, *Up* – and most recently *Toy Story 3*, which is the first ever Pixar film and first ever animated film to make $1 billion worldwide.

Pixar has been responsible for many important breakthroughs in the application of computer graphics for filmmaking, and a top talent school too. Technical and creative teams have developed a wide range of innovative production software used in-house to create its movies. This proprietary technology allows the generation of animated images of a unique quality, richness and vibrancy. However Pixar has continued to share its research and technology with the industry, not least by selling its RenderMan production technology.

In 2006, Pixar became a wholly-owned subsidiary of The Walt Disney Company in a $7.4 billion deal that saw Jobs, who was the majority shareholder of Pixar with 50.1%, take a seat on Disney's board of directors, and with 7% of all stock, the largest individual shareholder. A new brand name 'Disney·Pixar' was created, although Pixar and the Walt Disney Animation Studios continued to operate separately, with their own structures, processes and cultures.

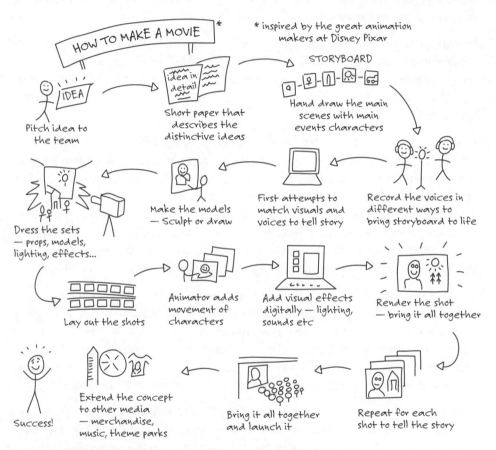

HOW TO MAKE A MOVIE *

* inspired by the great animation makers at Disney Pixar

IDEA

Pitch idea to the team

idea in detail

Short paper that describes the distinctive ideas

STORYBOARD

Hand draw the main scenes with main events characters

Record the voices in different ways to bring storyboard to life

First attempts to match visuals and voices to tell story

Make the models — Sculpt or draw

Dress the sets — props, models, lighting, effects...

Lay out the shots

Animator adds movement of characters

Add visual effects digitally — lighting, sounds etc

Render the shot — bring it all together

Success!

Extend the concept to other media — merchandise, music, theme parks

Bring it all together and launch it

Repeat for each shot to tell the story

Movie making: how to turn your ideas into engaging experiences

CHAPTER 6

Future back ... start with the impossible, then work out how

'Imagination is the beginning of creation. You imagine what you desire, you will what you imagine and at last you create what you will.'

George Bernard Shaw

Most innovation is incremental, imitated and quickly becomes irrelevant. It is limited by the priorities and conventions of today. The future is a much better place to start, and working backwards enables you to make better decisions about where to go, what to invest in and how to innovate.

'Future back' is less about imagining years ahead, more about simply 'thinking bigger': thinking about what is possible, or apparently impossible, and then thinking how to do it. The problem with looking from where you are today is that the most interesting things sit on the blurred horizon and getting to them is not easy. Physically we find the future hard to embrace because it requires new practices and behaviours, which can conflict with our shorter-term priorities. Mentally we find the future hard to adopt because we are conditioned by our prevailing attitudes and conventions, and because we lack courage to do so.

Another way is to take a giant leap forwards and then work backwards from the future. If you 'leap-frog' the limitations of today, you ignore the technology challenges or market regulations, all the thousands of reasons why you should not do something, and instead focus on what you could do. Only by having a clearer view of these possibilities, by understanding their potential impact and therefore their value to you, do you then have the motivation to find ways to overcome the reasons why you should not.

However, 'future back' is only practical if it is combined with 'now forward' thinking. The reality is that your customers need help in adopting new technologies, and technologies need more work in order to enable relevant applications. The key point is that you do the future thinking first, and then work backwards to understand which aspects you can make happen, when and how.

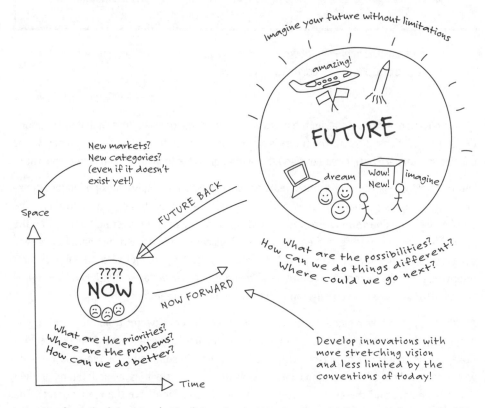

Imagine your future without limitations

amazing!

FUTURE

dream   Wow! New!   imagine

New markets?
New categories?
(even if it doesn't
exist yet!)

Space

FUTURE BACK

????
NOW

NOW FORWARD

What are the possibilities?
How can we do things different?
Where could we go next?

What are the priorities?
Where are the problems?
How can we do better?

Develop innovations with
more stretching vision
and less limited by the
conventions of today!

Time

Innovation from the future back: the future is a better starting point for creativity and decision-making

Timelines and wildcards

H.G. Wells' 1933 book *The Shape of Things to Come* was written in the form of a history book published in the year 2106. It could almost have been mistaken for a real history book, containing numerous footnotes and references to the works of prominent historians of the twentieth and twenty-first centuries – some real, others not.

Sci-fi authors use a storytelling device called a 'future history', a creative history of an imagined future, that serves as a background for their fiction. They might even create or imply a future history timeline to help the reader understand how the future evolved. To do this they must start at the end and then work backwards.

The Futurist, the magazine of the World Future Society, recently asked its readers to think up a series of wildcards. Richard Watson summarized some of the themes in his blog:

⇒ A new spiritual paradigm takes hold, changing values and behaviour.

⇒ Climate science is proven wrong – the world is actually cooling.

⇒ Mankind invents a new energy source comparable to oil.

⇒ Cloned humans threaten the entire population.

⇒ Intelligent life is confirmed in space.

⇒ Total collapse of the world's food supply chain.

⇒ A catastrophic weather event.

⇒ Rapid political shift to the far right or far left globally.

⇒ Widespread food or water poisoning incident.

⇒ Backlash against fundamentalism.

→ The Internet is disabled.

→ A disruptive new business model emerges.

→ President Obama is assassinated.

→ China collapses economically or politically.

Possible and plausible

Whilst wildcards are unlikely, but possible, there are many other emerging ideas that could provoke you to think differently about the future of your business. Consider some of these real, emerging ideas and how they could be relevant, either as parallel ideas, or direct applications, into your own business:

→ **Neurosecurity:** In a world of ideas, what's in your brain is much more valuable than documents or computer records. Companies such as MDSC can provide encryption implants that protect your conscience from 'neurobandits'. The digital security brand Kaspersky is even experimenting with updates in tablet form.

→ **Monster mash-ups:** Wikipedia is just the beginning of knowledge aggregation. Imagine being able to synthesize the best of any art, literature or music, customizing books, galleries and albums to your own whims or specialist interests. This is intelligent iTunes and more, editing and synthesizing a world where it is all too easy to be overwhelmed by the availability of everything.

→ **Crowd knowledge:** Bottom-up collaborations are mapping our streets and capturing our news, much faster than top-down developers such as Google Maps or News International. Aggregating individual news, photos and updates delivers a much faster and richer view of your locality. Look out for Open Streetmap or next-generation Twitter.

➡ **Backchannel media:** The story behind the story, rapidly growing in popularity on cable networks. Live blogging, status updates, photo and videostreaming enables audiences to gain a much faster, richer insight into what is driving events as they unfold. Tweetmeme and Collecta are dedicated to this task, which will eventually consume the controlled presentation styles of mainstream media.

➡ **Open evolution:** Forget your concerns about GM crops – nature is much more intermingled than the conventional evolution of species might suggest. Look at you own DNA and the diverse mosaic of genes that make you. Bdelloid rotifers, a type of freshwater invertebrate, gave up sex 80 million years ago because they found easier ways to extract genes from the animals they eat, and gerbils have recently been found to possess some snake DNA.

➡ **Digital relationships:** Gadgets are distracting, social networks suppress real social skills and emails lack emotion and literary richness. So they said. But instead our BlackBerrys and iPhones have brought us closer together, knowing more about each other, and the world around us, more responsive as individuals, and more powerful collectively, to events and causes.

➡ **HQ Africa:** Much of West Africa is small, poor and has little going for it. However, Ecobank in Togo is a continent-wide retail bank, growing at 100 branches a year, with a balance sheet of $8 billion in 2009 symbolizing the new pioneering spirit of African businesses, unfazed by a global downturn. As its CEO says, 'if Warren Buffett can be based in Nebraska, then it's not where you are but what you do'.

➡ **Renewable products:** Maximum ideas, minimum stuff – this is more of a way of thinking that recognizes the sustainable impact of everything we buy. Indeed, the value of a product is often inversely related to the amount of pollution it causes. Stop thinking how to make people buy more; start thinking how they can last longer. Bookcrossing encourages book-sharing and Howies have made a retro-virtue out of their 'hand me down' range of clothes.

➡ **Biobanks:** This is a bank not interested in your body, but something far more valuable – your DNA. Biobanks are springing up everywhere to store tissue samples, reproductive cells and blood. Instead of money, these vaults are liquid nitrogen deep freezers. Your materials can be saved for your future use, traded with others, contributed to testing or screened to anticipate future health needs.

➡ **Creative microfunds:** No longer do entrepreneurs need to waste most of their creative energies seeking out rich investors or venture capital funds. Microfunding of the best ideas is often a much faster and more useful way to get started. Ten dollars for a small piece of a cool start-up is much more attractive than anonymous share portfolios, and micro-investors are also a great source of ideas, capabilities and ultimately sales too.

➡ **Eco Intelligence:** More than IQ or EQ, we now need an EcoQ to understand the full impacts of the choices we make. Take a fairtrade, organic cotton T-shirt: what about the 10,000 litres of water required to make it (whilst locals went thirsty), the dye process (and polluting chemicals involved), the transportation costs (carbon not financial), and the local competitors (who have just gone bust)? Complex world, with non-obvious choices.

Whilst these are just a collection of ideas and innovations, plucked at random from around the world, they help you to stretch and they allow you to start imagining a different future for your business – and then thinking how you could apply that to today.

Muhammad Yunus ... Nobel prize-winning social entrepreneur

Muhammad Yunus was an anonymous professor of economics when he first wrote a paper about his vision for 'microcredits'. He envisioned a financial model where small loans were made available to entrepreneurs too poor to qualify for traditional bank loans, but with ideas and ambitions. Inspired by the vision, he soon founded Grameen Bank.

In 2006, Yunus and the bank were jointly awarded the Nobel Peace Prize 'for their efforts to create economic and social development from below'. He is one of the founding members of Global Elders, a network of people brought together by Richard Branson and Peter Gabriel to find better solutions to significant problems.

Yunus's entrepreneurial journey began in 1976 when he visited some of the poorest homes in Jobra, a central district of Bangladesh. He learnt how local women made bamboo furniture, but in order to buy the raw materials they had to take small loans at extortionate rates from local money lenders. They often gave away most of their profits, or ended in debt despite their enterprise. Yunus realized the need for a better way to give local people small loans to help them do business. 'I am a firm believer that all humans are entrepreneurs. Two-thirds of the world's population are not eligible for bank loans. What kind of system is that?' he told a recent gathering of business leaders at the World Economic Forum.

He began to give small loans himself, small amounts of around $25 from his own pocket. With similar loans to 42 Jobra women, they were able to start making a small profit on their furniture, and from that they were able to buy more raw materials and make more furniture – and their profits began to grow.

Whilst traditional banks were not interested in making such small loans available at reasonable interest rates to the poor, believing them to have too much risk, Yunus believed that, over time and with scale he could create a sustainable business model for himself and a means to help thousands of Bangladeshis to find a way out of poverty.

Twenty years later, Grameen Bank had issued more than $6 billion of loans to 7.4 million borrowers and now lends $1 billion-plus every year to small entrepreneurs. To ensure repayment, the bank uses a system of 'solidarity groups' that apply together for loans. Its members act as co-guarantors of repayment and support one another's efforts at economic self-advancement. More than 97% of Grameen loans have gone to women, who suffer dispro-portionately from poverty and who are more likely than men to devote their earnings to their families, and to eventually repay their loans. Before Yunus, only 1% of Bangladeshi bank loans were to women.

Yunus was asked in an interview with *Director* magazine about the secret of his innovation, responding:

> 'It was simple: all we did was look at how conventional banks do it and do the opposite. Conventional banks go to the rich – we go to the poor. Conventional banks ask for collateral, we say forget about collateral. And conventional banks use lawyers, we say forget about lawyers.'

CHAPTER 7

Creativity ... the extraordinary power of ideas

'To see a world in a grain of sand, and a heaven in a wild flower, hold infinity in the palm of your hand and eternity in an hour.'

William Blake

Arthur Koestler, author of *The Art of Creation*, reflects the process of creativity in three characters – the artist, the sage, and the jester:

→ **The artist** represents the traditional view, composing music, writing a novel, acting in a play or drawing a picture.

→ **The sage** represents the scientific or philosophical thinker, most relevant to business, and the inspiration to develop a new idea.

→ **The jester** represents challenging conventions, like the court jester was the only one willing challenge decisions of the king, but through humour and without offence.

All three matter in the business world of creativity.

Until the 1900s, creativity was thought of as a gift, an inherent ability, rather than something that we could all learn and embrace. It was Alex Osborn who made creativity an applied science, and therefore much more useful to business. He believed that people have vast amounts of experience and influence, but are only conscious of a small amount at any time.

He proposed that as a process, creativity was about helping people to access and apply this vast amount of conscious and unconscious knowledge. This also involved delaying our natural inclination to evaluate and dismiss our ideas too quickly, and thereby to suppress our creativity. This is even more the case with others, always ready to judge on ideas prematurely. Holding back enables refinement, and time to rethink.

To overcome this, Osborn created brainstorming: free associations, generated rapidly, without judgement. It was adopted by businesses, academics and consultants everywhere. But it was not enough; it assumes that future success can be found in a list of 50 ideas generated in ten minutes. It needs to go deeper: adapting, combining, rearranging, rearticulating. However, such concepts didn't capture the imagination in the same way, and to this day many businesses brainstorm their list and then go off to make a few of them happen.

Jane Henry defines different views on the sources of creativity in *Making Sense of Creativity*:

➡ **Grace** – out of the blue, something magical, you have it or you don't.

➡ **Accident** – good fortune, serendipity, when you weren't looking for it.

➡ **Association** – lateral thinking, connecting the unconnected.

➡ **Cognitive** – the logical process of observation and understanding.

➡ **Personality** – natural talent that can be developed and focused.

Whilst all of these matter, creativity is ultimately about 'creation' – creating something new.

New ideas

Creativity is a thinking process for discovering new ideas, or new associations between existing ideas, and fuelled by conscious or unconscious insight. It goes beyond ideas themselves, most commonly in art and literature – it is about creation, doing and making something. It can be influenced by a deliberate cognitive process, by environments, by your own personality traits and by chance, accident or serendipity. Some say it is a talent that we are born with, whilst others argue that it can be learned, and enabled with simple techniques. In the business world, it is the front end of innovation, but also fuels every other aspect of work.

Despite (or perhaps because of) the ambiguity and complexity of creativity, entire industries have spawned from the pursuit of creative ideas – ad agencies, design houses, ideas companies. Creativity has been associated with right or forehead brain activity, the side of the brain that sees things more holistically, intuitively and emotionally. However, creativity is best achieved by left *and* right brain thinking, by combining focus and the big picture, analysis and intuition, and logic and emotion.

Fusion

Out of all the creative techniques that you will come across, the one that I found most powerful is the ability to connect two unconnected ideas. Like the Medicis of years gone by, it is about bringing unfamiliar ideas, situations, talents, challenges and solutions together. Consider Ravi Shankar bringing together the music of India and Europe, Paul Klee combining the influences of cubism and primitive art, or Salvador Dali combining scientific perspective with random visualization.

One of the easiest ways to think more creatively in business is to apply existing ideas from outside your market. Look at what is happening in other sectors, countries or companies, and creatively explore how you can apply these to your business. The great thing about these ideas is that they are already tested: they can be produced and people buy them, albeit in a different context. The challenge is to find the relevant 'parallels' and to apply the lessons in new and relevant ways.

The simplest but most provocative questions are ones like 'How could we "do an iPod" in our industry?' This would encourage people to think of the whole business model by which

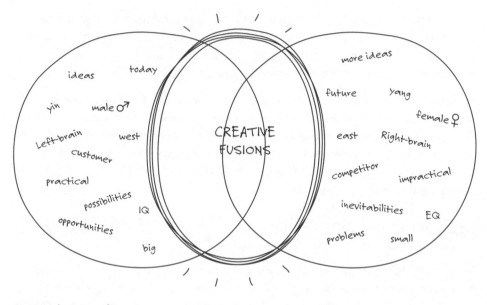

Creative fusions: making new connections is at the heart of creativity

devices, content, distributors and customers work together and make money. It might actually deliver an idea for digitalizing the basic products into components, renegotiating relationships with suppliers for exclusive content and letting customers select and combine them like iTunes, or it might be about creating the most aesthetically pleasing storage and usage device like the iPod itself.

Fusion might also be about more radical crossovers. Whilst it is many years since I studied particle physics, I still use some of the simple ideas in my innovation projects with clients. Understanding atomic structures is a model for thinking differently about how products and services work together. Applying the characteristics of astrophysics gives me a categorization tool for managing portfolios.

Donna Karan ... creative elegance in a chaotic world

Always energetic, sometimes a bundle of creative nerves, Donna Karan has been described as passionate, wild, insane, and sometimes even 'cuckoo'. She typically finishes her brochure notes for her fashion shows with the phrase 'To be continued,' reflecting her conviction that her styles and designs are an ever evolving process, and one that lives far beyond the runway.

She was obsessed with fashion from an early age. Donna Faske, as she started life, grew up in a rough part of New York City, her mother a model and her stepfather a tailor, and selling her first designs at a small store on Central Avenue at the age of 14. She studied at Parson's School of Design and then left to work for Anne Klein, making mid-priced sportswear. Ten years later, and with the support of her husband Steven Weiss, she founded Donna Karan New York.

Launched in 1985, her first collection created a new system of dressing, particularly for those used to Eighties power dressing. She combined elements of tailoring with sportswear to ensure clothes were luxurious and practical, and fitted well. Her clothes had a discrete style, rarely grabbing the headlines at fashion shows, but afterwards they were in high demand. She wanted them to be easy-to-wear in a luxurious blend of cashmeres and lycra, and typically discrete in blues and blacks. In particular, she was credited with introducing 'the body'.

Donna Karan was an innovator in styles, but also in developing derivative labels which were more accessible to more people. DKNY created a business model of bridge lines which generated huge demand for labels influenced by their premium sister brands. DKNY was initially inspired by her daughter, Gaby who wanted something cheaper but just as stylish. The Donna Karan and DKNY labels rapidly diversified into menswear, jeans, accessories, hosiery, fragrance and cosmetics.

In April 2001, she sold Donna Karan International, to the French luxury goods house LVMH for around $250 million. LVMH had already acquired the license-holding company, Gabrielle Studio, meaning that in total she received $643 million. Having moved the company to Italy, Karan quit within five years but remains honorary chairwoman and designer in charge of the Donna Karan brand.

Today the label is overseen by Peter Speliopoulos, a former Cerruti designer, with Karan contributing ideas and tweaks. The DKNY line is looked after by Jane Chung who was with Karan since her early days. Most other items are licensed to partners – for example, Liz Claiborne for DKNY Jeans, Van Heusen for DKNY men's shirts, Esprit for DKNY children's apparel, and Estee Lauder for cosmetics.

At a recent event at her new-age, Japanese-furnished West Village loft space in the heart of Manhattan, she describes to a small audience her approach to creativity and design, and the five principles that have served her well:

→ 'Work where the consumer is' – nothing replaces natural intuition, which stems from being with real people as they look at clothes, try them on, and take the deep plunge to buy.

→ 'Celebrate artistry and creativity' – these are the wellspring of design, and when combined with instinct and passion can turn the most mundane into the most inspired design.

→ 'Look for the void' – the bright shining light, as she describes it, of unmet consumer needs, which can never be found through conventional research – you have to find it yourself.

→ 'Use world cultures' – this is her greatest inspiration, combining ideas from every part of the globe, with a particular fondness for Balinese and Australian cultures.

→ 'Make the difference outside and inside' – she sees a breed of conscious consumers, who see fashion beyond a statement, and instead feel it more personally, and what it does for society too.

Karan remains passionate about fashion, people and style – studying different cultures and disciplines, fascinated by Eastern philosophies on spirituality, and yoga devotee who is consumed by alternative medicines and practices. She set up her Urban Zen foundation which explores the intersection between the complex reality of our busy lives and the simplicity and focus of a more spiritual existence. 'It's about finding the calm in the chaos', she says. It almost describes her signature style too.

CHAPTER 8

Design ... the fusion of function and form

'We have to replace beauty, which is a cultural concept, with goodness, which is a humanist concept.'

Philippe Starck

From coffee pots to high-heeled boots, digital user interfaces to soaring skyscrapers, wallpaper to newspaper, design is all around us. As James Dyson said in Ford's customer magazine, 'good design is about looking at everyday things with new eyes and working out how they can be made better. It is about challenging existing technology.'

As a verb, 'to design' refers to the process of originating and developing a plan for a product, structure, system or component. As a noun, 'a design' is used for either the final solution or the result of implementing that plan – the final product of a design process. It is about function and form, rational and emotional, process and solution.

Designing requires a designer to consider the aesthetic, functional, and many other aspects of an object or a process, which usually requires considerable research, thought, modelling, adjustment and redesign. Tim Brown, CEO of a leading design firm IDEO, promotes the concept of 'design thinking' as an essential discipline for anyone in business. That it is a process applicable to every aspect of business: innovation is essential to differentiation and growth, but design adds the real difference – adding simplicity and elegance, stimulating all the senses.

Historically, design has been treated as a downstream step in the innovation process, argues Brown – the point where designers come along and put a beautiful wrapper around the idea. Whilst this approach has stimulated market growth in many areas by making new products aesthetically attractive, design is much more than the cosmetic finish.

Looking back over recent decades, design has become an increasingly valuable competitive asset in, for example, consumer electronics (remember those first iMacs), cars (the iconic styling of a Porsche 911) and consumer packaged goods (everything from Nike Air to Tetra-Pak's drink cartons). But, in most others, it remained a late-stage add-on. Now, however, Brown believes that rather than asking designers to make an already developed idea more attractive to consumers, companies are asking them to create ideas that better meet consumers' needs and desires. The former role is tactical and results in limited value creation; the latter is strategic and leads to dramatic new forms of value.

Samsung ... innovative design, inspired by the Tae Kuk

'It's our aim to develop innovative technologies and efficient processes that create new markets, enrich people's lives and continue to make Samsung a trusted market leader. Everything we do at Samsung is guided by our mission – to be the best digital e-company', said the company's enigmatic chairman, Kun-Hee Lee, in his annual report.

Samsung – which means 'three stars' in Korean – was founded by Lee's father in 1938 as an exporter of rice, sugar, and fish. Based in Taegu, South Korea, it remained a commodity company well into the 1990s. Its managers cared little about customers and innovation, design or branding.

In the mid-1990s, Samsung revolutionized its business through dedication to making world-class products. The brand changed rapidly in terms of perception from cheap import to premium design, and 17 different products – from semiconductors to computer monitors, LCD screens to colour picture tubes – entered the top five players in terms of category share.

Soon after, Lee started to look around the world for new inspiration. On visiting a downmarket electronics retailer in Los Angeles, Lee found his company's products gathering dust on the store's back shelves, ignored by even the salespeople. US consumers, he realized, regarded the Korean company's goods as cheap, toy-like knockoffs. He asked his design adviser, Tamio Fukuda, to assess the state of Samsung design. Fukuda concluded that Samsung lacked a design identity: its product development process was primitive and its top managers discounted the value of design. Building a 'sustainable design culture' became a priority.

Lee decided on fundamental change. He reduced his workforce by 50,000 and sold off many of Samsung's non-core subsidiaries. To shatter old work habits, he ordered that, henceforth, every Samsung employee must report for work two hours early. He issued a manifesto to his top managers and repeated this in the book, *Change Begins With Me*: 'management is still clinging to the concept of quantity at the expense of quality ... We will become a third-rate company. We must change no matter what.'

Lee's ultimate aim was simple and audacious. To seize the future, Samsung would have to catapult to the uppermost ranks of the world's first-class brand. It would have to become a company whose vast array of digital products not only met people's needs but also captured their imaginations. He demanded that design become a core asset in the company's bid to transform itself. He sent a team of executives to the Art Center College of Design, in Pasadena, California, to work out how to launch an in-house design school back in Korea. It resulted in the $10 million, state-of-the-art Innovative Design Lab situated in the heart of downtown Seoul.

Samsung's in-house school gave its designers the tools and confidence to risk thinking differently. But it still needed an ethos, a distinctive style that wasn't Apple or Nokia. It found it in the *Tae Kuk*, the yin-yang symbol found on the South Korean flag, which represents the simultaneous unity and duality of all things. From there, the brand developed its ethos: 'the balance of reason and feeling', combining simplicity and complexity, technology and humanity.

The result was a 'softer' Samsung – intuitively simple but still embracing the latest technologies. Whilst Apple embraced simplicity and Sony delighted in complexity, Samsung believed in both. Squares became rounded, buttons were decluttered and the Koreans found their new language of innovation and design. Samsung has been calculated over the last five years to be the world's fastest-growing brand, supported by bold and beautiful products. Lee describes its transformation as 'opening itself to the outside world, and looking deep within its Korean heart.'

Samsung has come a long way in a decade. Whilst it is by no means perfect (taking knocks recently for its pricing strategies and tax issues), it now has Apple and Nokia in its sights with an ethos of yin-yang design driving its business. It has a leading share of the world's markets for colour televisions, flash memory and LCD panels. In 2008–9 it delivered $10.3 billion in earnings on $55.3 billion in sales, making it the world's most profitable technology company.

CHAPTER 9

Innovation ... making life better for people

'Great things are not done by impulse, but by a series of things brought together.'

Vincent Van Gogh

Innovators are rarely motivated by the thought of the final product, or even the money and fame that very occasionally come with successful products. Alexander Graham Bell's invention of the telephone transformed the world. Yet he was just a tutor of the deaf, keen to help them succeed. His favourite student was Mabel Hubbard and, as weeks went by, they grew closer. Her mother was not keen on a relationship.

Bell, turning up at Mabel's Nantucket home one rainy night, but it was made clear to him by Mother Hubbard that he was not welcome. He left despondent, but soon resolved to use his technical ingenuity to find a different way to reach Mabel. Whilst the telegraph was not new, lines were singular and expensive. He set about finding a way to jam many distinct signals down one line, instantly revolutionizing the applicability and economics of the phone line.

The multiplex telegraph was born out of a young, Scottish, immigrant boy's love of a Nantucket girl, and the world became a different place because of it.

'Nova' means newness

As Theodore Levitt said, 'creativity is thinking up new things, innovation is doing new things'. Innovation is about making ideas happen – involving incremental or revolutionary changes in thinking, products, processes or organizations. It is the total process, embracing creativity and design as well as the implementation and commercialization of ideas. It is the opening up and closing down process, and can also be used to describe the outcome of that process – the innovation.

Innovation might include invention, which is making an idea real. But to be innovative, the invention must be applied practically and successfully. Innovation is most often applied to areas of significant change. Whilst objects are more significant when described as innovative, the innovation process is often swamped with incremental rather than breakthrough ideas.

The goal of innovation is positive change, to make someone or something better. Innovation leading to increased productivity is the fundamental source of increasing wealth in an economy. In business, innovation seeks to increase value for customers, as well as for business – or, to return to that phrase, to make people's lives better.

Most new ideas fail

However, most new ideas fail. 3M estimates that it needs around 3000 clearly specified ideas, from which emerge around 300 prototypes, from which they get 30 strong concepts, which are eventually whittled down to three market entries, in order to get one successful innovation.

Ideas fail for many reasons. Most common is that they emerge from mediocre beginnings. A quick brainstorm is not enough; creativity takes time. It is an opening-up process requiring stretch and challenge, time to see perspectives, time to think. The acceleration part is the process that makes the great ideas happen. Even the best ideas can fail because:

➔ Leaders are not open to new ideas or changing what they do.

➔ Organizations have too many 'sacred cows' – things nobody wants to change.

➔ Nobody cares about innovation in some companies – it is not tangible.

➔ There are no boundaries to focus on – no urgency, no 'burning platforms' to address.

➔ There is no structure or method – no consistent process has been adopted.

➔ Not enough time is allowed – thinking is seen as a luxury and is not urgent or important.

➔ The organization hasn't thought creatively about how to do it.

➔ They are not seen as a priority – the short-term matters more.

➔ Generating new ideas is seen as another fad – something the textbooks talk about but real companies don't.

Opening up and closing down

The simplest model of innovation is one that makes ideas happen by embracing the disciplines of creativity, design and implementation. It is about opening up the possibilities through creative thinking, exploring the future potentials, generating ideas from many different perspectives, stretching the context and exploring the extremes.

It is then about closing down, focusing in on the best ideas and maybe making connections between them, evaluating them in terms of impact and practicality, understanding how they would work and how they would make money, where best to target them, and what is the

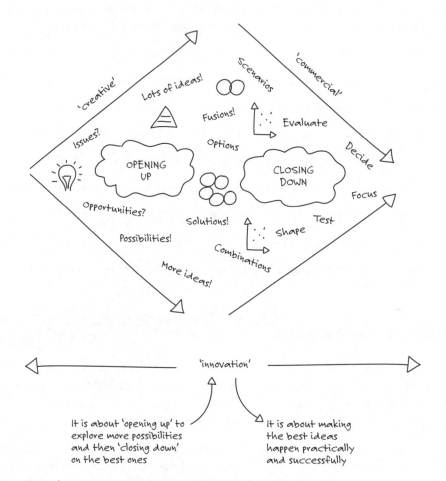

It is about 'opening up' to explore more possibilities and then 'closing down' on the best ones

It is about making the best ideas happen practically and successfully

Innovation makes the best ideas happen profitably, by 'opening up' and 'closing down'

compelling proposition by which they will stand out from a sea of commodity, noise and competition.

In our context of innovating from the future back, opening up is more about the future and how it could be shaped in our vision; closing down is more about working from the future backwards to connect it to now, in the most practical and profitable ways.

Degrees of innovation

Breakthroughs in business are rare, but they are the moments you live for. In 20 years I've experienced a few: flat beds in airlines, phones that do more for you, drinks that entertain you, paper that is about health, cement that is about growth, fertilizer that turns muck into green ...

Innovation can also be applied at many levels, both in terms of its intensity and its scope. The intensity of innovation relates to how ambitious it is – how much time, resource, cost and risk it embraces – and how great the impact we see in the market and bottom line as a result. There are three levels of innovation intensity:

➡ **Incremental:** Innovation as improvement, keeping pace with change and expectation, adapting designs and applications to evolving needs. In the car market we see a new version of the same car emerging frequently, maybe with slightly enhanced features.

➡ **Next generation:** Innovation as change, moving ahead of the competition to define a new level of performance, tapping into emerging needs and exceeding expectations. In the car market, this is a significantly new model, launched every few years, with a new brand name.

➡ **Breakthrough:** Innovation as revolution, changing the rules of the market, challenging the behaviours of customers, maybe redefining the market altogether – 'game-changing'. In the car market, this is the SUV or the hybrid engine creating a new genre or category.

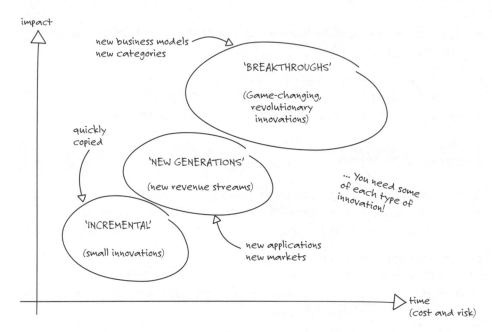

The three levels of innovation – a mixed portfolio of projects balances impact, risk and time

You need a balanced portfolio of innovation projects at each of these levels being developed simultaneously. Incremental innovations keep you in the market, little noticed and quickly imitated; next generations get you ahead for a short time, maybe opening up a new revenue stream. Breakthroughs are what make you famous, shaping your markets: they inspire customers, attract investors and deliver leaps in value creation.

The scope of innovation relates to how you apply innovation: which aspects you should consider, a new product or service that will be delivered by the existing organization, or an entirely new business model that creates value in new ways. There are four types:

➡ **Market innovation:** Creating new sectors and geographies, new audiences within the market, new channels to reach them, new applications for existing products, new propositions to reposition and communicate them, and new experiences to deliver and support them.

➡ **Product innovation:** Creating new products and services, new components within them, new solutions that bring them together in different ways, new fashions and styling to make them more attractive, and new ways to package and deliver them.

➡ **Organizational innovation:** Creating new processes and structures inside the organization, new ways to improve profitability and effectiveness, new partners to collaborate with, new suppliers, new tools and techniques, and new ways of managing and rewarding people.

➡ **Business model innovation:** Creating new ways of doing business, with new revenue and cost streams, new ways of working with customers and partners, and even creating new market models – the ways by which customers buy and use products and services.

Again, it is about balance – considering which levels of innovation are most appropriate to your market, demanded by your customers, acceptable to your stakeholders. Business model innovation can be most disruptive and change the game, but also involves most risk. These four types of innovation also work together, supporting each other for greater advantage and impact.

The world's most innovative companies

Business Week's annual ranking of the world's most innovative companies has become the definitive league table across sectors. It is compiled primarily based on the views of almost 3000 business leaders, and also on financial results (80% weighted on peer perception, 10% on shareholder return and 5% each on revenue and profitability growth).

There is perhaps little surprise in which companies lead the table, with the likes of Apple and Google consistently on top. Rising stars include Amazon, South Korean electronics giant

LG and Chinese electric vehicle maker BYD. Leaders are also asked to say which aspect of innovation they admire the companies for. Increasingly, products are the least common way through which companies achieve significant innovation.

Rank	Company	Focus of innovation	Revenue growth, (%) 2006–9	Profitability growth, (%) 2006–9	Shareholder return, (%) 2006–9
1	Apple	Product	30	29	35
2	Google	Experience	31	2	10
3	Microsoft	Process	10	-4	3
4	IBM	Process	2	11	12
5	Toyota	Process	-11	–	-20
6	Amazon	Experience	29	6	51
7	LG Electronics	Product	16	707	31
8	BYD	Process	42	-1	99
9	GE	Process	-1	-25	-22
10	Sony	Product	-5	–	-19
11	Samsung	Product	17	-9	10
12	Intel	Product	0	12	3
13	Ford	Process	-12	–	10
14	RIM	Experience	75	-6	17
15	Volkswagen	Business model	0	14	8
16	HP	Process	8	9	9
17	Tata Group	Business model	–	–	–
18	BMW	Experience	0	–	-8
19	Coca Cola	Experience	9	1	9
20	Nintendo	Experience	22	3	-8

Source: Business Week, 2010

James Dyson ... 'dual cyclone' inspired by running up sand dunes

As a teenage runner, James Dyson became a fan of Australian Herb Elliott, the 1960 Olympic 1500 metre champion, and his coach Percy Cerutty, who was famous for his training on sand dunes. Compared to roads and tracks, the beach was more fun, freer and built up more strength and endurance. As Dyson reflected in an interview with *Runner's World*, 'interacting with nature seemed to be what running was about. I latched onto that.'

From this came a wild side, a love of nature, and a relentless determination to do things different and better ... and sand spilling out his shoes when he arrived home, for which he needed a better vacuum cleaner.

Most vacuum cleaners still used bags or filters, which clog and lose their suction. After 15 years of tinkering and 5126 prototypes, Dyson famously developed a bagless, 'dual cyclone' vacuum – the first that doesn't lose suction. Inspired by the cyclone technology he'd first spotted on a sawmill work, he ripped the dusty clogged bag from his old vacuum and replaced it with a prototype that he slowly evolved to perfection. It was quirky but also stylish – function and form at its best – and can even be found in most museums of modern art as well as in many homes around the world.

Dyson studied architecture at the Byam Shaw School (now Central Saint Martins College of Art and Design), specialized in furniture and interior design at the Royal College of Art, and then focused on marine engineering. His first invention was named the 'Sea Truck', launched in 1970 while he was at the Royal College of Art. The wheelbarrow hadn't changed for 2000 years, but Dyson designed a smooth-edged plastic bin that, unlike the normal metal bin, didn't rust or cause damage. He replaced the wheel with a ball that gave it stability and stopped it sinking into soft ground. He called it the 'Ballbarrow'. But then things went wrong. He assigned the patent to a partner company who would make and market it. Although a shareholder, he soon found himself diluted by frequent cash calls as the business sought to grow. Eventually he was overruled by other shareholders who wanted to sell his invention, and the business was no more.

Out of frustration he was slowly learning from mistakes and to take risks, whilst his passion to create a successful invention fuelled his creativity both technically and commercially. The bagless cleaner took another five years to develop.

By 1985, Dyson had perfected the 'G-Force', a bagless upright cleaner that used a spinning technology to better keep its suction constant. However, no manufacturer or distributor was prepared to launch it in the UK, feeling that it threatened the current, profitable market. Instead he launched it in Japan through a catalogue channel. It was bright pink and sold for $3500; it also won the 1991 International Design Fair prize in Japan. At the same time, his designs began to be imitated by competitors – including Hoover, who he sued for $5 million in damages. He had learnt the importance of protecting his ideas.

In 1993 he opened his research centre and factory in Malmesbury, Wiltshire, and launched 'the Dyson' in the UK market. Interestingly it was the 'say goodbye to the bag' advertising strapline that proved much more appealing to consumers than an emphasis on technical performance, such as greater suction. The product became the fastest selling vacuum cleaner ever to be made in the UK, outselling many of those established brands that previously had rejected his idea, and by 2005 became the market leader in the US based on value.

He continued to work on his vacuum designs. New models emerged with more suction. He achieved this by adding a smaller diameter cyclone to give greater centrifugal force, which allowed 45% more suction than a dual cyclone and removing more dust by dividing the air into eight smaller cyclones, calling it the 'root cyclone'. He even made use of one of his original ideas, adding a wheel ball from his Ballbarrow concept into a vacuum cleaner, creating the 'Dyson Ball', enabling more movement and suction.

Looking beyond cleaning, he expanded his appliance range to include a washing machine. Called the ContraRotator, it had two rotating drums that moved in opposite directions and came in his usual bright colours. Whilst claiming it washed better and saved water, the invention did not take off and was quietly discontinued. In 2006 he launched an ultra-fast hand dryer called the Airblade, which produced an air stream flowing at 400 mph through a 0.3 millimetre gap, whipping moisture from hands. It claimed to dry hands 87% more effectively than other dryers and was soon a hit.

Most recently, he has been lauded for his fan without blades, known as the Air Multiplier. Without any visible movement, and no blades or motors, it draws in air and amplifies it 15 times. It took four years to develop – much faster than with previous designs because much of it was prototyped using computer simulations – and was recently launched to great acclaim.

'Anyone developing new products needs one characteristic above all else. Hope.' said Dyson in an interview with *The Daily Telegraph*. 'This comes down to having high expectations that you will succeed despite any setbacks, having the sense to break down an imposing task into smaller, manageable ones; and believing that you are able to achieve your goals'.

Remembering back to his days running up those Welsh sand dunes, he believes innovators need to be 'dogged and determined', and never afraid to be different.

CHAPTER 10

Creative genius ... welcome to 'the Genius Lab'

'The test of a first-rate intelligence is the ability to hold two opposed ideas in the mind at the same time, and still retain the ability to function.'

F. Scott Fitzgerald

Genius is expressed in many different forms. It may show itself in early childhood as a prodigy or later in life by natural talent or by hard work. Either way, geniuses eventually differentiate themselves from the others through great originality: they often have crisp, clear visions of situations in which interpretation is unnecessary, and they build or act on the basis of those facts, usually with tremendous energy.

Inspiration and perspiration

Thomas Edison famously remarked that 'genius is 1% inspiration and 99% perspiration'. To illustrate this, consider these outputs:

➡ Shakespeare penned 154 sonnets.

➡ Bach wrote a cantata every week of his adult life.

➡ Mozart produced more than 600 pieces of music.

➡ Einstein published 248 other papers in addition to his first and most famous.

➡ Darwin wrote 119 other publications beyond his theory of evolution.

➡ Maslow produced 165 papers, despite only being remembered for a triangle.

➡ Rembrandt created 650 paintings.

➡ Edison filed 1093 patents for inventions.

➡ Picasso delivered an incredible 20,000 pieces of art.

Not all of these were great, but were maybe part of their greatness.

Research collated by Malcolm Gladwell in *Outliers* illustrates just how much sweat and toil it actually takes. Studies of top sportsmen, musicians and chess players show that it takes someone around 10,000 hours of lifetime practice to reach the top in their chosen discipline. Talent and lick are important, but it is practice that makes the difference between being good and being brilliant, argues the research. Gladwell describes practice as the key to The Beatles' success, pointing to their early career when they would play eight hours a night, seven days a week while in Hamburg. By the time they hit the big time, they had performed live an estimated 1200 times – more than most modern bands play in their careers.

Welcome to 'the Genius Lab'

No book can promise to make you a 'creative genius'. However, the rest of this book gives you the building blocks and offers a sprinkling of inspiration to do significant, maybe even remarkable things. Whilst creativity, design and innovation are the practical disciplines, it is really about problem-solving, positive change personally and in business, and making people's lives better. Over the last 20 years I have worked with many organizations, addressing challenges both obvious and abstract. Some have long, complicated processes for innovation; for many others, there is little structure. Innovation isn't part of their business – it rarely has a dedicated manager or resource – yet companies are unanimous in recognizing innovation as essential to their future.

The best ideas are usually already inside a business – inside the heads of people who know their markets best, inside the many documents and databases which sit unexploited, and maybe inside the heads of their customers and partners too. The problem is how to unlock them in a fast and effective way.

'The Genius Lab' is an approach to accelerated innovation. The approach has three phases that bring together established (and some new) processes and activities for accelerating your ideas into practical action. Much of it can be done in-house, bringing together the right teams and disciplines from across your business, but it works best with a little added structure, facilitation and stimulus.

Over those two decades I have worked on all kinds of innovation challenges. What have I learnt? That innovation needs leadership and a cross-functional team that is committed to doing something significant. It needs energy and pace to cut through the organizational treacle, and it needs a clear and simple structure so that people know what's happening and where they are going. I have also learnt that most companies spend too much time on research and too little thinking about the insights and using them. They struggle to think bigger, from the future back or outside in. They lack the confidence to turn the big ideas into actionable projects and are often too scared to even propose them. And they fail to engage the decision-makers until the last moment, when it comes as something of a surprise, which is usually compromised or halted.

Innovation needs a guiding hand to give it direction and momentum, space to explore and create, and structure to focus on the best ideas and practical actions. Small improvements always help, but it's ultimately about doing extra-ordinary things (yes, anything but ordinary) in extra-ordinary ways.

The three phases of the Genius Lab define the rest of this book: the ideas factory, the design studio and the impact zone. It's a simple process but with much underneath, taking ideas from the future back, as well as the inside out and outside in, using left- and right-brain approaches, creativity and innovation to make the best ideas happen 'now forward' and deliver extraordinary results.

| THE IDEAS FACTORY | THE DESIGN STUDIO | THE IMPACT ZONE |

The three phases of the Genius Lab to achieve more significant, accelerated and successful innovation

Phase 1: The ideas factory

This is about insights and ideas – from the future, in partnerships with customers and experts, and our own imagination – from which we develop understanding and inspiration, direction and hypotheses.

We explore the possibilities, based on future scenarios, customer immersion, parallel worlds, emerging trends and creative ideas. Insights emerge out of the collation of knowledge from different perspectives – 'flashes of inspiration' or 'penetrating discoveries' – that are then fused with creative thinking.

Insights are much more than information, and create new platforms from which to generate stronger ideas. Ideas are much more than actions, but concepts for making life better. By understanding the problem or opportunity better, we have more chance of creating success-ful solutions. By focusing on real insights, we develop better ideas that are distinctive and powerful.

Phase 2: The design studio

This is about creativity and design, shaping the best ideas into more concepts that are com-pelling, practical and profitable – articulating, testing and evaluating each of the best con-cepts.

We work at the best ideas and hypotheses, reframing the context in which they are posi-tioned, fusing ideas together into richer molecular structures, considering the function and form of these bigger ideas, enhancing their practical usability and aesthetic appeal.

Concepts work beyond products and services. They emerge as propositions, solutions and experiences, perhaps requiring new business and market models. It is then about evaluating each of the best concepts for their value potential for customers and business, how they will make people's lives better, and how we can make them happen distinctively and profitably.

Phase 3: The impact zone

This is about development and commercialization: making the ideas happen, launching them into the right markets, making them contagious and sticky, and ensuring they deliver sus-tained results.

We focus creatively on the opportunities that will deliver the most return and the best markets, customers and solutions. Don't try to do everything for everyone; do things that are significantly different and better. And we don't stop at market entry – that is the starting point for bringing ideas to life, changing people's attitudes and encouraging new behaviours.

Delivering sustained results is about finding space in the market that you can make your own, defend and grow. That is achieved by telling your story in ways that are compelling and contagious, and shaping markets in your own mind rather than being a slave to somebody else's vision, stretching and evolving ideas so that can have even more impact, and staying a step or two ahead.

Steve Jobs ... the reality distortion field

In today's world of innovation there is nobody more inspiring than Steve Jobs.

He has not only redefined the world of technology but the music and entertainment industries too. From the early days of Apple's Macintosh to Pixar blockbusters such as *Toy Story 3*, and back to the 'i' world of Apple, he is a revolutionary, intelligently making sense of markets, and applying technologies to existing and emerging consumer needs.

Jobs grew up in the Californian apricot orchards that later became known as Silicon Valley at a time when technological innovation and psychedelic music were competing local influences. He studied physics and literature but dropped out to found Apple Computer with his friend Steve Wozniak in 1976, based in his parents' garage and financed by the sale of his VW campervan. By the age of 23 he was worth more than $1 million; more than $10 million by 24; $100 million by 25 ... and now a billionaire many times over.

He grew the business by focusing on niche markets, charging a premium for his novel products. However, 1985 saw him lose out in a power struggle with John Sculley as Apple began to crumble under the competitive might of Microsoft. This led him to Pixar Animation Studios, which has since created some of the most successful and loved animated films since the early days of Walt Disney.

Apple was struggling, and turned to Jobs in 1997 to come back. He was uncertain that the business could survive, recognized that the computing world was changing quickly. In the same way that Pixar had transformed movies, the likes of Dell had disrupted the computing world. But Jobs saw the future of technology differently from others. He realized that technology needed to learn something more from Pixar – how to connect with people emotionally, and to have a story that endures over time.

He re-kindled his passion for well-designed computers, this time with open systems, and the launch of his funky coloured iMacs – blueberry and tangerine instead of plastic grey. People loved them and they became the icon of a new generation of individuals and businesses. He kept working on every aspect of design: launching the Mac OS X user interface in 2000, he told *Fortune* magazine that 'we made the buttons on the screen look so good you'll want to lick them'. He focused relentlessly on innovation and marketing, outthinking rather than outspending his peers. 'Innovation has nothing to do with how many R&D dollars you have. When Apple came up with the Mac, IBM was spending at least 100 times more R&D. It's not about money. It's about the people you have, how you're led, and how much get it,' he added in the *Fortune* interview.

More significantly, Jobs recognized that the music industry was in desperate need of innovation. In 2001 the iPod was born, with the staggering ability to hold 1000 songs. iTunes closely followed – the real innovation, since its transformed the way people buy music and therefore changed every other aspect of the industry. New iPod releases were ever smaller but more powerful.

Pixar became part of Disney in 2006, in return for $7.5 billion, making Job's Disney's largest shareholder, and taking a seat on the board. And a year later came the iPhone, a sensation that threatens to transform the communication world not least through its open platform for apps. The MacBook Air brought the magic back to computing in 2008 and then came the iPad, heralding the tablet computing revolution of 2010.

Jobs takes a deeply personal approach to business. He is also a phenomenal communicator, the master of the message, rehearsing for hours to perfect every line that he will speak in public. Yet Jobs is a business superstar, voted by *Fortune* at the end of 2009 as 'CEO of the Decade'. Bringing together his contributions to Apple, Pixar, Disney and others, *Fortune* estimated that he has created more than $150 billion in shareholder wealth.

He has become the dominant personality in four different industries, transforming the world of music, movies, communications and computing. He is admired by his leadership peers across the world, and by many more of us who use his products, and he leads the most awe-inspiring, creative, and arrogant team of innovators around.

We know little about what makes Jobs tick, but perhaps the best insight came in his 2005 Commencement Address at Stanford University, which can be viewed and read online. In it he encourages his audience to believe in themselves, to grasp every opportunity, just like he does:

> 'Your time is limited, so don't waste it living someone else's life. Don't be trapped by dogma ... living with the *results* of other people's thinking. Don't let the noise of other's opinions drown out your own inner voice. And most important, have the courage to follow your heart and intuition.'

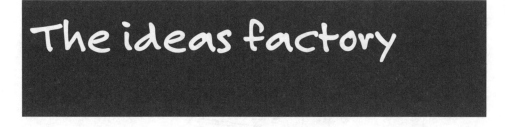

The ideas factory

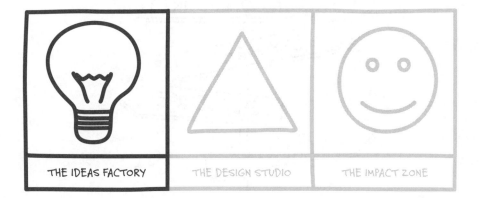

THE IDEAS FACTORY

THE DESIGN STUDIO

THE IMPACT ZONE

CHAPTER 11

Getting started ... the fuzzy front-end of innovation

'You can't solve a problem with the same thinking that created it.'

Albert Einstein

It is easy to rush into innovation, driven by the pursuit of 'time to market', harnessing the energy created by an initial idea, and seeking to see the new revenue streams as soon as possible. But speed is not always the priority. It's important to start running in the right direction, even if you are not yet sure where it will take you. Having an initial sense of the business objectives – the problem to solve, the possible scope of the solution and any parameters to work within – are all important starting points.

Guy Claxton's *Hare Brain, Tortoise Mind* explores the way people respond to situations:

➡ **very fast** – instinctive and intuitive;

➡ **fast** – driven for logic and speed, or as Claxton calls it, the 'hare brain'; and

➡ **slow** – immersive and thoughtful, this time labelled as the 'tortoise mind'.

Instinct is spontaneous and immediate, without deliberate consideration. However, our default is our 'hare brain' mode. It is conscious, deliberate, purposeful and clear, about solutions not questions and solution-finding, and the one we prefer to use in business.

However, this default mode is less effective when the problem is complex or not obvious. Claxton suggests that a slower and more thoughtful third mode of thinking is required, particularly at the start of a new project. It is as much about understanding the problem or the question, than seeking a quick solution. He calls it 'slow thinking', where there is more time to explore and reflect on the problem, develop new insights and hypothesize, and let new thoughts sink in.

Innovation is so often about speed that it is easy to miss the real problem that the product or service is seeking to solve. The 'hare brained' pursuit of time can increase the chance of incrementalism and imitation, relying on existing habits and knowledge, whereas taking a few pauses to reflect can lead to more considered and more remarkable outcomes.

Fuzziness

The 'fuzzy front end' is the messy 'getting started' part of innovation, where everything is a little unclear. It takes time – useful time – to get, and feel, oriented. It is where the problem and even potential solutions become clear, and where stakeholders become engaged in a way that is not possible near the end, particularly at a point when you are asking for implementation budget. It is the phase between developing limitless ideas and when design and development really take hold.

It can also consume significant time – maybe as much as 50% of the development time – but it is still an essential part of the process. Whilst the fashion is to reduce time to market by shrinking development time, it is still better to have some fuzzy time to reflect on what you are trying to do, build the right team, get decision-makers brought in and ensure you are heading in the right direction.

Problem-solving

Understanding the problem is a useful starting point. However, it is often said that 90% of the problem is defining what the problem is. Indeed it is all too easy to start creative problem-solving or even solution development without fully thinking through what the issue or objective really is. We rush to develop ideas without really understanding why, and can end up with imperfect solutions, failure or making the situation worse.

In journalism, the 'Five Ws' – which are actually five Ws and one H, and therefore sometimes called 'Six Ws' – is a concept in research and reporting that is regarded as the essential blueprint for information gathering. It is a formula for getting the 'full' story. In order for a report to be considered complete it must answer these six questions:

➡ **Who** was involved?

➡ **What** happened? (What's the story?)

➡ **When** did it take place?

➡ **Where** did it take place?

➡ **Why** did it happen?

➡ **How** did it happen?

Each question should produce a factual answer and, importantly, none can be answered with a simple 'yes' or 'no'. Editors would expect reporters to include the Five Ws in their 'lead', or the first two or three paragraphs of the story, after which more detail follows.

Napkin diagrams

The history of business is littered with crumpled white napkins with black ink jottings that evolve into new businesses and some of the best innovations. Just like Leonardo da Vinci's, they are informal and often unfinished. So why napkins? Why not a decent piece of paper or maybe a PowerPoint presentation?

You are rarely in your office, sitting alone at your desk, or deliberately seeking to be creative, when the best ideas emerge. Dinner gives you time to reflect, talk and listen. You are with somebody else, the food tastes good, and a great glass of Tempranillo is relaxing and inspiring. The ideas just begin to flow, your confidence builds and everything is possible. It is spontaneous rather than planned – it can't be scheduled or postponed. Pictures work better than words in describing new ideas and engaging people by building the picture up in stages.

And the best ideas are often simple enough to fit on the back of a napkin.

Philippe Starck ... enfant terrible of design

Philippe Starck is the *'grand fromage'* of contemporary design. From architecture to furniture, utensils to fashion, Starck puts his mark on around 100 products every year. 'Everyone should be pondering, asking themselves questions about life, money, desire, war, themselves,' he suggests in his blog at starck.com.

The son of an aircraft designer, Starck inherited his father's love of technology and spent his childhood underneath his father's drawing boards, playing with paper and glue, taking anything to pieces and rebuilding it: remaking the world around him. After dropping out of school, he founded his design firm in 1968. After a brief role as art director with Pierre Cardin, he moved on to independent interior and product design. He started by redesigning two Parisian nightclubs – which caught the eye of President Francois Mitterand, who asked him to refurbish the Elysée Palace in 1982.

This led to the spectacular interior design of the Café Costes in Paris, which acted as a prototype for the Paramount Hotel in New York, the Manin restaurant in Tokyo and the Felix restaurant in Hong Kong. Yet some of his most inspiring designs are everyday objects: the long spider-legged juice squeezer for Alessi and the witty Louis Ghost polycarbon chair. His designs are now everywhere, partnering with brands in every sector. Wake up to his alarm clock, use his Target toothbrush, wear his space-age Puma boots and Fossil wristwatches, carry his Samsonite luggage, work with his Microsoft mouse, dine at Asia de Cuba restaurant, drink the stylish bottled beer from Kronenburg 1664, or go to work in his office blocks like the Asahi Building in Tokyo.

With Pramac, an energy company, he designed windmills that also function as wind instruments. 'Ecology is not just an urgency of the economy and protection of our world, but also creativity and elegance,' he explained to *The New York Times*. He has also created a personal power-generating windmill in polymer and wood that costs around $600. It is, typically, a beautiful yet functional design, claiming to generate up to 60% of a home's energy needs.

Starck champions creativity with purpose, art that is practical and insight that is innovative. His collaborations turn average products into practical and essential objects of desire, and can easily triple the profit margins of the brands he works with. Much of his early work was more akin to fashion and novelty, whereas he has now moved on to more serious design and pieces of timeless value. His success has been built on his ability to translate his sometimes prophetic insight into social and cultural changes in society into objects, spaces and buildings. Unlike most modern designers, Starck's work does not focus on single, provocative and expensive pieces. He prefers his designs to be functional, affordable and mass-produced household items.

Starck inspires us with his striking reinterpretations of the world around us. He is subversive, intelligent and always interesting – an *enfant terrible* in his head, and court jester with others. He thinks without boundary, rejecting our conventions and challenging our tolerance, creating objects that are good and beautiful.

CHAPTER 12

Seeing things differently ... ideas, imagination and intuition

'The real act of discovery consists not in finding new lands, but in seeing with new eyes.'

Marcel Proust

Da Vinci believed that to understand a problem you had to restructure it. Your initial view is probably too conventional, full of prejudice and assumption. With each additional view he understood more, and moved toward the essence of the problem, and a better solution. He called this approach '*saper vedere*' – 'knowing how to see'.

Innovation requires new perspectives: seeing things differently, thinking different things and finding new insights, better ideas and the best opportunities. Whilst the future offers most stretch forwards, there are many other perspectives or 'worldviews' worth considering – both separately and then collectively – considering the viewpoints of customers, businesses, competitors, parallel markets, technology, responsibility, finance and the future.

Having clearly defined an issue or opportunity – an emerging customer need, declining share in key markets, a new technological application, a convergence of markets, an underperforming distribution channel or the need for a new style of service – then consider the possible ways of addressing from the different perspectives. What would Virgin do? What would customers love? What would Einstein have done? What might it look like in the future? What new technologies could help?

The eight 'worldviews' to help us see problems and opportunities in broader, richer and new perspectives are as follows:

➡ **Future world:** Future scenarios based on emerging trends, pattern recognition and random possibilities that might be driven from science or sci-fi.

➡ **Customer world:** The needs and wants of diverse individuals, their experience of you and your competitors, their frustrations and aspirations, trust and loyalty.

➡ **Business world:** The drivers of business performance, key issues and opportunities, assets and capabilities, assumptions and employee ideas.

➡ **Competitor world:** The strengths and weaknesses, postures and differences, strategies and potential actions of direct and indirect competitors.

➡ **Parallel world:** How companies in different markets address (or have addressed) similar issues; who won and who lost, and what did they do; and even extreme situations.

➡ **Technological world:** The emerging fields such as networking technologies, computing, mobile technologies, artificial intelligence, biotech and nanotech.

➡ **Responsible world:** The increasingly vital issues of environment, ethical practices, fair trading, human rights, local communities, well-being and transparency.

➡ **Commercial world:** The consequences of changing price, costs, profits, market share and the wider implications of changing regulation, governance and competition.

These perspectives provide a wealth of discontinuous and complementary insights. They can also be fused with existing knowledge: customer behaviour, market research, employee surveys, boardroom thinking, business performance, industry reports, technological insights, analyst reports and catalytic thinkers.

Collectively, they synthesize to provide the basis for rich insights:

➡ new viewpoints about the future;

➡ patterns that start to reoccur across the different perspectives, synthesized into scenarios for what it might be like;

➡ identifying the trends that will be most influential; and

➡ business value drivers that will be key to turn innovations into commercial performance.

Imagination

Albert Einstein said that 'imagination ... is more important than knowledge. Knowledge is limited. Imagination encircles the world.' Imagination forms new images in our minds that have not been previously experienced, or at least only partially or in different combinations. It is free from objective restraints.

The same limitations beset imagination in creating a hypothesis. Progress in scientific research is due largely to provisional explanations that are constructed by imagination, but such hypotheses must be framed in relation to previously ascertained facts and in accordance with the principles of the particular science.

The world as we experience it is an interpretation of all our senses, perceived as real compared to our thoughts and imagination. Some cultures and traditions view the real world as an illusion of the mind, as with the Buddhist *maya*. Others go to the opposite extreme and see dreams as important as reality, as do the Australian Aborigines with their concept of dreamtime.

Getting out there

Don't forget Leonardo da Vinci and the power of just 'getting out there'. Imagine two managers with similar backgrounds and experience being given one week to come up with a new solution to address a market opportunity. Imagine that one would work alone, sit at their desk, analysing the issues and thinking through optional solutions. The other manager would get up and out by doing the following:

→ Writing down the question and then continually challenging it. Why, who, how ... what is the real problem? What are the issues and opportunities behind it?

→ Talking with many different people: maybe an engineer, designer, retailer, single mum ... and some *really* different people, like a musician or a librarian.

→ Visiting other businesses, particularly start-ups, in related but different sectors, chatting to people and understanding how they approach similar challenges.

→ Going shopping to find similar but different products, observing how they are promoted, who buys them and what they are like.

→ Drawing pictures of emerging ideas and getting a colleague to build a very simple prototype that they show to people, who get interested and add more ideas.

Who do you think would develop the more creative and practical ideas?

Tim Berners-Lee ... weaving the World Wide Web

'If you think about it, it doesn't need the //. I could have designed it not to have the //.'

That was Sir Tim Berners-Lee, creator of the World Wide Web, confessing that the two forward slashes in Web addresses were unnecessary. Compared to the impact of his innovation, most people will forgive him for his slight over-complication. The man and his machine changed our world.

Berners-Lee began his work in 1989 at CERN, Europe's particle-physics laboratory on the French–Swiss border. The Internet was just beginning to emerge as a commercially available service, but lacked standardized systems for formatting, storing, locating and retrieving information. Berners-Lee solved these problems by creating a new computer language – the hypertext transfer protocol (HTTP) – for communicating documents over the Internet and designing a system to give documents addresses. He also created the first browser, calling it the WorldWideWeb – as well as another language, hypertext markup language (HTML), for creating Web pages and the first server software allowing those pages to be stored and accessed by others.

Unlike so many of the innovations that have moved the world, this one truly was the work of one man. Thomas Edison got credit for the light bulb, but he had dozens of people in his lab working on it. William Shockley may have fathered the transistor, but two of his research scientists actually built it. And if there ever was a thing that was made by committee, the Internet – with its protocols and packet switching – is it. But the World Wide Web is Berners-Lee's alone: he designed it and has, more than anyone else, fought to keep it open, non-proprietary and free.

While he was an independent contractor at CERN in 1980, Berners-Lee proposed a project based on the concept of hypertext, to facilitate sharing and updating information among researchers. While there, he built a prototype system named Enquire. He left when his project ended, returning to work in England as a software engineer. In 1984 he returned to CERN, which had the largest Internet node in Europe, and Berners-Lee saw an opportunity to join hypertext with the Internet. 'I just had to take the hypertext idea and connect it to the transmission control protocol and domain name system ideas and – ta-da! – the World Wide Web,' he recounts on w3.org.

The world's first website went live in late 1991 at the address info.cern.ch and contained pages describing Berners-Lee's project. Visitors could learn more about hypertext, technical details for creating their own webpage, and even an explanation on how to search the Web for information, updated daily but with no graphics. However, his vision was:

➡ **detailed** in how the languages and interfaces would all work together; and

➡ **stretching** in that much of what he initially suggested has still not happened – such as the 'semantic web', which begins to take on an intelligence of its own.

In 1994, Berners-Lee founded the World Wide Web Consortium (W3C) at MIT. It brought together various companies that were willing to create standards and recommendations to improve the quality of the Web. He made his idea freely available, with no patent and no royalties due. W3C decided that its standards should be based on royalty-free technology so that they could easily be adopted by anyone – an attitude that proved incredibly successful.

In November 2009, Berners-Lee launched the World Wide Web Foundation in order to 'advance the Web to empower humanity' and promoting more inspired use of digital resources by everyone to make their lives better.

CHAPTER 13

Patterns and paradoxes ... making sense of uncertain futures

'The future is already here, it's just unevenly distributed.'

William Gibson

The future is uncertain and unpredictable.

Speed and complexity add to this challenge – complexity because there are more variables and few straight lines; global economies and mind-boggling technologies can shape our futures in unimaginable ways. Speed because of the pace of change, relentless innovation and a perception that the future is coming at us faster than ever.

At the same time, history is littered with the remnants of organizations that failed to think ahead:

➡ In the 1970s IBM stumbled by letting others take the lead in microcomputing, blinkered by its leadership heritage in mainframes.

➡ In the 1980s the CIA failed to see the weakness of the Soviet economy and the imminent collapse of the USSR.

➡ In the 1990s Microsoft dismissed a new invention, the Internet, as a passing trend, letting small but more visionary rivals get ahead.

So how do we make sense of this world? How can we plan amidst such uncertainty?

The future has not been decided. We influence it by the decisions we make every day, and we shape our destiny within it. And given that it is unlikely to be like today, then our current world is insufficient evidence to anticipate a future world.

Pattern recognition

Our mind tends to recognize patterns without us being consciously aware of them. There-fore, it is important to develop skills in recognizing patterns, keeping an open mind, making sense of complexity or using hypothesis rather than assumption. Leaving behind our exist-ing beliefs, assumptions and prejudices is one of the hardest challenges in developing new insights.

Largely invisible to our everyday lives, often in the margins rather than in the mainstreams, patterns hint at our future. They are the forces that are shaping the more observed changes – trends, fashions and fads – and being shaped by how these collide, and how we respond. They are the behaviours of people who reject social norms.

We see all different kinds of patterns in our markets and social behaviour, largely short-term ones, but still important in helping us to see more invisible directions:

➡ Trends are ideas that evolve: a line of development and change that is enduring.

➡ Fashions are ideas that have a place in time and are usually part of a trend, but are associated with a certain moment and a particular style.

➡ Fads are ideas are embraced by a small audience, followed with extreme interest, and rarely part of a longer-term trend.

➡ Crazes are ideas that catch on incredibly quickly, spreading through groups and then go as quickly as they came, not part of a trend.

In business we live for the short-term too. Driven by short-term incentives or unable to take a longer view, we rarely look beyond a few years. Even strategic planning is reduced to one- to three-year horizons. But sometimes we need to look further, which is traditionally done in pharmaceutical R&D, developing new technology platforms or exploring new partners or markets. In every sector, future thinking is becoming more important.

Paradoxes

Perhaps the most interesting places to look for newness is where there is currently ambiguity. The inability to make two choices at the same time leads to frustration and demand. Where once we saw alternatives, we now want both. We want to be youthful and experienced at the same time. We want to speed things up, but also slow down. How could you resolve these paradoxes?

⇒ **Global and local:** Able to reach new markets, but human and relevant too.

⇒ **Connected and unconnected:** Phones are always on, but we like to switch off.

⇒ **Young and old:** Today's youth gets the new world, but experience still matters.

⇒ **Organizations and individuals:** The best people are rarely in the big companies.

⇒ **Real and virtual:** Building genuine relationships whilst living in social networks.

⇒ **Transparency and responsibility:** Putting your life online whilst seeking privacy.

⇒ **Activists and pessimists:** Some who care about the world, others who accept it.

⇒ **New media and old media:** The future is digital but we still need and like real things.

⇒ **Innovation and imitation:** the more ideas are copied, the more we need innovation.

Paradoxes are often the most fertile ground – the best whitespaces – for innovation. Brands have largely resolved the paradox of quality and price now, and so people pay for other factors. Consider how you could let people have the best of both worlds in whatever you do.

Futurology

Futurology is the science and art of proposing the future or, more correctly, alternative futures. Rather than choosing one, where the probability is that it won't happen, futurists explore possible and preferable futures, focusing on the drivers and events that make them more likely, and the consequences, risks and opportunities if they do happen.

Futurology does not generally include the work of economists who forecast movements of interest rates over the next business cycle, or of managers or investors with short-term time horizons. Most strategic planning, which develops operational plans for preferred futures with time horizons of one to three years, is also not considered futures. But plans and strategies with longer time horizons that specifically attempt to anticipate and be robust to possible future events are part of a major sub-discipline of futures studies called strategic foresight.

Strategic foresight seeks to understand what is likely to continue, what is likely to change and what will be new. It involves a systematic, pattern-based understanding of past and present to determine the likelihood of future events and trends. A key part of this process is understanding the potential future impact of decisions made by individuals, organizations and governments, and thereby to support more effective decision-making.

Three factors usually distinguish futurology from other kinds of research. First, futures studies often examine not only possible but also probable, preferable, and 'wild card' futures. Second, they attempt to build a holistic, system-based view based on insights from many different sources. Third, they challenge the assumptions behind existing views of the future.

The futurists

We would all love to be able to see the future. Will she marry me? What will happen to house prices? How will I die? The urge goes back to the oracle in the temple at Delphi, to Nostradamus staring into the flames and uttering his gnomic predictions, and to the Victorians attempting contact with the afterlife through a séance or a Ouija board.

But where the Romans consulted the entrails of slaughtered bulls, futurists depend on a different set of interconnected systems – fringe newsletters, trendspotter networks, extreme users and enlightened thinking about the world around us.

It would be easy to dismiss them as new-age palm readers, astrologers and tea-leaf gazers, yet they are more than researchers – part social anthropologist, part business consultant. Unlike conventional advisors, they focus on a longer time-truth, consideration of a greater range of alternatives and a willingness to think out of the box. They bring together fact and fiction, and become expert storytellers.

They are also in high demand: companies such as Nokia. P&G and Philips invest considerable resources in future thinking. The UK government has set up a 'horizon scanning' centre as part of its Foresight project, and the city of Bilbao plotted a route out of economic disintegration by envisioning a future around 'cultural centrality' out of which a new underground railway and the Guggenheim emerged.

Futurists are a rare breed of pseudo-researcher-scientists who seek to make sense of the possible futures and their implications for business and society. They typically have three strategies through which they develop their futures:

➡ **Deeper immersion** in the world around them, looking for the patterns that might go unnoticed amidst short-term fads or trends that are largely invisible in our daily lives.

➡ **Scenario building,** where they develop a number of optional futures, based on different causes and effects that might be diverse and seemingly unconnected.

➡ **Vision sharing,** articulating the story in relevant and practical ways, often using stories to explain big ideas, whilst also highlighting key drivers and impacts.

But, as futurist Richard Watson says, adapting a list from *The Evil Futurist's Guide to World Domination,* being a futurist is also about giving people confidence in your visions. He suggests that to be accepted as a futurist you should:

➡ Cultivate the look of an expert (glasses are always good).

➡ Sound really certain about things (people love precision).

➡ Go against any traditional wisdom (always pick the opposite position).

➡ Say things that are very difficult to substantiate.

➡ Be hazy about when things will happen.

➡ Never reveal your sources.

➡ If any prediction ever comes true, make a lot of noise about it.

➡ If anything doesn't come true keep really quiet about it.

➡ Take a big position on big issues ... then wait until you are right.

➡ Steal things from all over the place.

Honda ASIMO ... bringing the future to life

'Kon-nichi wa' it says, offering tea and then making a deep bow.

'ASIMO' is the most sophisticated humanoid robot yet created. It walks, talks, runs, dances, can kick a football and even climb stairs. Its creators, Honda, claim that ASIMO (Advanced

Step in Innovative Mobility) could eventually be used as an essential part of every office or home – cooking, cleaning – and advanced engineering in deep oceans, or in outer space.

ASIMO was first created in 1986 at Honda's Research & Development Wako Fundamental Technical Research Center in Japan. Weighing 54 kg and 1.3m tall, the robot's size was chosen to allow it to operate freely in the human living space and to make it people-friendly. This size allows the robot to operate light switches and door knobs, and work at tables and work benches. Its eyes are located at the level of an adult's eyes when the adult is sitting in a chair.

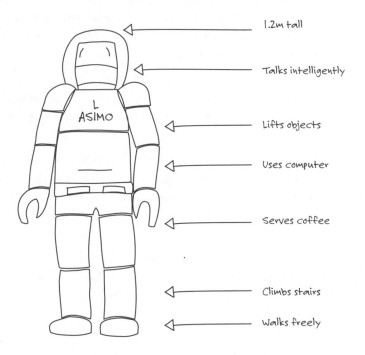

1.2m tall

Talks intelligently

Lifts objects

Uses computer

Serves coffee

Climbs stairs

Walks freely

Robotics, as demonstrated by Honda's ASIMO, are ready to create significant impact

There are over 100 ASIMOs in existence, each one costing just under $1 million to manufacture and some units can be hired out for $166,000. They travel the world and demonstrate their advanced robotics. One ASIMO even conducted a symphony orchestra in Detroit. Each task that ASIMO performs must be programmed by his team of software programmers who operate him wirelessly. He can run at nearly 4mph, and perform the most precise operations, like pouring tea from a traditional teapot into a china cup.

Honda does not reveal the amount spent on developing, but sees him as both a promotional device for the brand and as a prototype for eventual commercialization. An all-new ASIMO was launched in 2005, with more advanced physical and intelligence capabilities that enabled it to be more intuitive and responsive. It can interpret the postures and gestures of humans and move independently in response.

The newly developed technologies, which enable ASIMO to operate in an environment with people and other ASIMOs, bring Honda one step closer to the development of a humanoid robot that can be put to practical use in a real world environment requiring coexistence with people.

However project leader William de Braekeleer says that initially it must form the basics of understanding its environment, so that if it goes into a room where it sees a kettle and toaster, it will understand that it is in the kitchen. Honda sees the robot's main application as being a domestic aid for the elderly and unwell, a robot nurse and carer but without emotion.

That could take at least a decade. ASIMO still needs to learn simpler things, like how to get up if it falls over. For the moment ASIMO is a vision of the future, but one by which Honda can learn much, and inspire its customers, from the 'future back'.

CHAPTER 14

Future scenarios ... building visions of alternative futures

'Logic will get you from A to B, imagination will take you everywhere.'

Albert Einstein

Scenario planning was first developed in the 1950s by Herman Kahn, a highly influential Cold War analyst at the RAND Corporation. It begins with the observation of the current and emergent world, about what is happening in the margins as the mainstream. Kahn said 'if you stare at things long enough, you can eventually see the fundamental forces driving it.' These same fundamental forces are likely to drive the future, but in different ways conditioned by changing surroundings.

Scenarios enable companies to identify warning signals and then watch the real world for hints that one of the foreseen futures is beginning to unfold. They can prepare for different scenarios, ready to seize new opportunities or to mitigate significant risks.

In the late 1990s, Visa feared a challenge from the new online payment systems such as PayPal. It built a number of scenarios, including one in which a new start-up launched a new Web-based payment system that fundamentally challenged Visa, and another where such rivals fizzled out and failed. Visa started to track the signals that would indicate this first scenario was coming to life, monitoring factors such as the number of online merchants signed up to the start-up, capital raised and advertising spend. By 2001 all these measures were declining and Visa had avoided the need to retaliate, saving millions.

Scenario planning

In the past, strategic plans have often considered only the 'official future', which was usually a straight-line graph of current trends carried into the future. Often the trend lines were generated by the accounting department and lacked discussions of demographics or qualitative differences in social conditions. This has led to bad decisions, poor investments and developments, missing many of the biggest opportunities and risks for the future.

Scenario planning is used to make flexible long-term plans, adapted from classic military intelligence methods, to simulate possible ways of beating opponents. Early methods involved groups of analysts building simulation-based games for policy makers. The games combined known facts – such as demographics, geography, political and natural resources, and commercial information – and matched them against social, technical, economic, environmental, educational, political and aesthetic driving forces.

In business, scenarios are much less about 'gaming' the behaviour of opponents or competitors, and much more about the use of natural resources and evolution of markets and economies.

Scenario planning is built on systems thinking, the recognition that many factors may combine in complex ways to create surprising futures due to the non-linear 'feedback loops' of causes and effects. Rather than simulating futures based on today's factors, scenarios can also embrace new technologies, deep shifts in social values, new regulation or disruptive innovations. Systems thinking used in conjunction with scenario planning leads to plausible 'stories' based on relationships between the many factors.

The process starts by clearly defining a challenge or opportunity to address. It then brings together two types of knowledge: things we believe we know something about and things we don't. The first, typically in the form of trends, is based on projecting the past into the future. In the second, the uncertainties include interest rates, fads and fashions, and politics. The art

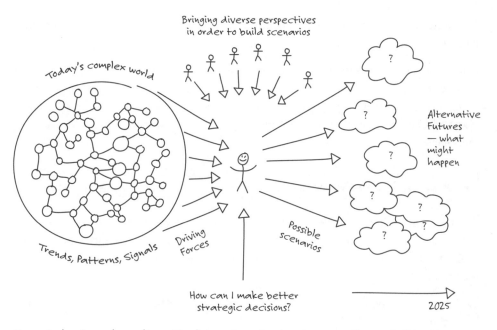

Bringing diverse perspectives
in order to build scenarios

Today's complex world

Alternative
Futures
— what
might
happen

Trends, Patterns, Signals

Driving
Forces

Possible
scenarios

How can I make better
strategic decisions?

2025

Scenario planning explores alternative futures based on trends, perspectives and wildcards

of scenario development is in blending known and unknown knowledge into a limited number of views of the future that together embrace a very wide range of possibilities.

Step 1: Future drivers

The first stage is to bring together all the potential drivers of change – all those factors that are variable and are therefore uncertain. This is about bringing together a team of strategic thinkers from different perspectives and all of the existing knowledge from future studies, trendwatching, business forecasting and other places. These might be in the form of ideas, pictures, statistics, graphs, videos or whatever.

Using a workshop, the group is encouraged to leave its existing thinking behind: to think about a ten-year time horizon – more than what it is used to and could reasonably predict – and build a wall map, often using sticky notes of all the potential drivers. Drivers can be clustered together as appropriate until the team focuses on the ones that it feels are the most important.

Step 2: Making connections

The drivers, sometimes called 'event strings', are brought together into related clusters. This is largely an intuitive process; some connections will be obvious but others will be more difficult. The sticky notes might move around many times, trying to find the most relevant connections:

➡ a change in the environment that will change social attitudes and maybe drive new political policies;

➡ a new technology that will drive market change, with new competitors emerging and economic growth in certain markets; and

➡ a new regulation that will reduce a current behaviour, but provoke another and the associated demand for new products to support it and technologies to enable them.

In more rigorous processes, the drivers might be simulated in a systems model, understanding their cause and effects and attaching probabilities to their influence and impacts. However, scenario planning is largely a creative process and such modelling is there to support the creative decisions, not replace them.

Step 3: Clustering themes

Having created between, say, seven and twelve clusters of related drivers, we now need to make more sense of them: articulating what they mean in terms of a narrative and their implications/size of impact. Giving them names starts to build their identity, rather than them depending on the original language of the drivers. This might be related to an animal or other phenomena: the 'brown bear' scenario (warm but scary, big and strong) or the 'Manhattan' scenario (dense and vibrant, commercial but chaotic).

The uncertain drivers are the ones to focus on because these factors will shape our futures most of all – they can be harnessed to our advantage but should be watched carefully because they could influence the greatest risks.

Step 4: Emerging scenarios

The challenge here is to converge the different clusters into two or three more powerful visions of the future. Ideally these are not extremes, as in good and bad scenarios, since managers would immediately reject the bad one. Instead they should be complementary; both are possible and could even co-exist. As in Step 3, this is not easy and might even involve untangling some of the previous clusters.

What matters most in this process is the discussion: the process of forced choices stimulates a lively debate where participants understand the drivers better, find new ways to describe them and begin to recognize which ones are the most important. It is useful to document this process; indeed, the tensions and debates should become part of a final report. Standing back, the team can now evaluate their emerging scenarios, asking whether they make sense more than whether they are likely.

Step 5: Interpreting scenarios

The scenarios have been developed for use by managers. Therefore, it is crucial that they are communicated in ways that are clear and compelling to them – so that they engage with them and respect their content – but also that they are simple to decipher and practical to use. Most companies articulate their scenarios in written reports or future essays. These might include bullet point lists of the characteristics, drivers and possible implications. They might be graphically represented, perhaps brought together onto a one-page 'rich picture'.

More creatively, scenarios might be retold as stories, the narrative showing how they might evolve, putting emphasis on certain factors and anticipating what comes next. Stories are more compelling but are typically told face-to-face. They might include characters who live in these future worlds or indeed the worlds themselves might be given names – like living on a different planet. The scenarios might be turned into short movies – available on the intranet – or might 'live' as dedicated spaces or scenario rooms, constantly updated and accessible to managers and their teams.

Step 6: Better planning

Scenarios become a tool to support managers across the organization – in strategic planning, making big decisions such as investments or acquisitions, in stimulating creativity and driving innovation. They therefore become part of other processes. The scenarios are examined to understand which are the most critical outcomes, where the significant junctions are when different futures unfold and what issues will have most impact on the future of the organization. Strategies should then take these factors into account, finding ways to mitigate risks and building contingencies for alternative futures.

The scenario planning process can take days or months. It can be done as a one-off exercise to support a significant decision, or can become part of the fabric of the business, continually updated with living scenarios that are informed by real events that shape our possible futures in unpredictable and sometimes dramatic ways.

Burt Rutan ... rocket scientist to the stars

Burt Rutan is the brains behind the spaceships of Virgin Galactic. He and his colleagues at Scaled Composites, located in the Mojave Desert, have produced more than 300 experimental aircraft designs. He is almost single-handedly shaping privately funded space travel.

Forty-seven years to the day after the USSR's Sputnik satellite began the Cold War race to the moon, Rutan's SpaceShipOne became the first commercial craft to complete two trips into space within 14 days. Designed and built in three years for less than $25 million, SpaceShipOne carried a pilot and the weight equivalent of two additional passengers. Over the course of a 90-minute flight it reached a height of more of than 367,000 feet, enabling Rutan to clinch the $10 million Ansari X Prize, an award created specifically to spur space tourism.

He is a maverick, an innovator and incredibly competitive. Minutes after the world's first privately funded spacecraft touched down, Rutan was overjoyed to beat the big aerospace companies at their own game. Interviewed by *Business Week*, he explained that 'the Boeings and Lockheeds of the world probably thought we were a bunch of home builders. I think they're looking at each other right now and thinking that they're screwed!'

Rutan is an aerospace industry veteran, involved in the design of more than 40 planes, and is famed for his originality in designing light, strong, unusual-looking, energy-efficient aircraft. He is often described as the 'second true innovator' in aerospace technology, following in the footsteps of Hugo Junkers who pioneered the design of all-metal aircraft in 1915.

Rutan displayed an early interest in aircraft design; by the age of eight he was designing and building model aircraft. His first solo flight in a full-scale plane came at 16 in an Aeronca Champ in 1959. Following an aeronautical engineering degree in 1965, he worked for the

US Air Force as a flight test project engineer. In 1974 he launched his own business, Rutan Aircraft Factory, where he designed and developed prototypes. His first design was the Rutan VariViggen, a two-seat pusher. Within eight years his business was renamed Scaled Composites and became one of the world's pre-eminent aircraft design and prototyping facilities.

Whilst his greatest success may well still lie ahead of him, his roll of honour is extensive. He received the Presidential Citizens Medal from Ronald Reagan in 1986 and was named by *Time* magazine one of the '100 most influential people in the world' in 2005.

CHAPTER 15

Deep diving ... immersing yourself in the customer world

'If a man looks sharply and attentively, he shall see Fortune, for, though she is blind yet, she is not invisible.'

Francis Bacon

Innovation requires stretch and depth. Once we have stretched forwards to understand the most likely directions we could and should be heading, then we can look more deeply at what drives people in those areas. This is not about standard research that largely measures attitudes and behaviours influenced by the past; it is more about looking at what people seek into the future. It requires more intuitive and immersive approaches.

Intuition

Blink! The Power of Thinking Without Thinking is Malcolm Gladwell's unravelling of the adaptive unconscious, mental processes that work rapidly and automatically from relatively little information, and how they affect our attitudes and behaviours in the world today.

From crime scenes to speed-dating, *Blink!* describes the idea of 'thin-slicing': our ability to gauge what is really important from a very narrow period of experience. It suggests that spontaneous decisions are often as good as (or even better than) carefully planned and considered ones. He also explains how this ability can be corrupted by our likes and dislikes or prejudices and stereotypes – even unconscious ones – and overloaded by too much information. Two particular forms of unconscious bias are 'implicit association tests' and 'psychological priming'. He also reveals our instinctive ability to mind read, which is how we can get to know what emotions someone is feeling just by looking at their face. In what Gladwell contends is an age of information overload, he finds that experts often make better decisions with snap judgments than they do with volumes of analysis.

Sometimes having too much information reduces its effectiveness or our ability to form insights and decisions – you might call it 'analysis paralysis'. The challenge is to focus on only the most critical information to make a decision. Gladwell explains that better judgments can be executed from simplicity and frugality of information rather than with volumes of analysis. In most cases more information reinforces our judgment but does not help to make it more accurate. If the big picture is clear enough to decide, you don't need a magnifying glass.

Immersion

The best way to learn about customers is to spend time with them.

No surprise there. But when was the last time you sat down and had a proper conversation with a customer, or even better a potential customer? Not just when they have a problem to sort out or as part of your training – a real conversation about their world and how you can be a more useful part of it. See the world as they see it, try out the alternatives as they see them. Observe how they behave, what is difficult or frustrates them, how they use and store things – all the irrational things we all do.

A.J. Lafley, the CEO of Procter & Gamble, encourages every one of his people – including his busiest executives – to spend time every week with families, living in their homes and shopping in their supermarkets. The point is to see, feel and think like a real person – not like a prejudiced, product-centric executive who is conditioned by industry conventions.

More formally, this is known as ethnography – qualitative research through observing and talking to people. It tends to be more holistic, exploring people's motivations more broadly, what drives them and what they want to achieve. Rather than being filtered by limiting contexts and predefined questions, it has the flexibility to explore much more and so is better at discovering the margins – deeper motivations, broader applications and future aspirations.

Learn about their broader needs and wants or frustrations and ambitions. Dig for ideas. Listen to the language they use. Capture the quirky findings – don't disregard them as the craze of one person. Ask your customers about themselves, their lives, their hopes and fears, what they love and what they hate, what they are trying to achieve day by day or in the longer term. Understand what influences them and how they make choices. Understand how the products and services you might provide fit into their lives.

And don't just leave this as a task for your research department. Make it a regular activity of everybody – the CEO, the finance director, the HR manager, the non-executive directors, the data processing team, the customer service team – helping them to understand customers more deeply, to show customers a human face to the business, to rediscover the passion of your people for why they are in business.

The dive

Such immersions into the customer world are often called 'deep dives' – diving deep to discover new, richer, broader insights. Another way is to share experiences with a peer in another company in a different sector – for example, if you want to customize your cosmetics, go and learn from the people at Nike ID. Such companies are not competitive, but you may well share the same customer.

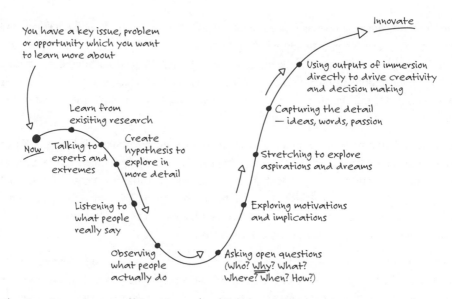

You have a key issue, problem or opportunity which you want to learn more about

Innovate

Using outputs of immersion directly to drive creativity and decision making

Learn from existing research

Capturing the detail — ideas, words, passion

Now Talking to experts and extremes

Create hypothesis to explore in more detail

Stretching to explore aspirations and dreams

Listening to what people really say

Exploring motivations and implications

Observing what people actually do

Asking open questions (Who? Why? What? Where? When? How?)

The dive – immersing yourself in customers' worlds for new insights and ideas

Some of the formats of a deep dive include:

➡ A 30–60 minute one-to one conversation with a customer.

➡ Observing a customer task, e.g. watching how a customer shops.

➡ Doing a customer task yourself, e.g. the weekly shop at the supermarket.

➡ A 30–60 minute one-to-one with a peer in a company in a different business.

➡ Being a customer of your own company, e.g. shopping online or by telephone.

➡ Comparing being a customer of your own company to being a customer of a competitor or benchmark company.

It is important to have an 'opening up' conversation: asking open questions, learning about the broader view and listening openly to what customers say, capturing the unusual or marginal things they mention rather than mainstream, predictable things.

Discovering new spaces

We have discussed time and space at a big picture level, and the emergence of new 'whitespace' in markets. The same is true of customers' needs and wants, and, equally significant, of non-customers' needs and wants.

Renee Maubaugne and Chan Kim describe similar ideas in their book *Blue Ocean Strategy*. The metaphor of red and blue oceans describes the market universe. Companies need to go beyond competing to seeking new opportunities for growth.

➡ **'Red oceans'** are existing market spaces within conventional boundaries and heightened competition, inevitably getting into price battles and locking horns for share. Growth and profit potential are limited, products become commodities, and few companies survive longer-term.

➡ **'Blue oceans'** are the opposite, the new opportunity spaces, where the focus is on developing customers and growing the market space. Competition is largely irrelevant, and there is significant scope for profitable growth.

The point of value innovation, as they describe it, is to find spaces that will deliver mutual value for customers and business, solving significant problems and delivering sustained profitable growth.

Ratan Tata ... making life better for scooter riders

Ratan Tata is chairman of Tata and Sons, the holding company for the sprawling Indian conglomerate Tata Group. He describes the inspiration for the Nano, the ultra-cheap people's car that he launched in 2009.

He was standing on the streets of Mumbai watching a family trying to share one small scooter – the father driving, hanging on his side, the mother sitting, with a baby in her arms. Such a common site in India, where such families could not even dream of buying just an old car, should not happen, Tata thought. He gave his design team the challenge to build a small, modern and stylish family car that would cost no more than 100,000 rupees (around $2000). He estimated that this price could allow millions of people in the developing world to drive in more comfort and safety.

Competitors dismissed the idea. The Maruti 800, the Nano's closest competition, sells for at least twice as much. Yet Tata was as good as his word and, on 9 April 2009, the Nano was launched in 470 outlets across India priced at 100,000 rupees.

Even more interesting than the price tag was the process that achieved it. Designers, engineers and suppliers sat down together with a white sheet of paper, recognizing that to achieve this and make money, they would need to think very differently – rethinking every component to minimize cost and weight without sacrificing basic performance, comfort and style.

The Nano is basic. It has incredibly small 12-inch wheels, tyres with no inner tubes, a single wiper on the windscreen and only one side mirror. Dashboard instruments weigh less than half that of other small cars. Light but rigid body panels were developed in Japan, with an exterior finish that had a high-gloss appearance. The Nano weighs just 600kg, around 60%

less than a Honda Accord. With four seats and four doors, it is efficient and certainly a lot more comfortable than being perched on the back of an overloaded scooter.

For Tata, the project is not expected to deliver rapid profitability, but to at least break even in four to five years. For an automotive industry fighting to survive, it challenges conventional thinking about audiences, products, new markets and business models.

CHAPTER 16

Crowdsourcing ... harnessing the power of people

'Dust as we are, the immortal spirit grows. Like harmony in music; there is a dark inscrutable workmanship that reconciles discordant elements, makes them cling together in one society.'

William Wordsworth

Could you strike gold from your armchair?

The Canadian gold mining group Goldcorp encouraged people to do exactly that. Struggling to locate new deposits, and overwhelmed by data, it made 400MB of geological survey data about its Red Lake, Ontario location available to the public over the Internet. The company offered a $575,000 prize to anyone who could analyse the data and suggest places where gold could be found. The results were astonishing, producing 110 target sites, more than 80% of which proved productive and together yielding eight million ounces of gold, worth more than $3 billion.

In *The Wisdom of Crowds*, James Surowiecki describes how many are smarter than few and how the aggregation of information in groups results in decisions that are often better than could have been made by any single member of the group. He proposes that a diverse collection of independent individuals is likely to make certain types of decisions and predictions better than individuals or even experts. He breaks down the advantages he sees in disorganized decisions into three main types, which he classifies as:

➡ **Cognition** – using crowd judgments, which he argues can be much faster, more reliable and less subject to prejudice than the deliberations of experts or expert committees.

➡ **Coordination** – influencing behaviour patterns such as traffic flows, store layouts or locations of coffee shops based on the likely actions of individuals and how they will be copied.

➡ **Cooperation** – helping people to voluntarily come together in networks of trust in order to create some form of content or action.

Getting crowds to work for you

'Crowdsourcing' is a term coined by Jeff Howe in *Wired* magazine. It is a form of outsourcing to a group of people or community, but different from 'open sourcing' since it is initiated by an organization (open source is initiated by any member of the crowd itself). It is a distributed problem-solving and production model. Problems are broadcast by the 'crowdsourcer' to an unknown group of solvers in the form of an open call for solutions. Users (the crowd) typically form into online communities and submit solutions. The crowd also sorts through the solutions, finding the best ones. These best solutions are then owned by the 'crowdsourcer' and the winning individuals in the crowd are sometimes rewarded with prizes or recognition.

The crowd could be invited to contribute new ideas, share experiences or feedback (like Tripadvisor), provide answers to questions posed by others (like Apple), participate in an innovation process (like Lego), or help sell it to others. Threadless is probably the best example of a successful crowdsourced business model today.

Crowdsourcing reaches out to people with a diversity of backgrounds – people who:

➡ Are passionate about the brand or products and how they are used.

➡ Might have experience in specialist fields such as materials science or related industries.

➡ Have more time because they are students, at home or retired.

Ten red balloons

In late 2009, the US defence agency tested the ability of social networks to locate hidden objects by running an experiment using ten red balloons across the nation. They could have represented all sorts of real-life challenges, such as lost children, suspected terrorists or consumer trends. Whoever found them would win a $40,000 prize. Many teams set about the search, but all were trounced in just nine hours by a smart-thinking team from Massachusetts Institute of Technology.

In the past, finding ten red balloons across a vast continent could have taken ten years. But the speed of the Internet and the power of networks to gather information rapidly and accurately within it have transformed capabilities. We just need to find the reasons and incentives to use them to their true potential.

The MIT team's networking strategy was to encourage participants by saying it would share the winnings along the lines of a pyramid selling system: giving $2000 per balloon to the first person to send the correct coordinates, but also giving $1000 to the person who invited them, $500 to whoever invited the inviter and $250 to whoever invited them, and so on. The website to do this was incredibly simple and, once launched, thousands of volunteers joined the MIT search in return for a small slice of their reward – even if they themselves never saw a balloon.

The simple experiment made an entire government think differently about how they collect and share information, and how collaboration with citizens could be incredibly efficient.

Threadless ... crowdsourced T-shirts, nude no more

Threadless began when Jake Nickell and Jacob DeHart entered an online T-shirt design competition that encouraged wild and personal designs for fellow entrants to vote on. Soon after, the two friends decided that this was how all T-shirts should be made. In 2000, with $1000 start-up money, they developed an online store called threadless.com that became an instant hit with online designers and everyone else who was bored with the limited ranges of T-shirts found in current stores.

Their business model focused on online networks, user-generated design and voting, low-cost production and high margins. Every week, contestants upload their shirt designs to the site and the staff selects winners from the most popular entrants. Winning artists each get $2000 in cash plus a $500 gift voucher (which they can trade in for $200 additional cash if they prefer); the company gets a vote-winning design. Every selected design sells out within a week. Nickell and DeHart say that their skill has been to never stop thinking like users – about the experience, the products and site features that they would love to see.

The priority for the business is to drive growth, which keeps the pool of potential designers large and fresh, and the audience large for new and distinctive T-shirts. Of course, networks work by connecting customers together, so every designer is emailed an online marketing kit to help them recruit their family and friends to vote for their shirt, and maybe buy it too. To keep people returning, Threadless has a viral marketing programme with a range of rewards. Upload a photo of yourself wearing a Threadless T-shirt, for example, and you receive $1.50 off your next purchase. Refer a friend who buys a T-shirt and you get $3 off. Visitors are encouraged to sign-up for newsletters, watch the regular vlogs, start their own blogs and leave comments, which all results in a rich online community that also buys T-shirts.

Threadless began creating weekly video logs called Threadless Tee-V in 2008, streamed through its site and on YouTube. The grainy and irreverent home-made style, with inputs from users, rapidly gained a huge following. In 2009 Threadless started working with Twitter, encouraging people to submit tweets that were then voted on by other tweeters and printed onto T-shirts. Winners received $400 and $140 gift vouchers.

Threadless is a shining example of a crowdsourced, user-generated participation business. People want to be part of something, to express themselves more personally. They want a piece of the action much more than a cheap T-shirt.

CHAPTER 17

Extremes and parallels ... learning from border crossers

'Leave the beaten track occasionally and dive into the woods. Every time you do so, you will be certain to find something that you have never seen before.'

Alexander Graham Bell

One of the best ways to get new ideas is to look to other sectors, geographies and extreme users. Once you know what you want to do, consider where in the world people do the same thing well. Explore what they do and how you can apply it to your business.

A wounded blood-soaked warrior limps into view. He has just risked his life protecting his cow from the jaws of a ferocious leopard and needs medical attention. The visiting European business leaders, who have just flown 6000km to the heat and dust of the Masai Mara, are horrified.

What can Kenyan tribesmen tell them about innovation? The four-day 'Warrior School' teaches ancient tribal wisdoms as well as life skills for the modern day Masai. They will witness charging elephants and tribal dancing, irrigation techniques and charity in action, the medicinal qualities of aloe trees, and the nutritional value of a bowl of *ugali*, a thick, polenta-style corn-meal porridge. Most importantly they will understand the simple structures of tribes, and the lessons that can be applied to their complex organizations and marketplaces back home.

They may well find creative ideas for product innovation too. Famed for producing many of the world's greatest long-distance runners, Nike wanted to test their shoes on the Masai.

However, the executives were astonished when the athletes shook their heads and said they preferred running barefoot or in their primitive sole pads made out of old tyres. From this insight, a new shoe concept was born: the Nike Free, the shoes that are as natural as running barefoot.

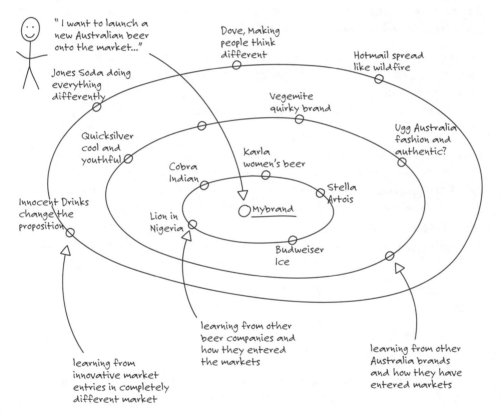

Learning from extremes, parallels and adjacent markets

Companies typically look to the centre of the market to drive innovation; with their penetrative questions to and analysis of this market, manufacturers think they can discern what to do in terms of innovative product development initiatives that meet consumers' needs. Professor von Hippel proposes that innovation does not come from the centre of the market; it comes from an extreme market fringe driven by localized users and early adopters pushing the limits of an original device or prototype.

Extreme users come in many forms. Ford's braking system engineers were looking for better technologies to improve their braking performance. They thought about who had the most extreme need to slow down. They decided to talk to NASA's braking engineers after watching the Space Shuttle and, within a year, the Escort and Mondeo were sporting spaceship brakes.

Similarly, parallel markets are a great source of insight. If people respond to an innovation in one sector – such as buying goods online – then you can learn from those successes to replicate similar behaviours in your own sector. Look at the flywire technology on the latest range of Nike running shoes inspired by the structural engineering of the Golden Gate suspension bridge in San Francisco. Or visit a branch of Umpqua Bank, the innovative bank based in Portland, Oregon. Here you will find a bank that calls itself a store, has merchandise inspired by Gap, coffee and interiors inspired by Starbucks, and service inspired by Ritz Carlton.

Not only are parallels a useful source of ideas, they are also a great way of anticipating the future:

➡ Look at the deregulation in one sector ten years ago and it might hint at how your currently deregulating market might evolve.

➡ Look at a merger between leading players and you can learn what to do and what not to do if you are about to embark on the same journey.

→ Learn from others who have entered a new market but with a different product, or introduced a similar service but in a different sector. Which distribution channels or promotional incentives do over sixties best respond to? How can you offer home delivery or mass customization efficiently?

→ Talk to your peers in the relevant organizations. They are not competitors, so are likely to be much more open and could learn as much from you as you can from them.

Paul Smith ... classic tailoring with a distinctive twist

Paul Smith had only one ambition when he left school at 15, to become a racing cyclist with Beeston Road Team. However, his father thought otherwise and found him a job in a clothing factory. He had no real interest in the work except for the cycle journey to and from his home. However, a bad cycling accident put an end to his ambitions, and a career in fashion design began. During the six months in hospital Smith made some new friends and when he eventually recovered, he arranged to meet them at a local pub that was popular with art students. From that moment he knew that he wanted to be part of this exciting, energetic world of ideas and creativity.

He attended evening classes for tailoring and joined the bespoke tailor Lincroft Kilgour in Savile Row where his designs were worn by celebrities including the footballer George Best. With the help of his fashion college girlfriend, and now wife, Pauline, and £600 of savings, he headed north to Nottingham to launch 'Paul Smith Vêtement Pour Homme' and opened his first shop in 1970.

By 1976 he was ready to promote his first menswear collection in Paris, under the label 'Paul Smith'. His network of stores grew, offering an combination of clothes and eclectic objects more often found in an antique shop: old *Beano* annuals, model racing cars, first edition books and, after he began travelling to Japan in 1982, comical Japanese toys and gadgets. He describes his quirky approach in his book *You Can Find Inspiration in Everything*:

> 'I take ingredients from upper-class tailoring, hand-made suits and so on, and bring them together with something silly ... So I might bring together a beautiful suit with a denim shirt. Or use floral prints inspired by old-fashion seed packets for men's shirts, or line tailored jackets with flamboyantly coloured silks, or ask a factory which specializes in V-necked school sweaters to knit them in crazy colours.'

Over the years he has become the UK's most consistently successful fashion designer. His products are sold in more than 200 shops worldwide and through 500 wholesale customers in Japan alone, where his label out-sells every other European designer. 'It is as though he possesses some inner equivalent of the Houndsditch Clothes Exchange – not a museum, but a vast, endlessly recombinant jumble sale in which all the artefacts of his nation and culture constantly engage in a mutual exchange of code,' wrote William Gibson about Smith's style.

Smith remains fully involved in the business, designing clothes, choosing fabrics, approving the shop locations and overseeing every development. He combines the skills of designer and retailer, which both embrace his slight eccentric fusion of tradition and quirkiness. He calls it 'classic with a twist of individuality'.

CHAPTER 18

Rule-breakers ... embracing discontinuity and disruption

'Those who have changed the universe have never done it by changing rules, but always by inspiring people.'

Napoleon Bonaparte

We live by rules made by others. Some are based on values of fairness and humanity, whilst others – such as data protection or anti-competitive pricing – have evolved as markets have changed. Then there are mental rules, which we more often adopt as standard practices or conventions – such as vacuum cleaners needing bags, or 30-day payment terms.

Rules are there to be broken. Not in some unfair or irresponsible way, but in a creative way. The majority of 'rules' or limitations that we impose on our solutions could reasonably be changed if you could come up with something better.

Opportunities for 'rule breakers' might come in many different forms:

➡ Discontinuities are dramatic situational changes where new things are possible, such as the availability of a new technology platform or deregulation of a market.

➡ Disruptions are dramatic responses to change, such as using a new technology to transform a market and/or changing the attitudes and behaviours of customers.

Innovations disrupt conventions.

The disruption might be a challenge or even a reversal in the received wisdom of the market. Every vacuum cleaner manufacturer automatically assumed that a dust bag was a pre-requisite within their designs – until James Dyson came along. Every airline thought it unrealistic to put a bed on a transatlantic aircraft – until British Airways met a yacht designer. Every analyst thought it was impossible to make money out of free information online – until Google created a fundamentally different business model.

Hotbeds of disruption might be something that creates a high level of customer frustration (e.g. how to remortgage your home), complexity (e.g. how to integrate your many computing devices), or paradox (e.g. how to shop in bulk when you have no space in your home to store it). Think of your DVD player, mobile phone, camera or PC – they have far more functionality than you will ever need. What if we removed all the non-essentials to significantly reduce production costs and offer a much lower price? Think about the Smart car, or more extreme the Nano – small cars that meet basic needs at a fraction of the normal price. Think about the Asus netbook and many others – a laptop for internet access and little else but at a fraction of the size and price of conventional laptops.

Technology can quickly distract us, with its constant ability to do more. But customers will only use technology up to a point: most electronic devices do far more than you ever do, most software on a PC remains largely unutilized, most new gizmos are reflections of aesthetic aspirations rather than functional need. 'Disruption', as Clay Christensen, author of *The Innovator's Dilemma* describes it, happens when this progress is far ahead of what customers need and can use. This overshoot creates the opportunity for a new entrant to come in with something cheaper, simpler and 'good enough' for a significant number of customers. Once this new entrant has carved out a niche at the lower end of the market, they can rapidly persuade more customers that they are good enough for them too. The disruption might be product-related, as in Dell's disruption of the PC market, or market-related, as in eBay creating an entirely new marketplace.

Commercially, it is not really about technology but about the business model. Small, agile companies can succeed with business models that would be unattractive to larger companies. An existing company may need to deliver a 40% margin in order that a new product is attractive; to a smaller company, a 20% margin might make them extremely profitable.

Capabilities and culture are also limiting factors for larger companies. If BMW prides itself on its design and manufacturing excellence, it is difficult to accept 'inferior' products – not because they don't work, but because they are not the best they can be. Similarly, British Airways struggled to compete against the new low-cost entrants such as Ryanair and easyJet partly because culturally a full-service airline that prides itself on its customer service finds limited service a difficult concept to grasp.

But larger companies that do embrace disruptive thinking can be successful too. Jack Welch's parting gift to GE was a programme known as 'destroy your business', where he encouraged staff to think like internet entrepreneurs: to disrupt their own business before somebody else blows them out the water.

Disruption enables more radical creativity, as shown in the table below. Once you have disrupted the status quo, a better, more creative solution is required in its place.

Example	Area of disruption	Comment
Digital media	Music industry	In the 1990s the US music industry phased out the single, leaving consumers with no means to purchase individual songs. This market was filled by file-sharing technologies such as Napster, which were initially free, and then by online retailers such as the iTunes music store and Amazon.com. This low-end disruption eventually undermined the sales of physical, high-cost CDs.
Mobile VoIP	International telecoms	Voice over IP technology, or Internet phone calls, can cost next to nothing for the user and the network used compared to the standard GSM network – especially for international calls. Where GSM providers would charge ludicrous prices, installing a small application on compatible mobile phones or laptops can cost the user nothing. The only downside is that it still needs an Internet connection.
Solid state drive	Hard disks	The solid state drive has many benefits over its disk-based rivals – speed, size and security. SSDs have begun to appear in laptops, although they are more expensive per unit of capacity than hard drives. The SSD has replaced the hard disk drive as the boot disk in the high-end market, whilst USB memory sticks have rapidly taken over from CDs and floppy disks.

Of course, creating a disruption is only the starting point. It requires creativity to exploit it in some useful and different way: thinking radically about why markets exist like they do, or about future market models and how they should work. Pure creativity is fun and energizing, but must be structured in order to deliver meaningful results.

Damian Hirst ... the shark, the sheep and the skull

Damien Hirst, the artist infamous for creating ridiculous works of art that were notable for nothing but their monetary excess, is now knocking out pieces for $5.

Hirst has always had a genius for gauging the zeitgeist. He came to prominence with works calculated to shock: sharks and cows cut open and preserved in huge tanks, a pickled sheep, and a diamond-encrusted skull that he sold for $150 million. He even sold an entire exhibition collection for close to $250 million. Now he has opened his own store full of his own creations, from $5 key rings to prints at a cool $6500 (the originals sold for around $20 million). He likes to shock and to court publicity that raises notoriety and prices – but most of all, he likes to surprise.

In 1990 Hirst curated two ambitous 'warehouse' shows, Modern Medicine and Gambler, in an old East London biscuit factory. Charles Saatchi arrived at the second show and stood open-mouthed with astonishment in front of *A Hundred Years*, Hirst's first major 'animal' installation consisting of a large glass case containing maggots and flies feeding off a rotting cow's head. Saatchi bought it immediately. Hirst said at the time, 'I can't wait to get into a position to make really bad art and get away with it. At the moment, most people would look at my work and say eff off, but with a reputation you can get away with anything.'

His first major international presentation was in the Venice Biennale in 1993 with the work *Mother and Child Divided*, a cow and a calf cut into sections and exhibited in a series of separate vitrines. Two years later he won the Turner Prize.

With a personal wealth in excess of £235 million, Hirst sees the real creative act as being the idea – creating and shaping the concept, which is then conveyed through any media – much more than the act of painting or construction. Whilst most of his early works were his own, he has now built up a team of assistants who do most of his actual painting and modelling. He compares it to Andy Warhol's 'factory' or the studios of many Renaissance painters.

'Art goes on in your head,' he says. He sees his inspiration in everyday surroundings – some of them instant, others that grow on him over time, 'like how to create a rainbow within a gallery'.

His store is a reflection of his commercialism to match his creativity. He has developed 'Other Criteria' as his merchandising arm, producing objects and books created by himself (or at least his team) and other artists. He aims to sell 'affordable art of the highest quality to everyone who wants it.'

CHAPTER 19

Ideation ... igniting the power of creativity

'Only as high as I reach can I grow, only as far as I seek can I go. Only as deep as I look can I see, only as much as I dream can I be'

Karen Ravn, author of 'Little Seeds of Wisdom'

Creative techniques encourage original thoughts and divergent thinking. Some techniques require groups of two or more people; others can be accomplished alone. Most use associations between the goal or the problem, the current state, and a form of stimulus. Some companies keep a box of creative tools at the ready at all times: IDEO have their 'Tech Box' in each of their workspaces; Lego use their plastic bricks as business tools, getting business people to throw away their inhibitions and construct models that represent ideas. Lego has even evolved this into a commercial proposition called 'Serious Play' for businesses.

Randomness is one of the simplest forms of stimulus. John Cage, an avant-garde musician, composed music by superimposing star maps on blank sheet music, rolling dice or preparing open-ended scores that depended on the spontaneous decisions of the performers. Randomness introduces new thoughts or ideas into a creative process.

Improvisation is a creative process that can be spoken, written or composed without prior preparation. It can lead to the discovery of new ways to act, new patterns of thought and practices, or new structures. Improvisation is used in the creation of music, theatre and other various forms. Many artists also use improvisational techniques to help their creative flow. Improvisational theatre relies upon the actor's skills of listening, clarity and confidence, and of performing instinctively and spontaneously.

Many of the great scientific breakthroughs have come from great thinkers able to think creatively. Albert Einstein, for example, used a form of provocation to trigger ideas that led to his new theories of relativity and electromagnetism. Alexander Fleming used association when he looked at his dirty instruments one night and saw a little mould growing, which led to the invention of penicillin. Charles Goodyear found newness when he was not looking for it – spilling some hot rubber led to the vulcanization process – and Roy Plunkett was trying to invent a new refrigerant, but came up with a glob of white waxy stuff, which he called Teflon.

Types of creativity

There are two main approaches to creativity:

➡ **Logical thinking:** This is structured and programmed, following clear and consistent processes, and is enormously effective in making things better. Because it is easy to define, it is the more usual form of creativity found within structured product development and innovation processes. It can then be codified, managed and deployed across organizations.

➡ **Lateral thinking:** Popularized by Edward de Bono, this is less structured and includes randomness and brainstorming. It helps us to break out of a patterned way of thinking and come up with startling, brilliant and original solutions – and is therefore an essential part of innovation. Lateral thinking recognizes that our brains are pattern-recognition systems that do not function like computers. It takes years of training before we learn to do simple arithmetic – something computers do very easily. On the other hand, we can instantly recognize patterns such as faces, language and handwriting, whereas computers need to become much more powerful before they approach our ability to do this.

The benefit of good pattern-recognition is that we can recognize objects and situations very quickly. Imagine how much time would be wasted if you had to do a full analysis every time you came across a cylindrical can of sparkling liquid – most people would just open their can of fizzy drink. Without pattern recognition we could not cross the road safely, and we would starve or be eaten. Unfortunately, we get stuck in our patterns. Solutions we develop are based on previous solutions to similar problems. Normally it does not occur to us to use solutions belonging to other patterns.

Being creative may just be a matter of setting aside the time needed to take a step back and ask yourself if there is a better way of doing something. Edward de Bono calls this a 'creative pause' – maybe just a short break of 30 seconds – but as a regular part of thinking. Such self-discipline is easy to forget, particularly for creative people when they're in the thick of thinking.

Idea generation

The important challenge throughout 'the ideas factory' is to keep generating more ideas and to capture them so that they are not forgotten.

Creativity is a divergent process – the more ideas, the better – and indeed ideas are one of the best catalysts for having more or better ideas. The discipline of writing ideas on sticky notes is helpful because it forces articulation, in a brief way, and they can easily be moved around or brought together with others later. Whether the ideas emerge through future scenarios, mapping trends, observing customers, exploring extremes, considering parallels or simple creative techniques, they are all valid. They can be categorized into different aspects of the problem, or different types of opportunity, although too much structuring is unwise at this point.

More interesting is to begin to look for fusions, connecting ideas to create better ones: maybe a function of a product relates to a new service idea, or a channel partner could deliver a new service, or a quirky application for one audience would be interesting for another. Out of these ideas a hypothesis can emerge: possible solutions that are more structured, with more supporting argument and said with more conviction, that require more evaluation. They can be an easy way to get a team to stay focused, reach some form of agreement or feel like they are getting somewhere. It is also a way to propose a dramatic or unpopular solution without it getting shot down too quickly. At the end of the creative workshop bring together all the ideas and develop a number of hypotheses to start thinking more about and work on in more detail next time.

However, creativity also needs restraints, not just to ensure that it focuses on what matters but also to stimulate a better response. 'Give me your ideas' is one of the worst starting points for creativity and will typically yield small and marginal results. Asking people to address something specific is likely to generate much sharper, more relevant and deeper responses.

Throughout the creative process, it is important to retain energy – to retain motivation, interest in the challenge and people's willingness to keep pushing themselves) and pace (to bring urgency, force ideas out, make the most of the collective time and sustain momentum). Creativity workshops can and should be exhausting, but exhilarating too.

IDEO ... where enlightened teams beat the lone genius

'Our values are part mad scientist (curious and experimental), bear-tamer (gutsy and agile), *reiki* master (hands-on and empathetic), and midnight tax accountant (optimistic and savvy),' says David Kelley, co-founder of the world's leading design firm, at ideo.com.

As companies seek more and more help to find breakthrough products and speed up development, they're increasingly turning to design consultancies such as IDEO for more holistic support than just product styling. Computers, water bottles, cordless phones, fishing rods, toothpaste tubes – even the new Prada shop in Manhattan – have all been transformed by the Palo Alto-based company.

IDEO was formed in 1991 by a merger of three established design firms: David Kelley Design (founded by the Stanford professor), ID Two (founded by Bill Moggridge) and Matrix Product Design (which belonged to Mike Nuttall). Kelley had a background in everything from venture capital to special effects and was responsible for the mechanical whale in Free Willy, whereas Moggridge was focused on user-centred design and had invented everything, including contributing to the first personal computer.

David's brother Tom Kelley, IDEO's lead marketing thinker, described six IDEO attributes when I talked with him recently in Istanbul:

➡ Building empathy with potential users to understand their diverse and unusual needs and motivations. 'The best products embrace people's differences,' he says.

➡ Intently observing 'the right people' – those who do things a little differently – and then asking yourself 'Why?'

➡ Staying close to the action – 'inspiration comes from seeing, hearing, feeling ... being there'. Sensory immersion is a powerful source of innovation.

➡ Brainstorming it every day, 'weaving it into the cultural fabric' of the organization.

➡ Encouraging 'cross-pollination' – finding answers from unusual places, cross-training or spark people to think beyond the norm.

➡ Being a little bit crazy – playing games, having fun – and creating an atmosphere where you naturally take chances and solve problems.

David Kelley always believed in recruiting people who he liked, respected and would have fun working with, and thereby get more done. Pranks became second nature at the firm. Kelley's door was once glued shut during a pitch from a salesperson. There are frequent rubber band wars and even water balloons dropped out of the window. All this added more sense of belonging, more smiles and better ideas.

Traditional customer research is not part of IDEO. Instead of relying upon surveys and focus groups, it prefers to go to the source of real insights: the people who use the products, or something similar to what might emerge. They observe people's natural behaviours, what frustrates them, what they love to do and what they try to do but can't – yet.

Tim Brown, the current CEO, continues the mission to fuse design, business and social studies to come up with deeply researched, deeply understood designs. In an interview with *MIT World*, he says that a 'design thinker' must not only be intensely collaborative, but 'empathic, as well as have a craft to making things real in the world'. He sees three central 'buckets' in the process of creating a new design: inspiration, ideation and implementation.

'Design thinkers must set out like anthropologists or psychologists, investigating how people experience the world emotionally and cognitively' says Brown in his new book *Change by Design*. While designing a new hospital, IDEO staff put themselves through a patient experience to see what being in an emergency room felt like. 'You see 20 minutes of ceiling tiles,' says Brown, who realized that the 'most important thing is telling people what's going on.' The inspiration for solving a problem might come from anywhere – in this example, the team visited a car racing pit crew to come up with more effective designs for the hospital. After inspiration comes 'building to think', which can mean quickly creating 100 prototypes to test the design and create stakeholders in the process. Brown says that 'so many good ideas fail to make it out to market because they couldn't navigate through the system'. IDEO counts on:

➡ Storytelling to develop and express ideas, and buy key players into the concept.

➡ Constantly refreshing its sources of inspiration by bringing in bold thinkers.

➡ (Increasingly) focusing on socially oriented design problems.

The company uses conventional techniques but done in an enlightened way. Brainstorming is seen as fun and creative, but is also taken very seriously. 'The buzz of a good brainstorm can infect a team with optimism and sense of opportunity that can carry it through the darkest and most pressure-tinged stages of the project' says Kelley. In a company without many rules, IDEO has a very clear idea about what constitutes a brainstorm and how it should be organized:

➡ **Duration:** Sixty minutes in an optimum length. The level of physical and mental energy required for a brainstorm is hard to sustain for much longer than that.

➡ **Don'ts:** 'Brainstorming sessions aren't presentations or opportunities for the boss to poll the troops for hot ideas. Nor should they feel like work. And brainstorming is most definitely not about spending thousands of dollars at some glamorous off-site location.'

➡ **Idea engine:** 'Brainstorming is the idea engine of IDEO's culture. It is an opportunity for teams to 'blue sky' ideas early in a project or solve a tricky problem that's cropped up later on. The more productive the group, the more it brainstorms regularly and effectively.'

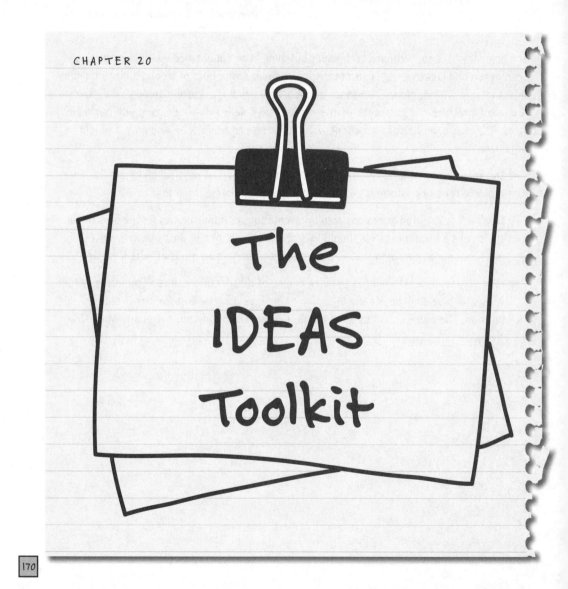

CHAPTER 20

The IDEAS Toolkit

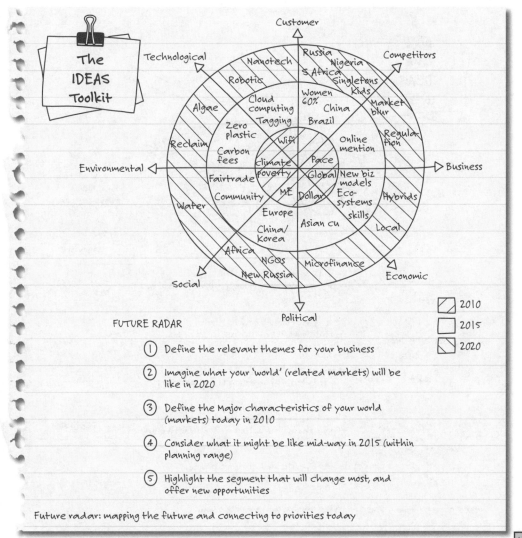

The IDEAS Toolkit

FUTURE RADAR

① Define the relevant themes for your business

② Imagine what your 'world' (related markets) will be like in 2020

③ Define the Major characteristics of your world (markets) today in 2010

④ Consider what it might be like mid-way in 2015 (within planning range)

⑤ Highlight the segment that will change most, and offer new opportunities

Future radar: mapping the future and connecting to priorities today

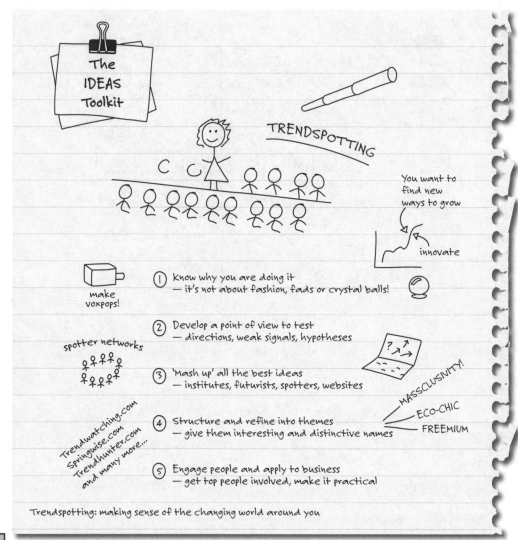

The IDEAS Toolkit

TRENDSPOTTING

You want to find new ways to grow

innovate

make voxpops!

① Know why you are doing it
— it's not about fashion, fads or crystal balls!

spotter networks

② Develop a point of view to test
— directions, weak signals, hypotheses

③ 'Mash up' all the best ideas
— institutes, futurists, spotters, websites

MASSCLUSIVITY!

ECO-CHIC

FREEMIUM

Trendwatching.com
Springwise.com
Trendhunter.com
and many more...

④ Structure and refine into themes
— give them interesting and distinctive names

⑤ Engage people and apply to business
— get top people involved, make it practical

Trendspotting: making sense of the changing world around you

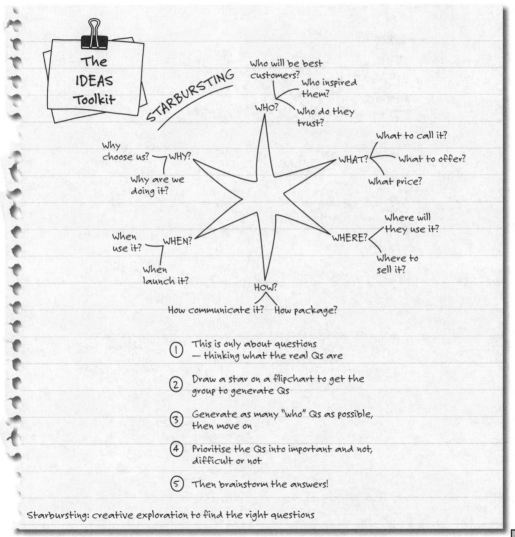

The
IDEAS
Toolkit

STARBURSTING

Who will be best
customers?
Who inspired
them?
WHO?
Who do they
trust?

What to call it?
WHAT?
What to offer?
What price?

Why
choose us?
WHY?
Why are we
doing it?

Where will
they use it?
WHERE?
Where to
sell it?

When
use it?
WHEN?
When
launch it?

HOW?
How communicate it?   How package?

① This is only about questions
— thinking what the real Qs are

② Draw a star on a flipchart to get the
group to generate Qs

③ Generate as many "who" Qs as possible,
then move on

④ Prioritise the Qs into important and not,
difficult or not

⑤ Then brainstorm the answers!

Starbursting: creative exploration to find the right questions

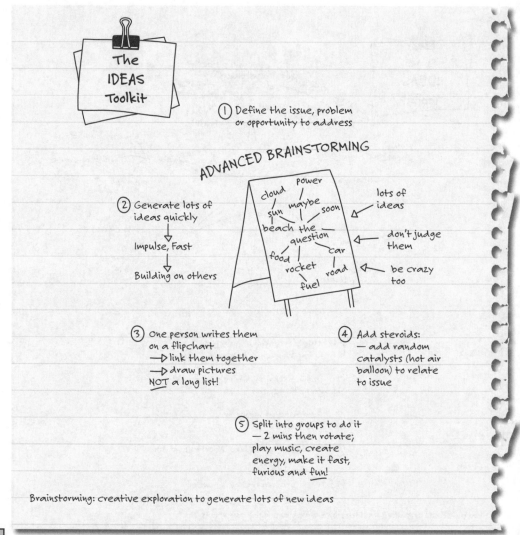

The
IDEAS
Toolkit

① Define the issue, problem or opportunity to address

ADVANCED BRAINSTORMING

② Generate lots of ideas quickly

Impulse, Fast

Building on others

cloud   power
sun   maybe   soon
beach   the
question
food   car
rocket   road
fuel

lots of ideas

don't judge them

be crazy too

③ One person writes them on a flipchart
  ▷ link them together
  ▷ draw pictures
  NOT a long list!

④ Add steroids:
  — add random catalysts (hot air balloon) to relate to issue

⑤ Split into groups to do it
  — 2 mins then rotate; play music, create energy, make it fast, furious and fun!

Brainstorming: creative exploration to generate lots of new ideas

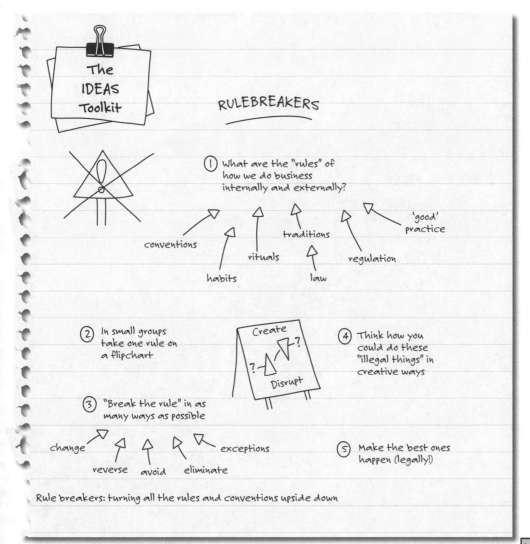

The IDEAS Toolkit

RULEBREAKERS

① What are the "rules" of how we do business internally and externally?

conventions

habits

rituals

traditions

law

regulation

'good' practice

② In small groups take one rule on a flipchart

Create

Disrupt

③ "Break the rule" in as many ways as possible

change

reverse

avoid

eliminate

exceptions

④ Think how you could do these "illegal things" in creative ways

⑤ Make the best ones happen (legally!)

Rule breakers: turning all the rules and conventions upside down

The design studio

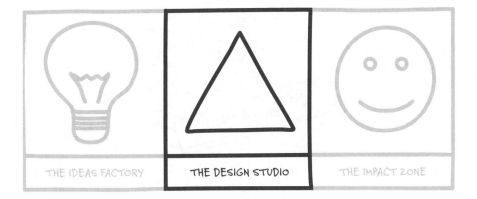

THE IDEAS FACTORY | THE DESIGN STUDIO | THE IMPACT ZONE

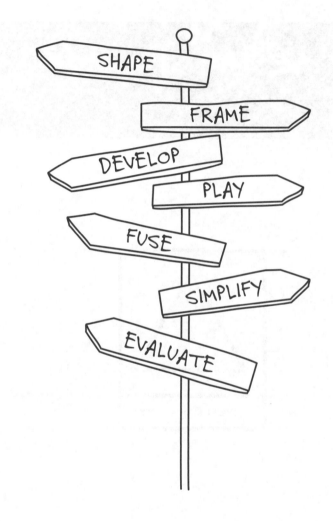

CHAPTER 21

Design thinking ... mindset for a creative business

'We don't have a good language to talk about this kind of thing. In most people's vocabularies, design means veneer ... But to me, nothing could be further from the meaning of good design. Design is the fundamental soul of a man-made creation.'

Steve Jobs, in *Fortune* magazine

When A.J. Lafley became the CEO of P&G, he described his vision to *Fast Company*: 'I want P&G to become the number one consumer design company in the world, so we need to be able to make design part or our strategy. We need to make it part of our innovation process'. Designers at P&G were historically called in at the end of the product development process to add some superficial decoration – a funky curve, a splash of colour. They now get involved from the beginning of any project, ensuring that the power of design is leveraged at every stage and in every aspect of the product, channel and consumer experience.

Design was originally the craft of a designer or creative person. The Industrial Revolution demanded more precision and commercialization, and resulted in a divergence of approaches – design as art and design as engineering. More recently, the Design Council has argued that successful products need both function and form – or to put it another way, engineering and industrial design.

Design, like creativity, has many definitions – sometimes because of imprecise thinking, but also because it has multiple components. Design is:

→ **The tangible outcome** – the product or service.

→ **A creative activity** – embracing function and form.

→ **The development process** – turning ideas into solutions.

Design is a deliberate, structured, thoughtful discipline, most commonly referred to as a process. As the understanding of design has evolved, so too has its scope – from products to services and experiences, and from cosmetic styling to a holistic business concept:

→ **'Style' design** – shapes, colours, graphics

→ **'Product' design** – also includes research, engineering, industrial design

→ **'Experience' design** – also includes marketing, communication, service, people

→ **'Business' design** – also includes business model, organization structure, operations.

'Design thinking' has become a new business mantra, in particular led by Tim Brown and IDEO. At a Technology, Entertainment, and Design (TED) event he described design thinking as 'a human-centred approach to problem-solving. It is a process built from people (inspiration gained from looking and listening to them), prototyping (making ideas tangible as soon as possible), and stories (getting things implemented by selling compelling narratives not concepts).'

Design thinking typically has four components:

→ **Customer centricity:** Understanding what customers or consumers really want – which is often not what they say they want – through immersion and ethnographic techniques.

→ **Team experimentation:** Exploring different possibilities and solutions, opening up before closing down, and then focusing on a smaller number of hot prospects.

→ **Rapid prototyping:** Rather than talking about it try building it, thereby enabling more discussion, understanding, enhancement and engagement.

→ **Emotional appeal:** Engaging people in the potential applications of the design through storytelling rather than glib product specifications or advertising slogans.

Jonathan Ive ... the real iMan of Apple

Jonathan Ive never made much of an impression when he trained at Newcastle Polytechnic or when he went to work on wash basin designs for Tangerine in London. He had design ideas that no one understood. Then he moved to California and began work at Apple, where he found the people who understood his passion for 'humanizing technology'.

Apple represents perhaps the most successful fusion of business and design, and Ive – with a little support from his CEO – has been largely responsible for its journey to global icon. Despite being notoriously secretive about its design process, Apple makes no secret of Ive's contribution.

The man who, after Jobs, is most responsible for Apple's amazing ability to dazzle us with iMacs, iPods, and iPhones believes in 'the craft of design'. He likes to focus on few projects and what matters most within them. He likes to understand his challenge deeply – the user, application, materials and tools – and he cares deeply about what he creates. He combines what he describes as 'fanatical care beyond the obvious stuff' with relentless experiments into tools, materials and production processes. Comparing Apple's challenge to what he sees in other sectors, he says that 'with technology, the function is much more abstract to users, so the product's meaning is almost entirely defined by the designer'.

Ive became Apple's design chief in 1996, at a time when Jobs was gone and the business was in deep trouble. A year later the co-founder returned, and immediately axed all but four of

Apple's sixty-plus products. Jobs saw design as the future for Apple and scoured the world for a design superstar, until realizing that he had just that under his nose.

A design synergy was born: Jobs set the direction and Ive made it happen. It started with the first iMac, turning the intimidating personal computer into something more fun. To understand how to make a plastic shell look exciting rather than cheap, Ive and his team visited a candy factory to study the finer points of making jelly beans. They also spent months devising new plastics-based manufacturing processes and then set about making the internal electronics look sexy, because now you could see them.

The casing cost $65 – three times more than normal – but it was the design feature that turned the business around. What sets Ive's designs apart is their 'fit and finish' – the impression that results from thousands of tiny decisions that go into a product's development.

Apple's design evolution with Ive

Four phases characterize the extraordinary fusion between Jobs and Ive, and the seemingly never-ending evolution of beautiful, iconic and mostly phenomenal product designs:

- **The translucent phase:** Inspired by the confectionary factory, early products such as the original 'Bondi blue' iMac (inspired by Sydney's Bondi beach) were characterized by translucent, contoured surfaces with colourful or milky-white colouring. Even the power cables had twisted wires visible within them.
- **The colourful phase:** The blue iMac was replaced with five fruit colours – blueberry, grape, tangerine, lime and strawberry – that continued into the first iBook. They set a new trend in consumer goods, from vacuum cleaners to alarm clocks. The brightly coloured 1990s models slowly gave way to translucent snow and graphite.
- **The minimalist phase:** The turn of the century saw a shift to metal, with the PowerBook G4 featuring titanium and then aluminium. The previous soft, bulging shapes became

streamlined, orthogonal and minimalist. The success of the iPod and its simple rounded-rectangle styling affected all other designs – even the iMac G5 was labelled 'from the creators of the iPod'.

➡ **The aluminium phase:** A move away from white plastics, replacing them with glass and aluminium, and seeking extreme minimalism. The iPhone debuted this new style, showing off darker aluminium on its back and a glass front, and other iPods and MacBooks followed.

Ive leads a small team of 12–15 designers. They work intensely in a large open studio with a huge sound system booming out music, indulging the team's creative passion and obsession for perfection. Ive says that many of Apple's products are dreamed up whilst eating pizza in the small team kitchen. The studio is guarded with great secrecy and off limits to most Apple employees.

'Apple is a cult, and the design team is an even more intense version of a cult,' concluded *Business Week*.

CHAPTER 22

Context reframing ... finding the bigger idea

'All our knowledge has its origins in our perceptions.'

Leonardo da Vinci

'Reframing' is about changing the frame of reference – the situation, occasion, context or purpose – in which an idea, problem or opportunity is considered.

Imagine a bottle of wine. Is it to be shared with friends, a device to get drunk, part of the ritual of eating a good meal, a gift – or something more? The frame alters the proposition – the audience, benefits, the alternatives and perceived value.

One of my most interesting projects was to work with a leading funeral company. 'Find new ways to grow our business,' instructed the CEO rather scarily. How do you grow a funeral business? Particularly when you are already the market leader and people are living longer, healthier lives. More difficult still is to make money out of funerals, since they are all essentially the same: you get buried or cremated, and beyond that there is less differentiation and therefore little profit. We talked to some customers – the partners and relatives who are usually left to make the essential choices and who often pay for the services. In a time of extreme stress, they are more concerned about what has happened, and doing the right thing, rather than thinking about much else.

But in The Netherlands, and a growing number of other markets, most people pay for their funerals well before they die. At an average cost of around €2500, it is an inevitable expense at some stage in your life – so people are including a funeral policy alongside their savings plans and life assurance policies, paying by instalments or as an insurance policy. They don't arrange this in a funeral parlour, with the slightly negative thought of dead bodies in the back room; instead, they buy these plans (often relabelled 'end of life' plans) through a financial advisor or insurance agent. And when they spend time thinking about it, they spend a bit more: organic burials, woodland cemeteries or having a better send-off, with a party for friends and relatives, good food and wine, their favourite band playing and maybe a fireworks display for a final goodbye.

By reframing a concept you can reach new audiences, redefine the competition, dramatically enhance the perceived value and maybe sell additional products and services as part of a bigger solution.

There are three levels of context to choose from. Choosing one of them as your 'frame' creates a far better position from which to innovate, or through which to bring together smaller ideas and rearticulate them in a bigger or different way:

➡ **Function:** What is it? The simple product or service as defined by its category, such as a laptop computer with the usual catalogue of technical features.

➡ **Application:** Why do people use it? The many different uses of the product or service, and the direct benefits, e.g. 'It enables me to work anywhere, anytime, faster and more effective.'

➡ **Enablement:** Broadly, what does it enable people to do? For example, 'It enables me to have a flexible lifestyle, be independent and more responsive to clients, and to make more money.'

Why is the Audi A6 compared to the almost identically priced BMW 3 series in reviews, rather than being seen as a peer of the much cheaper Volkswagen Passat, with which it shares a technical platform? Because Audi has made you think this way, promoting it as a mid-

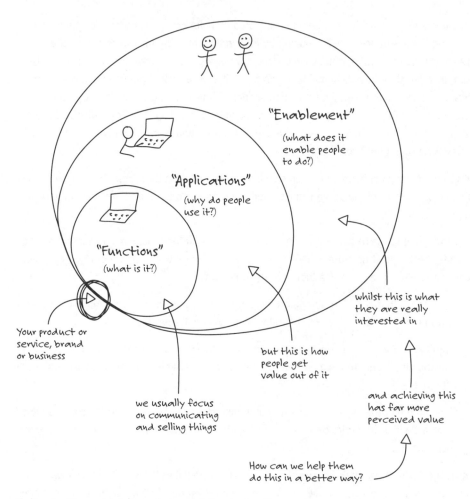

"Enablement"

(what does it
enable people
to do?)

"Applications"

(why do people
use it?)

"Functions"
(what is it?)

Your product or
service, brand
or business

whilst this is what
they are really
interested in

but this is how
people get
value out of it

we usually focus
on communicating
and selling things

and achieving this
has far more
perceived value

How can we help them
do this in a better way?

Reframing the context from what you do to what customers do

size executive car rather than a family car, in silver and chrome rather than bright colours, matching BMW rather than Volkswagen.

Banksy ... when graffiti becomes a work of art

His pictures fetch six-figure sums but the graffiti artist's identity remains a mystery. Banksy is an anonymous graffiti artist from the south-west of England.

His anti-establishment 'cool' has made him highly collectible, with Angelina Jolie, Brad Pitt and Christina Aguilera among his fans. Largely using stencils in black and white, one of his 'works' sold for more than £250,000 at auction – the only problem being that it was still attached to the white-washed wall of an immovable building. This is one of the main reasons why his art is so controversial and often political, inviting criticism and debate.

In 2005 he placed his own versions of well-known paintings in galleries including the Museum of Modern Art in New York and the Tate in London – they went undetected for several days. However, with permission, the British Museum added a Banksy to their permanent collection when they discovered his imitation cave painting depicting a caveman with a shopping trolley.

Several Banksy pieces have been painted over accidentally by unsuspecting workers – most recently, a scene from the film *Pulp Fiction* in which the characters hold bananas instead of guns. However, 97% of local people voted to save a controversial mural that suddenly emerged in the centre of Bristol in 2006. It showed a husband and wife looking out of a window while the wife's lover hangs from the ledge, painted on the wall of a sexual health clinic.

CHAPTER 23

Co-creation ... designing with customer 'ubuntu'

'Individually, we are one drop. Together, we are an ocean.'

Ryunosuke Satoro

'Co-creation' is development done collaboratively with others. Whilst these others could be other companies or individuals, employees or experts, the term is most often associated with customers.

➡ Lego Factory is a physical and online co-creation facility where consumers work with others and the Lego designers to build future products.

➡ Ducati's Tech Café is where bikers hang out and design the next generation of superbikes.

➡ Clients run facilitated innovation programmes at IBM's Innovation Centres.

➡ Samsung has a Virtual Product Launch Center where you can find the coolest newest devices.

Whilst some companies have hi-jacked the 'co-creation' word to redefine customer research techniques such as focus groups and immersion, others recognize that it is a bigger approach, engaging customers as partners in a journey from ideas to implementation:

➡ **Co-thinking:** Working with customers to understand their needs and wants, but also to develop new ideas using collaborative creativity techniques. This is similar to 'crowd-

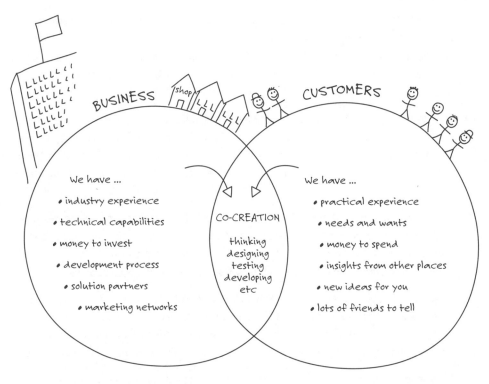

BUSINESS

We have …

- industry experience
- technical capabilities
- money to invest
- development process
- solution partners
- marketing networks

CO-CREATION

thinking
designing
testing
developing
etc

CUSTOMERS

We have …

- practical experience
- needs and wants
- money to spend
- insights from other places
- new ideas for you
- lots of friends to tell

Co-creation opportunities between business and customers

sourcing', but more personal. P&G take consumers away to hotels for weekends, or go to their homes, to explore better ways to do washing or cleaning.

➡ **Co-designing:** Joint problem-solving by better defining the issues and potential solutions, maybe encouraging people to submit new designs – both in terms of the business and the style of products. See how Threadless rewards the best submitted T-shirt designs or Jones Soda prints your photos on their bottle labels.

➡ **Co-evaluating:** Testing ideas with customers, building advance customer networks and getting their feedback for improvement whilst also turning them into lead-user ambassadors. This might involve extreme users; for example, Nike working with elite athletes to evaluate new shoes designs, or Gore working on new fabrics with emergency services.

➡ **Co-developing:** Customers can be as skilled and fanatical as your own technicians in being able to develop better products or specify better services. The Boeing 787 Dreamliner was developed in partnership with customers, Nike ID design studio is at the heart of Niketown and IKEA 'allows' you to find your products in its warehouse and build them yourself.

➡ **Co-communicating:** Customers can be your best and more trusted advocates. They might write reviews on your website or on other directory sites such as TripAdvisor for hotel customers. They might even develop user-generated advertising for you, like made possible with Scrmblr and demonstrated by Converse's social ads campaigns.

➡ **Co-selling:** People are much more likely to buy from friends and others like them, rather than some anonymous salesman. 'Customer get customer' in return for a case of wine or iPod is familiar to us all, as is the pyramid-selling models championed by Avon and Oriflame, which has even turned some of their most active customers into millionaires.

➡ **Co-supporting:** When something goes wrong – particularly when trying to use technological devices – you need help and fast. User guides are gobbledegook, so you get online and ask other users for help. Apple have utilized user communities to great effect, ensuring that you get an answer to your question in minutes and in language that you understand.

This is a creative process, tapping into a diversity of customer backgrounds and utilizing a range of innovation techniques. It also needs to be carefully facilitated, because it opens your business to customers in a way they have never seen before – so professionalism and reputation still need to be managed. It also helps you build relationships that no longer depend on direct mail or loyalty cards.

Best of all, customers will often give you all of this free. However, whilst tapping into the resources of passionate customers is cheap and often delivers better results, customers will increasingly become aware of their value. Incentives and discounts are increasingly expected, and the innovative co-creators will rethink business models in order to share the longer-term rewards with customers, either through pricing strategies or profit-sharing.

Procter & Gamble ... from product push to customer pull

In 2000, P&G needed to change: Profits were declining, brands were looking tired and consumers were disengaged. New CEO A.J. Lafley concluded that it needed three things: more speed and agility, a deeper understanding of consumers, and a more radical approach to innovation.

P&G has since experienced transformation internally and has absorbed some of its largest competitors too, buying Clairol for $5 billion in 2001, Wella for $7 billion and Gillette for $54 billion in 2005. He has replaced at least half of his most senior managers and cut many more jobs as part of his vision to turn P&G into a virtual brand-owning company, with brand-building and innovation its core business – much of the latter done in partnership with others.

Lafley's initial rallying call was incredibly simple – as he reminds people in meetings, 'the consumer is the boss'. With this phrase he is turning P&G inside out – or, more precisely, outside in.

Symbolically he tore down the walls of the executive offices, including his own. He moved people about, for example seating marketing and finance people together to drive faster, more collaborative, more commercial, customer-driven ways of working. He spent hours talking to real consumers in their homes around the world – about how they live and how they cook or clean. When his managers came to him with an idea, he was ready to respond with a consumer's mindset.

In particular, innovation has come under the microscope. Despite battalions of scientists and engineers and millions of dollars being pumped into internal ventures, P&G hadn't delivered a real innovation in decades. When it tried to innovate, it was always based on a technically advanced product offer rather than something consumers actually wanted. Two major initiatives drove Lafley's innovation agenda:

➡ **'Connect and develop'** – a co-creation approach to developing new ideas with partners and consumers.

➡ **'Design thinking'** – using those insights to create dramatically improved brand experiences.

'Connect and develop' started from Lafley's goal that at least 50% of new products should come from outside, compared to 10% when he began. This would require a huge culture change, and putting your future in the hands of others would be risky too: it meant that influence within P&G would shift from research scientists to ethnographers. The new approach was also about collaboration, with a diverse array of partners who had specialist skills and perspectives that P&G didn't and with consumers.

The initiative is P&G's version of open innovation – working in partnership with external expert companies to access their ideas and capabilities, and equally those of consumers. It works both inbound and outbound, and encompasses everything from trademarks to packaging, marketing models to engineering and business services to retail partnerships.

'Design thinking' has also become a core driver of P&G's culture change under Lafley. Business leaders have learnt to focus and listen rather than order and control. Teams work together

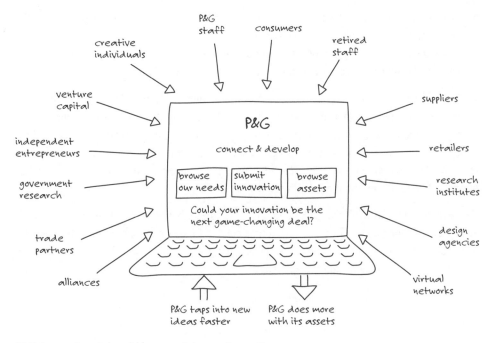

P&G's 'connect and develop' approach to open innovation

rather than apart. The best ideas come from customer immersion rather than research scientists. Business cases have been reduced to one-page posters, rigorous evaluation has been overtaken by rapid prototyping, and new products and services are rolling out like never before.

It was initially driven by Claudia Kotchka, VP Design, who was asked by Lafley to build 'design' into the DNA of the company. At P&G this would usually result in a complex, highly specified process, but she knew that good design needs a cultural pull rather than process push mechanism to work. At first, people wanted to know about the academic theory behind the process, which stifled thinking and behaviours. But slowly they embraced the more experiential approach and engaging in problem-solving rather than product thinking became intuitive to them, as did searching for new stimuli that led to creative solutions.

The resulting design thinking workshop structure became more of a fast-paced immersive experience that ended with a serious reflection point about what was different using a methodology. The main lesson was that people need to do design thinking rather than just think about it. People were initially scared to talk to real consumers or just build a prototype and try new ideas, but by doing it they found it worked – indeed, counter-intuitively, the less finished the prototype, the more feedback it got.

Net revenues have grown from $55 billion in 2005 to $79 billion in 2009, with 60% growth in profits over the same period. Forty-two per cent of P&G products now include an externally sourced component. It seems that P&G, with the customer as its leader and design thinking as its discipline, is doing very well.

CHAPTER 24

Creative partners ... collaboration, the spirit of Koinonia

'In the long history of humankind (and animal kind, too) those who learned to collaborate and improvise most effectively have prevailed.'

Charles Darwin

'*Koinonia*' is about mutuality, intimacy and participation, and about achieving more together.

Choosing the right partners for development or distribution gives you the flexibility, reach, capabilities and courage to thrive in fast-changing markets. Partners might offer some specialist component to your solution, essential to your success – the high-speed, ever-smaller microprocessor from Intel, for example – or they might complement what you do in some way – such as Rolls-Royce engines being an essential part of the Boeing design and manufacturing process.

Partners might improve your access to the market, such as iPhone working with exclusive network partners such as AT&T and O_2 for the first few years after launch. Or they might make your brand more compelling and relevant to your target audience – think of famous designers working with H&M to improve their designs and hugely enhance their brand kudos.

The table below lists the different types of partners you could work with.

Partner type	Timeframe	Positives	Negatives
Subcontract	Short term	Reduce costs, risks and time	Harder to ensure quality
Licensing	Fixed term	Use of a technology, brand or resource	Cost, constraints and future use
Consortia	Medium term	Expertise, shared funding and risks	Leaked knowledge, less differentiated
Alliance	Flexible	Market access, lower cost and risk	Leaked knowledge, inflexibility
Joint venture	Long term	Complementary skills and dedicated focus	Above, mismatch of purpose or culture
Network	Long term	Shared learning, market access	Above, inefficiency of participation

Few companies can survive, and even fewer thrive, without partners today. Such partnerships are rarely formalized as companies or even joint ventures, which they tended to be in the past. Increasing confidence in working with others means that most companies are now happy to work contractually but not structurally together. Licensing and franchising, brand alliances and affinity brands, endorsement and ingredient brands, exclusive distributors and guest designers – these are the new models of partnership.

Open innovation

Partnerships can be the source of innovation even before they start. Such collaborative approaches between businesses are typically called 'open innovation'. Henry Chesbrough first used this term in his book *Open Innovation: The New Imperative for Creating and Profiting from Technology* to include co-creation and crowdsourcing, collaboration and customization with customers, or collaboration and co-opetition (working with competitors) with other companies.

Chesbrough describes a world of widely distributed knowledge where companies cannot afford to rely entirely on their own research but should instead work with others; for example, buying or licensing processes or inventions from other companies. In a world of rapid change, this agility enables companies to adapt faster and seize new opportunities quicker, rather than being restrained by needing the capabilities to achieve this.

Open innovation also works in reverse, when a business seeks other partners to work with in order to exploit its own IP (ideas, patents and capabilities) through licensing, joint ventures and spin-offs.

Ideas exchanges

Several companies currently operate as open innovation intermediaries, including Inno-Centive – a global, online marketplace in ideas. Organizations searching for innovation can connect with a network of the more than 185,000 potential problem-solvers, all of them registered members of InnoCentive. Anyone with interest and online access can become a member: large corporations and small businesses, academics and experts, students and the retired. Solvers whose solutions are selected by the seekers are compensated for their ideas by InnoCentive, which acts as broker of the process.

The process works both ways – 'seekers' can also become 'solvers' for other companies. In this way they can find new opportunities to license products or practices, apply their in-house capabilities to external challenges, find new applications for technologies and devices, and, in so doing, open new streams of revenue.

Disney ... the enduring magic of a mouse called Mickey

Since 1923, The Walt Disney Company has remained faithful in its commitment to delivering the best entertainment based on its rich legacy of creative content and storytelling.

Since the early days the company has become the master of growth through adjacent markets, constantly developing the business into new but related businesses by using its characters, audiences and capabilities as springboards. If you can make animated films, you can make TV shows. If you engage customers with characters they love, they want to go see them. If you can run theme parks, you can run cruise liners. Whilst Walt grabbed the headlines, dreaming of magic kingdoms and a talking mouse, it was his brother Roy who made it all happen operationally. Today Disney and its 133,000 employees are divided into four major business areas, each bringing together a range of famous and integrated brands and activities, but linked across the group in order to maximize their exposure, engagement and impact.

Since Bob Iger replaced the embattled Michael Eisner in 2005, Disney's share price has climbed by almost 50%. According to investment analysts, this is partly because Eisner invested wisely and partly through Iger's more effective management style. He has ensured that Disney has brought together its diverse assets for real impact. Most crucially, he has ensured that content works harder in a multimedia, digitally enabled world. With so many different platforms, Disney can make a film, show or character work in many formats, taking it to many more people and creating an enduring revenue stream.

Record-breaking revenues of $34 billion was due to an impressive string of hits: *Pirates of the Caribbean: Dead Man's Chest* was the world's best-selling film and DVD, *Cars* the best-selling animated film, TV shows such as *Lost* and *Desperate Housewives*, and Disney Channel's *High School Musical* also delivered a best-selling album. Indeed, Disney as a brand has been so consistent and successful in its marketing over the years that it has gained 'ownership' of a handful of emotive words that perhaps define its brand better than any slogan: Disney words (where more than 80% of people associate the word with Disney, according to Martin Lindstom's *BrandSense*) include 'fantasy', 'dreams', 'magic', 'creativity' and 'smile'.

The four businesses that make these words come to life are:

➡ **Disney Studio Entertainment:** The studio is the foundation of the company, and includes subsidiary brands such as Touchstone Pictures and Buena Vista.

➡ **Disney Parks and Resorts:** Disneyland was first developed in Arnheim, California, in 1952. Now there are 11 parks, 35 hotels and two luxury cruise ships.

➡ **Disney Consumer Products:** The brand extends into every form of merchandizing, including toys, clothing, interactive games, fine arts, home décor and Baby Einstein – all available in Disney Stores and beyond.

➡ **Disney Media Networks:** Disney has brought together a vast array of television, cable, radio and Internet brands, including ABC and ESPN.

Disney is also benefitting from the boardroom arrival of Steve Jobs. When Disney acquired his Pixar animation studios for $7.4 billion, Jobs joined the board and also became the company's largest individual shareholder. Whilst Pixar is breathing new life into Disney's movie business, Jobs is having an even greater impact in encouraging the use of digital platforms.

In 2005, Disney's ABC became the first supplier of TV programmes to the iTunes store, selling episodes at $1.99 each. A year later it was the first to stream full episodes for free onto the

ABC website, upgrading the site's video player to something close to cinema standard. Viewers can vote online to shape the plot of TV programmes and engage much more deeply.

Whilst other media companies might be concerned about free content taking customers away from its TV audiences, and therefore from its sponsors and advertisers, Disney sees it as incremental – reaching new audiences or deepening relationships with them. It can partner with advertisers to create co-branded Web versions of shows, which have proved to have more impact than traditional TV advertising.

The results are impressive. By 2007, iTunes had delivered 21 million downloads of Disney/ABC shows, generating $41.8 million to be shared between Apple and Disney, with the majority to the content supplier. Meanwhile in the first year of free online downloads, 90 million episodes of Disney Channel shows were viewed on the disneychannel.com and 76 million episodes of ABC television shows were viewed on abc.com.

But it's worth remembering Roy: for every Walt, there needs to be a Roy. Innovation is about ideas and implementation, and commercial success like Disney's needs both. Whilst Walt was having all the dreams, it was Roy who was making the dreams come true.

CHAPTER 25

Experimentation ... prototypes, simulations, let's just try it!

'To invent, you need a good imagination and a pile of junk.'

Thomas Edison

New concepts are always uncertain. People are sceptical or unclear about what they actually are, others are technically uncertain as to whether it can be done, and others are worried about whether customers will buy it.

The best solution is to try it as soon as possible. Even the simplest prototypes make ideas tangible, giving people creative focus to make ideas better rather than creating more of them. With significantly improved computer modelling, most prototypes can be created incredibly quickly as virtual simulations. James Dyson describes how a process that used to take months can now take a few hours – a huge saving for industrial design processes where millimetres and angles can make a huge difference to performance.

Imagine designing a sports car where styling is crucial to the aerodynamics and therefore performance of the car. In the past, full prototypes would be constructed, tested in the wind tunnel and then demolished in order to do better. Today, the style can be tweaked until it reaches simulated perfection. The designer can find the right balance between factors such as weight reduction and crashworthiness.

When electronics retailer Best Buy decides to enter a new area, it initially invests $1 million in developing a 'lab store' to test different combinations of products, concepts and merchandizing, seeing who actually comes to the store and buys. In some locations, its home entertainment studios might be popular; in others, it might be its scrapbooking workspaces. The lab store process is an experiment that makes at least enough money to pay for itself. Once it has learnt enough, Best Buy tailors its store to sub-brands that work best locally.

'Test and learn' is a set of practices followed by retailers, banks and other mass-marketers to test ideas in a small number of locations to predict impact. The process is often designed to answer three questions about any tested program before rollout:

➜ What impact will the concept have if implemented across the network or customer base?

➜ Will the concept have a larger impact on some stores/customers than others?

➜ Which components of the idea work best, and which others improved?

The iterative approach to innovation has been systematically applied since 1988 by Capital One. The credit card company tests everything from product design to marketing to customer selection to collection policies. In a single year, it performs tens of thousands of tests, allowing it to offer thousands of different types of credit cards to customers, based on the knowledge gained from their tests.

Last year, according to *Fast Company* magazine, the company performed 28,000 experiments, such as live in-market tests of new products, new advertising approaches, new markets and new pricing structures and incentives. As a result, it can deliver the right product, at the right price, to the right customer, at the right time: 6000 kinds of credit cards, each with slightly different terms, requirements, and benefits, and each requiring a slightly different monthly statement.

El Bulli ... gastronomic creativity from the world's best restaurant

El Bulli – or elBulli, as it prefers to be branded – is the best restaurant in the world.

Restaurant magazine has voted the small Spanish restaurant run by chef Ferran Adrià its global favourite for five years. It is only a small restaurant, overlooking the Cala Montjoi and the Catalonian seaside town on the Costa Brava. It has been described as 'the most imaginative generator of haute cuisine on the planet', famed for its molecular gastronomy.

Ferran Adrià is the driving force, or gastroscientist, behind the restaurant's menu. He travels for six months every year in search of inspiration, and then returns to his Barcelona laboratory where he experiments with new tastes, temperatures and textures. His ground-breaking techniques have inspired other chefs throughout the world to experiment, including Heston Blumenthal of the Fat Duck in Bray.

'Taste is not the only sense that can be stimulated. Touch can also be played with though contrasts in temperatures and textures, as well as smell, sight in terms of colours, shapes and much more. The five senses become one of the main points of reference in the creative cooking process,' says Adrià.

El Bulli was founded in 1961 by German chef Hans Schilling and his Czech wife, who fell in love with the location. The name 'El Bulli' came from his French bulldogs. The restaurant won its first Michelin star in 1976 while under French chef Jean-Louis Neichel. Adrià joined the team in 1984 and took charge of the kitchen in 1987. Under him the restaurant gained its second Michelin star in 1991 and a third six years later.

The restaurant has a limited season from April to October, and bookings for the whole of the following year are taken in a single day after the closing of the previous season. The average cost of a meal is €250. During the closed season, Adrià can be found in his Barcelona chemistry lab, concocting his next surprise.

El Bulli employs around 40 chefs and has operated at a loss since 2000 – revenues come from branded recipe books and merchandise, and lectures and schools from Adrià. The 500-page recipe book is more suited to a coffee table than a kitchen and describes Adrià's creative methods, with a map that traces the development of his cuisine – a kind of historical and scientific anthropology.

Most of his 30 recipes included are beyond the reach of most people cooking at home, who probably don't have access to a Pacojet, freeze-dryer, liquid nitrogen tank, candyfloss machine, Superbags and other high-tech kitchen tools that Adrià relies upon – although he also uses a screwdriver and bike pump. Even the cocktail recipes involves Himalayan salt crystal and a microplane grater to make a margarita. Like the rest of this book, the recipes are to be marvelled at, rather than eaten.

In 2010, in a turn more akin to the most rebellious of artists, Adrià decided that in 2012 he would close his restaurant for two years whilst he recharges his creativity, searching for real change in his approach and making sure that Blumenthal and others don't catch up. Whilst recognizing that it means he will lose his three Michelin stars and two years of restaurant income, he feels that his art matters more. By January 2014 there is certain to be a long waiting list for his reopening.

CHAPTER 26

Concept fusions ... building molecular solutions

'New ideas come from differences. They come from having different perspectives and juxtaposing different theories.'

Nicholas Negroponte

Concepts are like Lego models.

Lego comes in packs of many pieces, including different colours and sizes – sometimes even with a motorized engine or a software programme. Similarly, business comes in packs of many ideas, manifest as products and services, propositions and experiences, or business models and marketing campaigns. Just as you can build an infinite number of Lego models, concepts come from the many different idea components, emerging in bigger and better combinations.

Concepts typically take on a molecular-like structure, fusing together the best ideas. At their core is a number of the most common items, just like carbon atoms, but from this an infinite variety of different atoms are attached in different ways. The molecules are far more distinctive than simple atoms, difficult to imitate by competitors and much more valuable to customers. The molecules might be unique, a one-off for a customer, or replicated many times because they prove appropriate for a whole workforce or for all customers with similar characteristics.

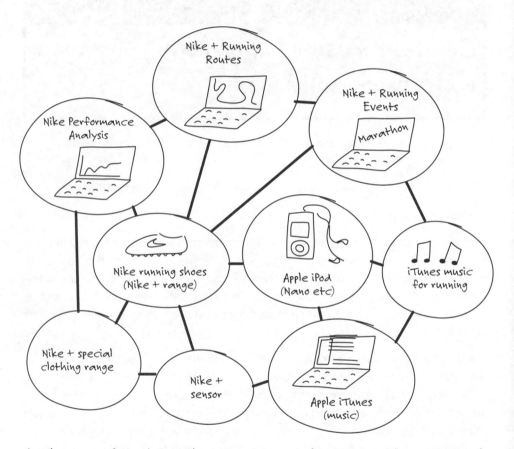

The Nike+ concept fusion that enables you to get more out of your running, with a combination of Nike and Apple's products and services

The molecules might be entirely home-grown (i.e. made of all the company's own products and services) or they could include components provided by a wide range of different suppliers, complementary brands and even the customer's own resources. The more diversely sourced the molecule – particularly through exclusive networks of partners – the more difficult it is to copy and the more compelling is the eventual innovation.

Concepts are the starting points of storytelling – ways to make people's lives better – but they can also be physical structures too.

Concept fusions, in the form of molecular idea structures, can be named and packaged in the same way as products and services – although by definition they represent a bigger idea that creates a total experience for the customer, enabling them to work better and achieve more. They can be scaled up into mass production if appropriate, or they might simply form an ongoing template from which a range of different models, maybe under different brand names, and targeting different audiences and applications are developed.

Platforms become a highly efficient route for innovation. The car industry is one of the simplest examples: consider, for example, Volkswagen's mid-size PQ35 platform, which is shared between its own Beetle, Golf, Scirocco and Touran, as well as Skoda's Octavia and Yeti, Seat's Leon and Toledo, and the Audi A3 and TT. In a market where new models can cost $1 billion to develop, this saves the group enormous speed and time whilst also creating innovations that are adapted to different markets.

Anish Kapoor ... cloud gates, sky mirrors and fishnet tights

The sculptor Anish Kapoor is creating the *Tees Valley Giants* in collaboration with structural engineer Cecil Balmond. The first giant, known as *Temenos*, resembles a pair of fishnet tights, stretched 110 metres in length between giant hoops, suspended 50 metres above the ground. The Middlesbrough installation will be joined by three others in the adjacent towns Stockton, Hartlepool, Darlington and Redcar. The £15 million project seeks to rise above the post-industrial wastelands, inspiring a new generation of creativity and entrepreneurship across the region.

Over the past twenty years Kapoor has exhibited all over the world. His exhibitions have sparkled in locations like the Kunsthalle Basel, Tate Gallery in London, the Haus der Kunst in Munich and Centre Georges Pompidou in Paris. He was awarded the *Premio Duemila* when representing his adopted UK at the Venice Biennale in 1990 and the Turner Prize a year later.

His sculptures are strikingly simple, using usually monochromatic and brightly coloured curved forms. He seeks to engage the viewer: inspiring them through size and simple beauty, evoking mystery through the works' shadows, encouraging them to touch the inviting surfaces, and fascinating them with reflections. Kapoor likes to play with 'dualities' –earth and sky, body and spirit, lightness and darkness, visible and invisible, conscious and unconscious, male and female, and body and mind. His most recent works are mirror-like, reflecting or distorting the viewer and surroundings.

A beautiful and timeless stone arch by Kapoor stands on the shoreline of a lake in Lødingen in Norway, whilst *Parabolic Waters*, consisting of rapidly rotating coloured water, sits outside London's O_2 Arena. *Sky Mirror*, a large mirror reflecting the sky and surroundings, was erected for the Nottingham Playhouse and later also for the Rockefeller Center in New York. And perhaps most inspiring, *Cloud Gate*, a 110-tonne stainless steel sculpture, captures the world above in Chicago's Millennium Park.

CHAPTER 27

Simplicity

'I dream for a living.'

Stephen Spielberg

Innovation is about making people's lives better.

Physicist Paul Dirac said that beauty should be the first thing to look for in a new scientific theory. Beauty, he said, is about elegance, naturalness, pleasure and simplicity. In design, we seek to create a beautiful solution – not only in its outward appearance but in the way in which it solve a problem and make life better.

Simplicity is about making things simpler (simple!) – sometimes simpler is the best possible way to be better. In his book *The Laws of Simplicity*, John Maeda reflected on the world around him to find that success was often about less rather than more, that people responded better to clear propositions even if they were less good than more complex ones, and making things faster or easier can often be when of the best ways to add value and stand out from the crowd. He developed ten principles:

→ **Reduce ... the simplest way to simplify:** Consumer electronics are intimidating because they can do so much, when all you want to do are the simple things. But sometimes you want to more. Finding the balance is achieved through thoughtful reduction, watching how users behave and thinking laterally, like Jonathan Ive did so successfully with his clickwheel.

➡ **Organize ... making lots appear like little:** There's nothing more annoying than a cluttered home or office. You could just throw everything out – think of the paperless office or brochure-image home – but that's often not practical. But it's amazing how organizing things can help. Sorting paper into five categories suddenly seems manageable; a wardrobe organized into shirts, trousers, jackets suddenly seems refreshed.

➡ **Time ... speeding up, saving time:** We typically spend an hour a day waiting in a queue. We hate waiting and because of that, we love speed: we marvel at FedEx's overnight delivery capability or the speed of the Drive-Thru McDonald's. Waiting time seems complex, saving time seems simple.

➡ **Learn ... knowledge beats ignorance:** There is nothing worse than spending hours trying to make a new device work: connecting it to the Internet, knowing how to use its applications or synchronizing it with other devices. We jump in with eyes closed, four different experiments all at the same time. Sometimes taking time to read the guidebook is time saved in the longer run.

➡ **Differences ... simplicity needs complexity:** Recognizing alternatives helps us to focus on what matters most. Contrast is good. We appreciate good food because we sometimes experience bad food. The more complicated the technology, the more we crave simplicity. The more complexity there is in a market, the more that simplicity stands out.

➡ **Context ... don't just focus on the obvious:** Looking to the periphery of what you are addressing is as important as the main thing. A good-looking product deserves a good-looking box. Excellence in customer service relates to the car park as much as the service desk. Looking more broadly across the customer's experience usually offers more scope to make things simpler.

➡ **Emotion ... be human and personal:** Empathy, body language, words, a smile – these can all take away the fear and frustration of complexity. Aesthetic and ergonomic design looks and feels good. Knowing that you are in it together is much better than feeling alone. Knowing that somebody is there to help is always reassuring. Add more human-ness, warmth and personalization to every interaction.

➡ **Trust ... in simplicity we trust:** We trust what we can understand, and we don't trust what we don't. We trust it to work without complex problems, but we like it more too. Bang and Oluffsen develops premium electronics devices that look simpler than any of its rivals, and we trust it more. Alessi turns complicated ideas into simple designs and we trust them more.

➡ **Failure ... some things can never be simple:** Google's algorithms, which enable us to make sense of the unbelievably complex networks of knowledge, are never going to be simple – but the complexity results in simple search results. The power of nanotechnol-ogy is too mind-boggling to even think about, but the results are simpler, easier tech-niques and applications.

➡ **The one ... subtract the obvious, add the meaningful:** Simplicity is incredible subtle. It depends how you see it, standing close up or from a distance. It depends on what else matters to you in your work and life. In a frantically busy and cluttered world, it only takes one or two things to make our lives so much easier. Simplicity should actually be quite simple – don't make it too complicated.

John Maeda ... the digital artist in search of simple ideas

At first glance, John Maeda doesn't seem all that amazing: quiet, easy-going, T-shirt wear-ing, maybe a technology geek. Yet he is also a world-renowned graphic designer, visual artist and computer scientist at the MIT Media Lab, and President of the Rhode Island School of Design.

Maeda is most famous for his pursuit of simplicity and using electronic media to express ideas through educational and beautiful graphic designs. He is part of a new generation of digital artists that connects creativity and technology in both innovative and aesthetic ways. Some see him as a twenty-first century Renaissance man, reconciling the design world's competing demands for creativity and pragmatism, uniqueness and mass-marketability.

The word 'genius' is often – although for him, embarrassingly – associated with Maeda. Whilst he sees MIT as the hub for left-brained technology research, Rhode Island is the right-branded antithesis for creativity and design. Inevitable, he loves the fusion. He recognizes the distinction and seeks to retain the polarity, but as a person wants to embrace both. Maeda believes that innovation in the future will be less about technology and much more about design: 'art humanizes technology and makes it understandable. Design is needed to make sense of information overload. It is why art and design will rise in importance during this century as we try to make sense of all the possibilities that digital technology now affords,' he wrote on his blog, giving Apple as the best example.

Like many others, Maeda believes that the business world has become too left-brain in its thinking, focusing on logic and reasoning – science, technology, engineering and maths, or 'STEM' as he calls it. He thinks that future economic development needs more right-brain thinking, or in his words, 'IDEA' – intuition, design, emotion and art. Simplicity, he believes, lies in the combination of both sides of our brains, and 'in our hands to make it real'. He muses on what it is that Apple has that others don't, the '*je ne sais quoi*' that draws us in:

'I'm beginning to think that it's not just that they understand the power of simplicity, or the power of software. It's that you can see they were born from a person, from two dirty hands, from just a little bit of technology, and from a massively powerful *idea*.'

CHAPTER 28

Experience design ... doing more for people

'I don't have to invent anything ... It's out there somewhere if I can just find it and integrate it ... Inventing is frustrating, it's dangerous, it's expensive, and inventors should avoid it whenever possible. Be a systems integrator'

Dean Kamen in *Code Name Ginger*

'It's one thing to have people buy your products, it's another for them to tattoo your name on their bodies ... What we sell is the ability for a 43-year-old accountant to dress in black leather, ride through small towns and have people be afraid of him.' That's how Harley Davidson's CEO Jeff Bleustein described the experience by which he seeks to bring his brand to life in his recent annual report.

Customer experiences are most memorable when they are like nothing else. The designed experience – having eliminated the negative moments and found ways to create a more positive emotional journey through streamlining, elaborating and maybe even a touch of theatre – can then be delivered uniquely for each customer.

This is not one person or department's challenge – it is a whole business challenge. It may even require the cooperation of suppliers, distributors and partners. It is not just about putting in place the tangible activities, products and processes; it is about attitude and behaviours, service and style, and acting as one.

However, experiences are emotional. To reflect the excellent book by Andy Milligan and Shaun Smith, it is about what customers *See, Feel, Think and Do*. They encourage managers to use their intuition, based on all their senses to make better decisions, and equally to enable customers to be multi-sensory too. We are familiar with the far greater impact of our non-aural senses – what we see, feel and touch – yet it is easy to dismiss these in the rush to maximize transactions.

Singapore Airlines will leave you with a lasting smile, but they will also sell you a bottle of their air. You will encounter the subtle fragrance as you board an aircraft and it relaxes you during your flight – its experience design team spend many hours working perfecting it. Similarly, when you test-drive a new Lexus car you are seduced as much by the scent and softness of the leather as by the acceleration and fuel efficiency of its hybrid engine.

In finalizing the design of your customer experience, consider how you can bring it to life, making it a multisensory experience rather than a sterile one. Add to your touchpoint map what you want customers to see, how you want them to feel, what you want them to think as well as what they do at each different interaction. You could offer a more personalized style of service, being more responsive to each customer, finding ways to connect with them, learning more about them from information in databases and previously expressed preferences rather than following a standard list of procedures.

The Ritz Carlton taxi driver will alert the hotel doorman and receptionist of the imminent arrival of a new guest so that they can greet the guest by name when they arrive. As soon as a regular customer calls the telephone bank First Direct, the incoming number will prompt a personal profile to pop-up in front of the person answering the call – summarizing the customer's details, preferences and financial background, and enabling a more informed and relevant experience.

The information and experiences of each interaction with each person can be useful in anticipating, improving or personalizing future interactions, be they moments or months later, by the same person or by different people across the organization.

Brands are not names or logos. They are distinctive concepts that become personal experiences. Don't forget the big idea of your brand – enabling people to run faster, make new friends, cook better food – and what makes you different from the others who also seek to do this. 'Bringing your brand to life' is about finding ways to make the brand come alive in relevant and personal ways at every interaction, whether it's through a recognized visual identity, distinctive language and exclusive features, or service delivered with a trademark attitude and style. Find ways to symbolize this at points throughout your experience – the 'brand gestures' that tangibly and emotionally bring the brand to life.

As you enter Disneyland, brand gestures are all around you – the music playing as you walk through the gates, Mickey Mouse waiting to greet you within the next few steps, the smell of fresh bread as you walk down Main Street, the smile and banter from the street cleaners, the surprise and delight as Pluto waits around the corner, or as Cinderella bursts into song.

Nobel-prize winning psychologist Daniel Kahneman has found, through research into people's experiences in all walks of life, that the quality of an experience is almost entirely determined by two events: how the experience felt at its peak (the best or worst moment), and how it ended. It suggests that the memorable experiences end on a high: spending as much time advising customers after their purchase as you do when helping them to buy or celebrating when a customer moves into their new home rather than just selling the house to them.

One approach to designing a better customer experience is to consider how you can add more significant value to customers by adopting an enhanced role rather than just being a supplier of products and services – how you can enable them to do more. Imagine you are a performer. There are different ways to interact with your audience, sometimes following a script, at other times being unscripted. Sometimes you allow the audience to passively enjoy your show, sometimes the show might require interaction with them.

In a similar manner, you can consider the types of performance, and therefore types of experience you seek to create for your customers at each interaction – will they be passive and scripted, or spontaneous and responsive to each different customer? This leads to a number of different roles, and potential new ways of enhancing the value you create for your customers:

→ **Entertaining experiences**, from sporting events to rock concerts, far more dramatic than when edited and viewed remotely; for example, the Red Bull Air Race absorbs you in the adrenalin rush of a canned drink.

→ **Educational experiences**, from historic monuments brought to life through re-enactments to training courses based on role-play and interaction; for example, Schwab Learning Centers demystify the investment world.

→ **Guiding experiences**, from art galleries that embrace all the senses to health spas that stimulate and pamper them; for example, Michelin Restaurant Guides take a lowly tyre manufacturer into a different context.

→ **Coaching experiences**, from adventure sports to videogames that take participants into extreme or imaginary worlds; for example, Subaru Driving Experiences teach drivers how to handle the toughest terrains.

Any business can embrace any of these types of experiences to enhance their proposition or exploit adjacent revenue streams, and to simply engage customers like never before.

Guggenheim Bilbao ... architecture that re-energizes a wasteland

Mention the Spanish city of Bilbao to a culture lover twenty years ago and you may well have been met with blank stares. Mention it today, however, and their eyes will light up. Not only will they know Bilbao, they may even have visited the former shipbuilding city in Northern Spain's Basque country.

Why? Because of the Guggenheim Museum.

The fantastic, futuristic structure contains works by late 20th century greats such as Mark Rothko and Andy Warhol, as well as avant-garde artists such as the UK's Gilbert and George. Just as big an attraction is the much-lauded museum building designed by the renowned architect Frank Gehry: with its unearthly curves and titanium 'fish-scale' surface, the Guggenheim has quickly become one of the most recognized buildings in the world.

The standard joke is that Gehry was sketching out a plan for an art museum in Bilbao, rejected it, screwed up the piece of paper, threw it down, looked at it and, realized he had his museum. Of course he did not do that and the building, which opened in 1997, is considered one of his most iconic creations.

When Bilbao decided it needed a spectacular building and cultural clout to lift it out of industrial decay, the site by the River Nervión was not inspiring – but Gehry loved the challenge. 'To be at the bend of a working river intersected by a bridge, and connecting the urban fabric of a dense city to the river's edge with a place for modern art is my idea of heaven,' Gehry wrote to the Guggenheim Foundation.

Beneath the titanium fish scales, stone and glass of the buildings canopy are three levels with 20 galleries plus a large area for art structures, two cafés, a renowned restaurant and a 300-seat auditorium. The outside entrance is dominated by Jeff Koons' huge floral *Puppy*.

CHAPTER 29

Evaluating concepts ... deciding what to do

'The winner is the chef who takes the same ingredients as everyone else and produces the best results'.

Edward de Bono

Innovations should be reviewed and evaluated from initial idea to market entry, and over time in the market too. However, the nature of this evaluation will differ depending on the objectives of the development phase:

➡ **Idea filters:** In the early discovery and ideation phase we are seeking to 'open up' as far as possible, challenging the conventions and searching for newness. Therefore the filters are less about right and wrong, more about making ideas clear and distinctive.

➡ **Concepts filters:** In the design and development phase we are looking for 'turning point' concepts that bring the best ideas together in coherent ways, addressing the problem as first defined or maybe a broader one that can be articulated more tangibly and have a practical applications.

➡ **Solution filters:** In the later development and preparing to launch phase, we need to 'close down' on the few best concepts that we (a) want to make happen, (b) see as practical and profitable, and (c) will invest huge sums in producing and marketing (and therefore the financial risks are greatest).

Evaluation in these different phases can be both rigorous and intuitive. Customers can generate fantastic ideas through deep dives and co-creation. Of course, this gives them great credibility in the organization: 'our customers say we want it' is often a much stronger position to win a debate than just believing in it yourself.

Whilst customers are a fabulous source of ideas, they can be wrong too – because they don't see that value yet in future possibilities and only look at things from their perspective rather than whether it works commercially too. Of course, you can always start with something they find compelling and find a way to make it profitable, but it is still not always the right answer.

The future is equally important in understanding the potential of new innovations. The whole purpose in looking for whitespaces, developing scenarios of alternative futures, and looking for patterns and paradoxes to exploit is to get a view as to which ideas are likely to deliver the best 'future-proofed' innovations and exploit emerging markets and future profit pools.

Then there is your own intuition as a designer or business leader. The great designer Alberto Alessi has perfected a simple scoring mechanism that helps him to filter the many different designs in his studio. However, he also uses his gut instinct to overrule his quantified methods if he really believes in it. Sometimes you just have to believe in an idea.

At the end of the design studio, I would typically get the team to evaluate their ideas themselves using what information they have such as market research and financial data, their own experiences in making things happen, and their intuition based on being absorbed in the project over recent weeks. I get each person to independently score the best concepts on three grids, using a simple high/medium/low system. The grids are:

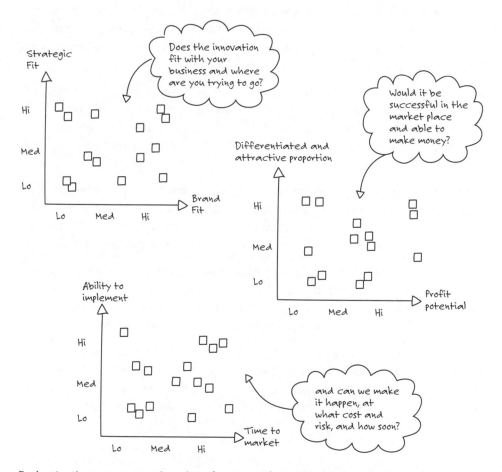

Evaluating the best concepts through qualitative analysis – in terms of strategic fit, market impact and practical implementation

➡ **Strategic fit:** How well do the emerging concepts fit against the business strategy, the purpose of the brand or the specific objectives set for the project? At Marks and Spencer, for example, its brand is about 'making aspirational ideas accessible to everyone', and so strategic fit was measured in terms of axes labelled 'Aspirational' and 'Accessible'.

➡ **Market impact:** How well the concept will perform in the eventual market once it has had time to get established with effective positioning and promotion. At Fosters drinks, for example, we evaluated concepts against competitive differentiation and anticipated price premium.

➡ **Practical challenge:** How easy it will be to make the idea happen in terms of capital investment and risk involved, and the complexity and time required for implementation. At The Cooperative Group, for example, the team evaluated the concepts against ball-park investment requirements and likely time to market.

We then reflect upon all three grids, finding the average score for each concept on each grid, and then overall. Ideally you want concepts that score highly on all three grids; however, if, for example, it scores well on two but not the third, you might consider how to modify it to get a better score.

The additional value of the team participants doing the scoring directly is that it is:

➡ Instant and personal.

➡ Doesn't require complex spreadsheets that are only as good as their assumptions.

➡ 'Owned' by the people who are making the decisions, and potentially also making the innovation happen – there is an emotional and rational logic to moving forward.

However the only way to know for certain is to make the ideas happen – launching them in a controlled experimental way, perhaps only in one or two locations, with clear monitoring and evaluation measures in place. Concepts could also be trialled in parallel to compare their impacts, learning from each of them, and maybe further combining the most responsive ideas from each into stronger concepts ready for full scale implementation.

Alessi ... bird kettles and funky tableware

Alberto Alessi leads the iconic design firm that was founded by his grandfather Giovanni in 1921. It is still based in Crusinallo, around 50 kilometres north of Milan, and remains privately owned. In Alessi's view, both the ownership structure and the location have helped to establish a strong tradition of artisanship and given its designers the freedom to create as they see fit.

Tradition and individuality have allowed Alessi to produce some of the most popular houseware designs of recent decades, as well as some of the most exclusive. The design firm is perhaps best known for its invention of the first home espresso maker, as well as its sense of humour with the design of common kitchen utensils.

His grandfather, initially founded the family business to make metal products. Alberto has built on that capability with the belief that familiar domestic items are as worthy of first-rate creative thinking as buildings, beinging together probably the world's finest collection of designers – people like Philippe Starck, Aldo Rossi and Ettore Sottsass – to design iconic pieces for his collection.

Many Alessi products seem to have something playful about them. In 1980, Alessi challenged 11 well-known architects to create coffee and tea sets in which the pots would mimic buildings and the tray would serve as a 'piazza'. The collection was a design sensation, and commercially viable too (the limited edition sets sold for as much as $25,000). He has built a successful business by selling the idea of design, and of designers, to consumers. The company relies entirely on outside designers for all design execution and for the majority of concept initiation activities.

Alessi also developed a formal set of assessment criteria that he applies to all new concepts before deciding if it should be developed for production. The formula measures the proposal on four criteria:

➡ **Function:** Does it work? Is it practical, functional and labour saving?

➡ **Sensuality, memory and imagination:** Does the design please the senses? Is it memorable? Does it engender emotion?

➡ **Communication and language:** Will the product give its owner status and fit with current trends?

➡ **Price:** Can the product be made and sold at a sensible price, both relative to substitute products and to the customer's sense of its value?

Items are given a score from 0 to 5 along each of these four dimensions. A prospective design must have an overall score of more than 12 (equivalent to four 'neutral' ratings of 3) to be considered worth taking forward to the next stage. After each subsequent stage, the evaluation is repeated. Many projects are frozen after the initial assessment, and their prototypes and production details are placed in the company archive. These products may be revisited in future if trends change.

Once an initial design idea has proved itself to be fit for production, it moves on to the next stage of the Alessi design process. This is managed with a variety of tools and techniques, not least the metal manufacturing tools Alessi has retained to produce metal items in-house.

Alessi applies his model across all types of designs, audiences and cultures. He sees little difference among core customers, arguing that they are defined by their attitude to design, and to life, rather than the city they live in.

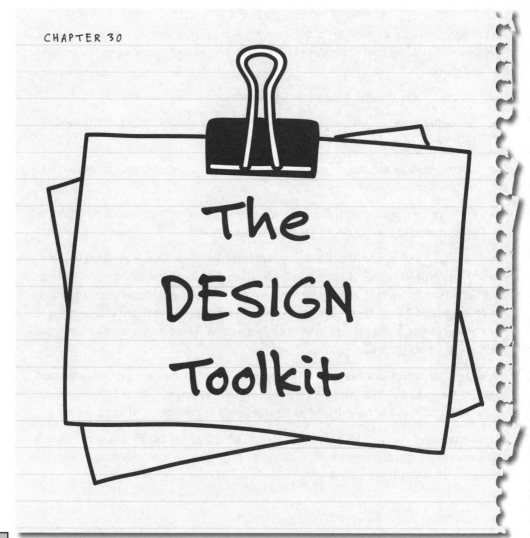

CHAPTER 30

The
DESIGN
Toolkit

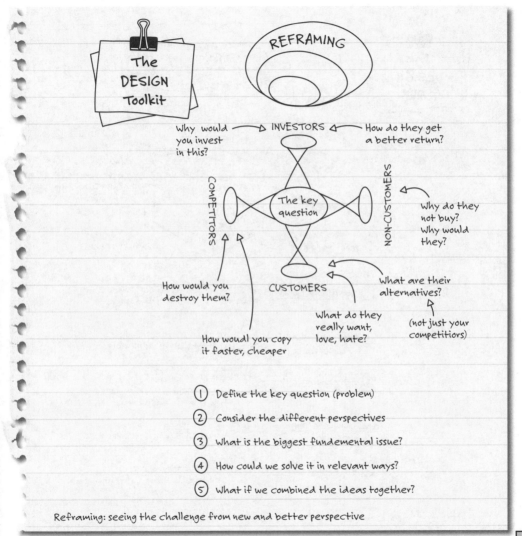

The DESIGN Toolkit

REFRAMING

Why would you invest in this? → INVESTORS ← How do they get a better return?

COMPETITORS

The key question

NON-CUSTOMERS

Why do they not buy? Why would they?

How would you destroy them?

CUSTOMERS

What are their alternatives?

(not just your competitiors)

How woudl you copy it faster, cheaper

What do they really want, love, hate?

① Define the key question (problem)

② Consider the different perspectives

③ What is the biggest fundemental issue?

④ How could we solve it in relevant ways?

⑤ What if we combined the ideas together?

Reframing: seeing the challenge from new and better perspective

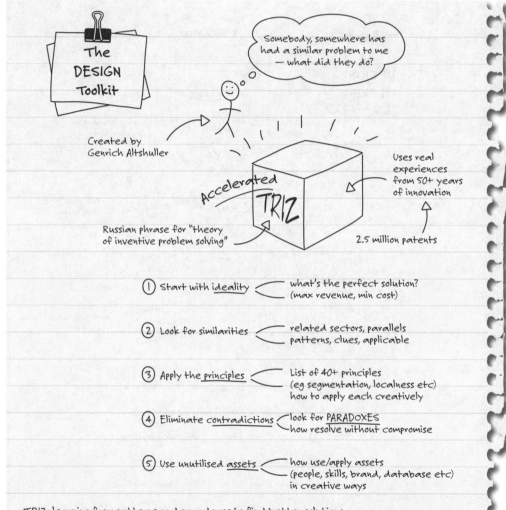

The DESIGN Toolkit

Somebody, somewhere has had a similar problem to me — what did they do?

Created by Genrich Altshuller

Accelerated TRIZ

Uses real experiences from 50+ years of innovation

Russian phrase for "theory of inventive problem solving"

2.5 million patents

① Start with ideality — what's the perfect solution? (max revenue, min cost)

② Look for similarities — related sectors, parallels / patterns, clues, applicable

③ Apply the principles — List of 40+ principles (eg segmentation, localness etc) how to apply each creatively

④ Eliminate contradictions — look for PARADOXES / how resolve without compromise

⑤ Use unutilised assets — how use/apply assets (people, skills, brand, database etc) in creative ways

TRIZ: learning from patterns and paradoxes to find better solutions

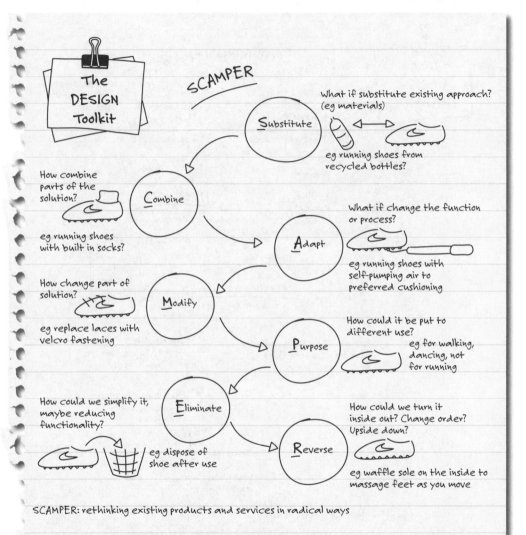

The DESIGN Toolkit

SCAMPER

Substitute — What if substitute existing approach? (eg materials)
eg running shoes from recycled bottles?

Combine — How combine parts of the solution?
eg running shoes with built in socks?

Adapt — What if change the function or process?
eg running shoes with self-pumping air to preferred cushioning

Modify — How change part of solution?
eg replace laces with velcro fastening

Purpose — How could it be put to different use?
eg for walking, dancing, not for running

Eliminate — How could we simplify it, maybe reducing functionality?
eg dispose of shoe after use

Reverse — How could we turn it inside out? Change order? Upside down?
eg waffle sole on the inside to massage feet as you move

SCAMPER: rethinking existing products and services in radical ways

227

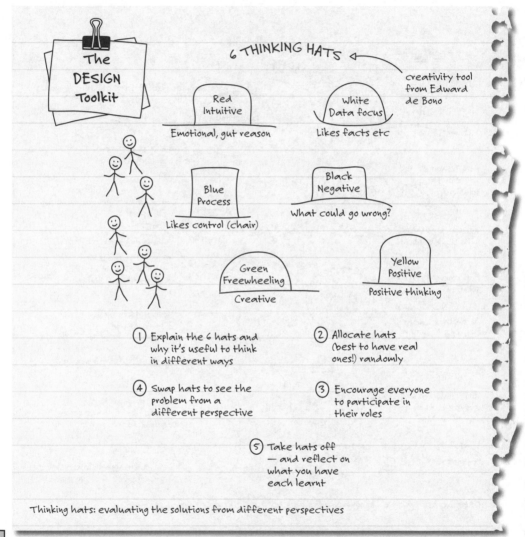

The DESIGN Toolkit

6 THINKING HATS ← creativity tool from Edward de Bono

Red Intuitive
Emotional, gut reason

White Data focus
Likes facts etc

Blue Process
Likes control (chair)

Black Negative
What could go wrong?

Green Freewheeling
Creative

Yellow Positive
Positive thinking

① Explain the 6 hats and why it's useful to think in different ways

② Allocate hats (best to have real ones!) randomly

④ Swap hats to see the problem from a different perspective

③ Encourage everyone to participate in their roles

⑤ Take hats off — and reflect on what you have each learnt

Thinking hats: evaluating the solutions from different perspectives

The DESIGN Toolkit

QFD

Quality Functional Deployment

① Define the customer needs and product attributes

Product attribute

								Customer priorities	Competitive advantage	Marketing priority
Customer needs	✓	✓✓				✓		3	4	8
"			✓				✓✓	7	3	9
"	✓	✓		✓	✓	✓✓		2	2	6
"		✓✓		✓✓✓			✓	3	1	7
"	✓✓✓		✓✓		✓			9	9	10
"	✓			✓		✓✓		1	10	4
"		✓✓✓			✓		✓	5	1	5

Current performances	8	7	6	2	4	3	9
Improvement opportunities	2	4	7	9	1	3	2
Innovative priorities	4	5	7	10	9	8	6

② Map the strong 'Matches' between customer needs and product attributes

③ Evaluate customer priorities and competition advantage

④ Evaluate product performance and improvement potential

⑤ Prioritise innovation and market opportunities and focus resources on best

QFD: matching customers and products to focus innovation

The impact zone

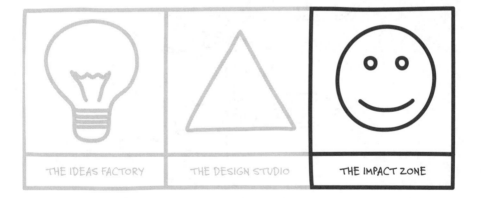

THE IDEAS FACTORY · THE DESIGN STUDIO · THE IMPACT ZONE

CHAPTER 31

Launch pads ... accelerating new ideas to market

'Everyone who has taken a shower has had an idea. It's the person who gets out of the shower, dries off, and does something about it that makes a difference.'

Nolan Bushnell

Launching an innovative solution, entering a new market or reaching out to new customers is in many ways the real starting point rather than the end of the innovation process.

Innovation is less about the creative idea or the inventive product but more about the ability to turn that idea into a practical application for customers – to make their lives better – and in doing so, turn the idea into profitable streams of revenue for the company too. Helping the customer achieve the full benefits of applying the solution to their particular problem might require new customer attitudes and behaviours both in how they use the solution as well as in buying it. This all requires innovative propositions, communications, distribution, pricing and incentives, sales and service, and support overtime.

On top of this, launching a new innovation can often lead to further innovation, or at least incremental ways of building on the step change. Toyota's Prius, one of the first cars to popularize the hybrid engine, was just the starting point of a new generation of models and developments for the brand.

This is a more strategic role for market entry rather than just 'getting it out there'. The skill by which Apple has relentlessly introduced new platforms for its continued innovations – with the iMac, iPod and iPhone as platforms for doing so much more – can be applied to all types of business.

Most market entry strategies start by targeting a niche audience of early adopters, the people who are most ready to embrace newness – either because of their more advanced usage behaviours (the emergency services for protective clothing, for example) or because they are already involved in some way (maybe as co-creators of the ideas, design and development). These early audiences are also key in establishing a positive reputation for the innovation, writing reviews, talking to others and being seen with it.

Everett Rogers called this phased roll-out the 'diffusion of innovations', where an innovation is communicated through certain channels over time among the members of a social system. He proposed that people adopt innovations in an S-shaped curve: few at first, then accelerating rapidly into the mainstream and then slowing down. He described adopters based on their innovativeness – how quickly they embrace new ideas. He identified five types:

1   **Innovators:** The first 2.5% of adopters are adventurous and educated, have multiple sources of information, and show greater propensity to take risks. They appreciate technology for its own sake and are motivated by the idea of being a change agent, willing to tolerate initial problems that may accompany new products or services.

2   **Early adopters:** The next 13.5% of adopters are social leaders. They are popular and educated, visionaries in their market, and are looking to adopt and use new technology to achieve a revolutionary goal – often to get an advantage. They are not very price-sensitive because they see great benefits in adopting a new technology, demanding personalized solutions and support.

3   **Early majority:** The next 34% of adopters have many informal social contacts, but are more motivated by evolutionary changes. They are more rational and cautious, wanting to be reassured that they are backing a technology winner rather than the latest fad, and take confidence by being part of the crowd – therefore, they are strongly influenced by peers.

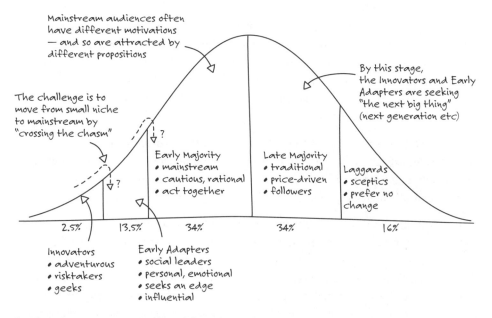

Mainstream audiences often have different motivations — and so are attracted by different propositions

By this stage, the Innovators and Early Adapters are seeking "the next big thing" (next generation etc)

The challenge is to move from small niche to mainstream by "crossing the chasm"

?

?

?

Early Majority
• mainstream
• cautious, rational
• act together

Late Majority
• traditional
• price-driven
• followers

Laggards
• sceptics
• prefer no change

2.5%　　13.5%　　　34%　　　　34%　　　　16%

Innovators
• adventurous
• risktakers
• geeks

Early Adapters
• social leaders
• personal, emotional
• seeks an edge
• influential

Accelerating new ideas to market whilst avoiding the chasms

4   **Late majority:** The next 34% of adopters are sceptical, traditional and often less wealthy, and are therefore often price-sensitive and want ready-to-use solutions. They are motivated by keeping up with the mainstream rather than getting an edge, often looking to advisors to help them or discounters who will sell it cheap.

5   **Laggards:** The final 16% of adopters are sceptics, often the oldest and least educated, who are most interested in maintaining the status quo. They are happy with what they have and don't believe that the new technology can really make a difference to them – indeed, they might even resist purchase.

One of the problems, however, is that the reason why early adopters are attracted to a new innovation might be significantly different from what motivates the mainstream. Worse than this, it might even put them off. They buy through different channels, have different price perceptions and respond to different messages. Ideally you want the early adopters to influence the others, but sometimes, particularly in consumer markets, they are the very people who others don't want to emulate.

In *Crossing the Chasm*, Geoffrey Moore describes how the visionaries and pragmatists have very different expectations, and that a 'chasm' emerges between the early and later adopters. He relates this phenomenon particularly to technology markets, illustrating it with the 'premature death' of many good ideas, but it can apply to any market.

Market entry strategies can be complex, requiring different approaches for different audiences. They need to be considered over time rather than as a one-off event: a sequence of horizons as the innovation reaches further into the market, supported by related but different propositions that evolve over time, embracing additional distribution channels and media to engage the additional audiences. As well as managing a series of progressive entries into the market, the actual mechanics for entry can be highly innovative too. Conventional launches are based around key events:

➡ **Tied in with sponsorship deals** – for example, of the World Cup.

➡ **Coinciding with industry gatherings** – such as technologies launched to coincide with the Consumer Electronics Show in Las Vegas.

➡ **Seasonality**, carefully timed at the moment when people buy gifts.

If you want to reach a new audience, perhaps the smartest strategies are those that 'piggy back' on a proven winner – ideally not one of your competitors, but from a related sector. Work with them through affinity branding or with joint promotions. You may even be able to share distribution networks and promotional activity.

Smart did this extremely effectively when entering the US market, but lacking the branded network to promote its car. Working exclusively with a mid-sized retail chain, it advertised the car with a reservation fee, which could be redeemed against a test drive at one of a number of locations. Compared to the usual push of car brands, this was a pull strategy, and had an incredibly high conversion rate from trial to purchase.

Most significantly of all, once you launch an innovation, you need to retain and build momentum. There is nothing worse than an initial heavy investment that suddenly runs out of ideas. Build your entry activities like a snowball, gaining pace, popularity and sales as it continues to roll, and be ready with your next idea.

Gü ... launching 'lüvly pots of güdness'

Gü makes the irresistible chocolate pots that melt in the middle.

They are inspired by the incredible chocolate desserts discovered by James Averdieck in a small patisserie on the Rue des Tongres, near the centre of Brussels. He was there working for St Ivel, the dairy business, when he fell in love with the little cafe's puddings.

He knew he was onto something in 2003 when he placed some Gü sample boxes onto the shelf of his local supermarket and saw the shoppers dive on them. He immediately launched the brand with a partner supermarket and a range of three products.

In an interview with *The Times* he describes his masterpiece product: 'It's a less sweet, adults-only chocolate with a high cocoa content. Belgian chocolate has anything from 53 to 70%. Our own products are made almost entirely from cream, chocolate and eggs. Of course, they're slightly wicked, but they're a small indulgence and that does you good.'

He believed there was a trend in people moving away from mass-produced products bought at low prices to something more individual with premium quality. He started working with two retailers, Sainsbury and Waitrose, and quickly developed the range to include brownies to chocolate truffles. And just in case chocolate isn't your thing, he has also created Gü's 'fruity little sister', branded as Frü.

Averdieck's mission is to build a brand that stands for seriously good chocolate. 'We are all about chocolate extremism with a dollop of fun,' as he puts it on his site. He estimates that a Gü pud is now eaten somewhere in the world every two seconds. Turnover by the end of 2009 had exceeded £22 million but with plenty more room for growth.

The small patisserie in Brussels is probably unaware that it sparked a chocolate pudding craze and a business worth £35 million – the price that Averdieck eventually sold his business for in early 2010. Noble Foods, a leading UK egg producer, now has the challenge of taking the melt-in-the-middle puds further.

CHAPTER 32

Creative scripts ... selling ideas, telling stories

'We are in the twilight of a society based on data. As information and intelligence becomes the domain of computers, society will place more value on the one human ability that cannot be automated: emotion – will affect everything from our purchasing decisions to how we work with others. Companies will thrive on the basis of the stories and myths. Companies will need to understand that their products are less important than their stories.'

Rolf Jensen in 'The Dream Society'

The stage was set. The lights dimmed, the music cranked up and we waited. Watched by thousands of disciples, partners and employees, consumers and fanatics, and millions more online, waiting for the moment when Steve Jobs walked on stage.

When he did, it was like the return of a conquering hero. In his uniform of washed-out jeans, black turtleneck and rather scruffy New Balance trainers, his first few words whipped the crowd into a frenzy. It another defining moment. We had waited months for this. When he eventually reached into his jeans pocket to pull out his latest innovation, the world took a deep breath and watched in awe – and then in mayhem.

The techniques that have turned the Apple CEO into one of the world's most extraordinary branded storytellers are useful to anyone who wants to sell a new idea, in a way that inspires people. For more than three decades, Jobs has transformed product launches into an art form. He spends hours perfecting the words like poetry, practising the gestures and jokes until they look effortless. Above all, his presentations are intended to do three things: to inform, to educate and to entertain. This is what we can learn from him:

1 **Tell a story:** He plans his presentations like a movie. He sketches and storyboards the scenes, plot and story. And with music, video clips, guests and interaction, there is never a dull moment.

2 **Keep it simple:** He finds simple, single-sentence descriptions for complex ideas. The MacBook Air was simply defined at 'the world's thinnest laptop' – nothing else. That was the headline he wanted everyone to write.

3 **Introduce the enemy:** Every great story has heroes and villains. Accepting that Apple is the hero, he starts by establishing 'the bad guy' – why a competitor such as IBM, Microsoft or Nokia is bad for customers and for the industry, standing in the way of progress.

4 **Focus on benefits:** Don't get caught up in features. Instead, focus on why your audience should care – what's in it for them? Why buy the iPhone 3G? Because 'it's twice as fast at half the price'. And different audiences seek different benefits, so keep thinking like them.

5 **The power of three:** There are three parts to his presentations, with three messages, three priorities and three benefits. Three is significant yet simple, dramatic and memorable.

6 **Sell dreams:** He doesn't sell computers and music players, he sells the promise of a better world. On introducing the iPod, he said that 'in our own small way we're going to make the world a better place'. He is passionate about his products, but even more about his customers.

7   **Use distinctive words:** He speaks in plain English, and uses wow words rather tech speak. He called the iPhone 'amazingly zippy' and 'incredibly cool' – not a mention of kilobytes per second.

8   **Add great visuals:** His presentations reflect the simplicity and humanity of the Apple brand. There are no bullet points, just stunning images and maybe one or two words like 'think different'. His messages are incredibly clear and are reinforced by the visuals.

9   **The big moment:** Every good presentation has one of these. 'Today, we are introducing three revolutionary products. The first one is a widescreen iPod with touch controls. The second is a revolutionary mobile phone. And the third is a breakthrough Internet communications device. An iPod, a phone, an Internet communicator. An iPod, a phone, are you getting it? These are not three devices. This is one device.' The audience erupted.

Wieden and Kennedy ... just doing it for Nike and the Coke side of life

It created 'Just do it' for Nike, 'The Coke side of life' for Coca-Cola and 'Grrrrr' for Honda, and even the yellow Livestrong wristband for Nike and cyclist Lance Armstrong.

W+K has proved time and again that it is an ad agency that really knows how to communicate. Founded in 1982 in Portland, Oregon, the agency still thrives on the unconventional energy of founder Dan Wieden. He regularly reminds colleagues and clients that 'no good idea ever happened without somebody sticking their neck out'.

The agency got its big break with Nike, which was still in its infancy at the time but growing rapidly on the jogging boom of the 1970s and bringing a hip, West Coast attitude to the previously serious Adidas-dominated world of running shoes. The fact that Nike's founder Phil Knight and his successors have stuck with the agency for more than 30 years is testament to the agency's ongoing creativity – most clients feel that they are getting diminishing returns from an agency after about five years and turn to others for some new perspectives and fresh thinking. From lines like 'There is no finish line' to the swoosh that no longer needs a name, W+K has grown alongside the sports giant.

At the end of 2009, *Adweek* announced its advertising awards of the decade. W+K, which had just exceeded $2 billion in billings for the first time, ran off with many of the awards, as did its clients. *Adweek* picked Honda's 'Grrrr' as its 'ad of the decade, period.' The 90-second animated spot, created by the agency's London office, features cute animals denigrating a polluting, gas-powered engine and celebrating a cleaner-burning, quieter diesel. It was originally shot for UK television but was then adapted for other media and rolled our worldwide. W+K's 'It's mine' ad for Coca-Cola in 2008 was *Adweek*'s 'Super Bowl spot of the decade'. It featured a horde of Thanksgiving Day parade balloons chasing an inflated Coke bottle and became the most talked about ad online, having a significant impact on Coke's reputation metrics through its carefully but creatively thought-through 30-second running time.

The agency is now seeking to expand beyond conventional advertising programmes. Nike, for example, has already invested significantly in the agency's development of a Broadway show entitled *Ball* and a film about Lance Armstrong entitled *Road to Paris*. It takes a soft-sell approach, not overtly plugging Nike (although the company's swoosh symbol is frequently seen Armstrong's cycling kit) and seeks to engage more deeply with a core audience – in this case, cycling enthusiasts. The agency recently hired a rock band to record a song called '6453/Freedom', the name of a new Nike shoe, which reached the Top 10 in Japan.

Wieden believes that 'the industry is at an evolutionary crossroads', explaining how he hopes that the agency's new ventures can do more for companies seeking to 'associate their brands with various forms of entertainment that go beyond the 30-second commercial'.

The W+K mantra is simple: 'Be useful. Be beautiful. Be thought-provoking.'

CHAPTER 33

Profit models ... business models for successful innovation

'To be successful you have to be lucky, or a little mad, or very talented, or to find your-self in a rapid-growth field.'

Edward de Bono

Ideas are your most valuable assets. The question is how to realize that value.

Whilst brands, relationships, patents and talent are often seen as the more valuable 'assets' in a business, it is the ideas behind them that has the ability to transform fortunes – driving revenue and profit growth, reducing risks, and sustaining growth over time.

It might appear obvious at first glance – 'turn the idea into a product or service, and then get people to buy it' – but there is more to it than that. Bigger ideas tend to embrace how people buy things, as well as what they buy. Therefore the added value, or at least the perceived added value, is not always in the product but potentially in other aspects of their experience too. This is where the business model comes in – that mystical buzzword, trotted out to impress peers but with little coherent definition. A business model is the way you make money.

Google makes its money from advertisers, typically charging for every click-through to their business, whilst for the user, this service is free. HP makes money by selling printers, but the real strategy is to sell the hardware cheap and then make money from the regular sale of ink cartridges. Tata is able to sell the Nano at $2000 because of its supply partnerships. FedEx command a price premium for overnight delivery that pays for the infrastructure to deliver it. In fact, almost every leading business has a different business model. When products and services are so easily copied, the business model is often the source of sustainable differentiation.

Therefore, business model innovation – rethinking the way you make money from your ideas – is a crucial aspect to innovation today. It starts by you thinking carefully about your audience and value proposition – how can you most effectively create value for them? – and then what products and services will deliver this promise, the capabilities and resources to support this, and the financial model by which revenue and costs flow. The business thereby creates value.

Innovation can be focused on any or all of these aspects of the business model.

→ Rethinking who the **audience** is, or the problem to be solved, as Nike did when seeking to engage females with Nike Women.

→ Refocusing the **value proposition** on different benefits that have more perceived value, as Dove did in moving from outer beauty to inner confidence.

→ Redesigning **products and services** to deliver the proposition, as BMW did when redesigning the Mini for a new generation.

→ Resourcing **capabilities** in different ways, internally or in partnership, as Boeing has done in developing its 787 Dreamliner.

→ Using a **revenue model** that balances different revenue streams to maximize income, as Disney does across audiences, media and geography.

→ Creating a **pricing structure** of how much to charge people, for what and when, as Hilton does to maximize its room occupancy.

→ Creating a **cost model** that balances direct and indirect costs, and scale and risk, as Amazon does to be profitable whilst offering significant discounts.

→ **Speed** of development ensures positive cashflow by managing revenues and costs, as Dell does by delivering made-to-order computing.

➡ Creating **processes** to deliver all of this effectively, as Air Asia does in order to grow rapidly in the low-cost airline market.

However, an analysis of major innovations in companies over the last decade shows that few have been business model-related – most are focused on products and the related product system. Yet those that have innovated their business models have delivered far greater returns.

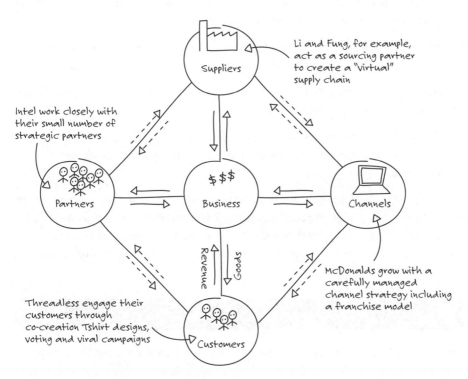

Suppliers

Li and Fung, for example, act as a sourcing partner to create a "virtual" supply chain

Intel work closely with their small number of strategic partners

Partners

$ $$
Business

Channels

McDonalds grow with a carefully managed channel strategy including a franchise model

Threadless engage their customers through co-creation Tshirt designs, voting and viral campaigns

Revenue   Goods

Customers

Designing innovative business models that do more for customers and commercially

Whilst new business model innovation is more frequent in start-ups, few larger businesses have the confidence or foresight to change. Here are five situations in which companies really should think about how to innovate their business model:

➡ Addressing large groups of potential customers who are currently not served because existing solutions are too expensive or complicated.

➡ Launching a new technology that requires new attitudes and behaviours (which are unlikely to be encouraged by charging in a conventional way).

➡ Redefining the perceived value of a solution, maybe by reframing the context and articulating a significantly different value proposition – including a higher or lower price.

➡ Responding to new entrants in the market, particularly discounters or low-end disruptors who would otherwise make your existing business model irrelevant.

➡ Responding to a shifting basis of competition – inevitably, what defines an acceptable solution in a market will change over time, leading core market segments to commoditize.

Of all of these, the use of business model innovation to reach new audiences is perhaps the most significant. And as C.K. Pralahad has predicted, and companies such as Air Asia are demonstrating, this is perhaps most relevant to those two billion potential customers, representing a $5 trillion potential revenue opportunity, who currently sit at what he calls the 'bottom of the pyramid'.

Giorgio Armani ... the designer who knew how to make money

Giorgio Armani is one of the world's most successful fashion designers, creating a niche for himself with his elegant, timeless designs. Although his fashion house is much smaller than many other fashion houses, it is one of the most profitable. Unlike most other houses, Armani headed both the creative and business sides of the company. Born in 1934 in the small Italian town of Piacenza, Armani initially aspired to become a doctor and for two years studied at the medical school of the University of Bologna, but hated the sight of blood.

Following his passion for the arts, and particularly fashion, he became a window dresser for La Rinescente, Milan's largest department store, and was soon promoted as a buyer where he sharpened his sense of style and design. In the early 1960s he joined designer Nino Cerruti, working on his Ungaro and Zegna labels.

Armani's breakthrough came in 1966 when he met architect Sergio Galeotti, who was impressed by his talents as a designer and encouraged him to set up his own label. Armani left Cerruti in 1970 and established his own business, bringing out his first line of menswear under his own name in 1974. The designs became so popular that he officially launched his own label a year later with money raised by selling his beloved Volkswagen Beetle.

In the mid-1970s, more women began to take office jobs. Armani targeted this professional market, bringing out a womenswear line using men's fabrics. It proved to be a huge hit.

Armani became known for his classic minimalist style, creating clothes that were elegant in their simplicity. Compared to peers such as Gianni Versace, who used bright colours and bold designs, he preferred a neutral palette with simple cuts, saying that 'fashion should evolve rather than change drastically from year to year'. He rose to fame with the introduction of his 'unstructured jacket' in the late 1970s, a little battered and creased but relaxed and flowing.

He continues to lead his house in his seventies, although some commentators (and particularly investors) have expressed concern that he does not have a natural successor. Some suggested that this highlighted a rich arrogance – partly a shortcoming, but also an attribute that enabled him to direct fashion trends and gave him the courage to be successful. Awarded the 'Superstar Award' for his lifetime achievements at New York's *Night of Stars* in 2004, Armani responded: 'Thanks for the kind thought. But don't imagine that I'm going to disappear, or that you'll get rid of me. I'll accept the award, but I'll keep on generating ideas.'

His fusion of creativity and business skills has served him well, guiding his company and brands through good times and bad. Over the years, he introduced several diffusion ranges, sub-brands that offered beautiful clothes at more affordable prices.

CHAPTER 34

Brand propositions ... making ideas relevant and distinctive

'Sex appeal is 50% what you've got and 50% what people think you've got.'

Sophie Loren

Value propositions, whether based around your brand or a specific product or service, are more about the customers rather than what you are offering: benefits they can achieve, not the features you supply; perceived value to them, rather than the price you charge.

The same product can be sold to different audiences in different ways much more successfully than trying to sell the same product to everyone in the same way. Value propositions will sometimes require entirely new products and services to fulfil their promises, or iconic components that bring existing products together as integrated solutions. They are articulated as themes based on the critical issues for the target customer, pulling customers towards you.

This provokes the audience's interest in something important and relevant to them, cutting through the noise and price obsession of your competitors, and you are in a position to shape a more personal and valuable solution. They are much more interested when the discussion is about them rather than you.

The theme sets a context beyond the product. More significant themes have more perceived value, allowing you to price them more profitably too. It might even be a more enduring theme that can stretch over time, enabling a richer relationship to develop. Cross-selling becomes easy, not at a discount but at a price premium because of the perceived additional value of the theme. It will also attract more, similar customers that potentially form communities around the issue too.

Propositions are about being relevant to specific customers – at an individual, segment or market level – by interpreting the brand and articulating products and services in a more relevant way. The conceptual value of a proposition can be articulated as the basic value of the commodity, plus the distinctive benefits not offered by others, less the price and alternatives, resulting in a net value to the customer that is hopefully superior to that offered by competitors or other alternatives. Whilst this all sounds obvious, the key is to focus on the benefits, not the features. Products describe features; propositions describe benefits. So '24-hour home maintenance' is a feature, but 'piece of mind at home' is a benefit of it. 'Wireless emails on your phone' is interesting, but 'stay in touch with clients anywhere' is more valuable.

The key parts of a value proposition are:

➡ **Who?** The target audience, their issues and motivations, and the key insight into the world of these customers that you are addressing.

➡ **What?** The primary benefits that you offer, supported by the key features of some of the products and services that can deliver these benefits.

➡ **Why?** The competitive difference in what you offer. How and why it is better or different from what others offer.

➡ **How much?** The price position relative to alternatives, given the superior benefits offered and compared to other ways of achieving the benefits.

➡ **What not?** The trade-offs the customer makes in choosing you over someone else, i.e. your competitors' differentiators (although you wouldn't communicate this!).

These dimensions together articulate the superior value that you offer customers (usually not expressed numerically, although it could be).

This would, of course, be an internal document that can be rearticulated externally for the customer in a compelling way. Key to marketing propositions is to link them to the customers for whom the issue-driven themes are most relevant. Whilst it might not be possible (or desirable) to 'push' the propositions through direct marketing to specific names and addresses, target customers will be attracted to, say, certain special events (conferences, exhibitions), membership networks (associations, hobbies), television programmes (specialist interests) or press (specific sections, special features). The self-selecting customer is therefore 'pulled' to you.

The propositions might be communicated through conventional advertising or by working with partners relevant to the particular theme. For example, the 'home buyer' proposition might be offered through real estate agents to engage customers before they start approaching other financial service companies.

Propositions are then fulfilled through dialogue, by bringing combinations of standard products together under the umbrella of the theme, or sometimes by also adding specific 'iconic' ingredients – a special guidebook or dedicated advisor for the home buyer, say, or unique diagnostic tools and industry forums for the high-growth manufacturers. These icons add value and differentiation, and provide a 'glue' to bring together more comprehensive and profitable solutions.

A better perception of comparative benefits, expressed through a value proposition, therefore enables you to increase price, maintain the same value for money and directly improve profitability.

Tesla ... high performance is not everything

The advertising copy begins 'Zero emissions equals zero guilt'.

Tesla Motors was founded in 2003 by Martin Eberhard and Marc Tarpenning with a mission to 'design and sell high-performance, super-efficient electric cars'. It is a small Silicon Valley-based manufacturer of high-performance electric cars. The company has around 1000 workers producing around 25 battery-powered sports cars per week, mostly customized vehicles designed to individual owners' specifications.

Tesla's primary goal is to increase the number and variety of electric vehicles available to mainstream consumers in three ways:

➡ Selling its own vehicles in a growing number of showrooms and online.

➡ Selling patented electric components to competitors so that they can accelerate their own electric developments.

➡ Being a catalyst and positive example to other automakers, demonstrating that responsible cars can also be fast and fun.

In a recent edition of the *New Yorker*, Robert Lutz of GM admitted 'All the geniuses here at General Motors kept saying lithium-ion technology is 10 years away, and Toyota agreed with us ... and then, boom, along comes Tesla. So I said, "How come some tiny little California startup, run by guys who know nothing about the car business, can do this, and we can't?" That was the crowbar that helped break up the log jam.'

The Tesla Roadster, the company's first model, is the first production car to use lithium-ion battery cells and the first with a range greater than 200 miles per charge. According to CEO Elon Musk, it accelerates from 0 to 60 mph in 3.9 seconds and is twice as energy-efficient as the Toyota Prius. It also has a base price of $109,000, well out of reach of the mainstream for now. However, Tesla has deliberately targeted 'early adopters' with customized models as it refines the technology before cascading it down to less expensive vehicles – perhaps learning from the way its technology neighbours launched their devices. The next platform, the Model S, is expected in 2012 with a price tag of half the original price.

Tesla does not advertise, instead relying on the media, word-of-mouth and Musk's love of the limelight at conferences and on chat shows. Tesla's Roadster made an appearance in 2008's *Iron Man* movie and added its coolness to recent ads for BlackBerry and California Tourism.

Owners include Governor Arnold Schwarzenegger, alongside a horde of movie producers and technology leaders. 'Our owners become our ambassadors,' says Musk. 'We're fortunate because we are at the centre of the confluence of a product with high sex appeal that in a sense helps save the world.'

CHAPTER 35

Contagious ideas ... memes, viruses and all that hype

'The universe is made of stories, not of atoms.'

Muriel Rukeyser

Nike's Phil Knight once explained his passion for endorsing sporting icons by arguing 'You can't explain much in 60 seconds, but when you show Michael Jordan, you don't have to. It's that simple.' Some words, symbols or icons can capture a thousand words, and be far more memorable.

Richard Dawkins coined the phrase 'meme' to describe 'a unit of cultural evolution analogous to the gene', arguing that replication and mutation happens within our culture – in the language or symbols we use, or the behaviours we adopt – in a similar way to way to genetic evolution. He considers memes as the units of information that reside in the brain, and we see memetic structures in everything from catchy pop songs to new fashion designs.

Memes help to turn brands and propositions into stories, symbols and slogans. They catch people's attention, stay in their minds and quickly spread virally by word of mouth, email or text. If value propositions and communications are to reach target audiences, leverage the power of virtual or physical networks, and be in people's minds at the point of purchase, they need to embrace memetics.

Memes are constructs of memory that are more memorable, recognizable and contagious:

→ **Slogans,** e.g. Nike's 'Just do it'.

→ **Colours,** e.g. the *FT*'s pink paper.

→ **Music,** e.g. Intel's five-note jingle or the 'Nokia tune' played by every Nokia phone.

→ **Designs,** e.g. Apple's translucent white computers.

→ **Numbers,** e.g. Peugeot's trademarked central '0'.

→ **Smells,** e.g. on Singapore Airlines flights.

→ **Typography,** e.g. the script and bottle shape of Coca-Cola.

Malcolm Gladwell defines a tipping point as 'the moment of critical mass, the threshold, the boiling point'. In his book *The Tipping Point* he explores what he calls the 'mysterious' sociological changes that mark everyday life, and how ideas and behaviours take off, from the rampant spread in popularity of Crocs within a year of their launch to the non-stop chatter around the latest antics of Lady Gaga.

Contagious ideas take off when three factors come together:

1   **Sticky ideas:** Ideas that are easy to pass on: supported by memorable messages and represented by iconic symbols or gestures. Al Gore's *An Inconvenient Truth* transformed attitudes to climate change, Lance Armstrong's yellow Livestrong bracelet became a fashion statement as well as a crusade against cancer.

2   **Relevant context:** Ideas that align with the times, with a broader situation or mindset that makes the idea more relevant and can be taken up as a simple way to respond to a complex situation. Gore's rallying cry came as climate change was rising in everyone's conscience; Armstrong launched his bracelet at the same time as the Tour de France headed for the Alps.

3   **Crowd connectors:** Ideas taken up by the relatively small number of people who are well-connected, sharing their expert knowledge with others – they are salespeople who have natural gift to influence people. It's an echo of Stanley Milgram's concept that everybody is connected by "six degrees of separation".

Physical and virtual networks have made disseminating ideas fast, interactive and non-linear. Word of mouth is trusted and powerful, but when it is replicated in the fast-evolving world of social and professional networks – Baidu, Facebook, LinkedIn, MySpace, Xing and many others – its impact can be phenomenal.

One of the best examples of this was Barack Obama's campaign for the 2008 US Presidential elections. Obama rose from relative obscurity through his novel use of network technologies. His fundraising did not rely upon large cheques from elite dinners, but much smaller sums for many thousands of normal people. His messages reached people every morning by emails and SMS messages, rather than relying on reported broadcasting. And his supporters were able to actively engage in debate and two-way dialogue, rallying around the simple themes of 'hope' and 'change'.

Dave Stewart ... from rockstar to change agent

Dave Stewart is most famous as one half of Eurythmics alongside Annie Lennox, as well as songwriter to the likes of Gwen Stefani, Jon Bon Jovi, Mick Jagger, U2 and Katy Perry. He has sold more than 80 million records worldwide and produced a feature film, *Honest*, that premiered at the Cannes Film Festival. His photographs have been displayed at Paris Museum of Modern Art and the Saatchi Gallery in London.

But it's the rest of his CV that is most interesting. He started the consulting company Deep-Stew with Deepak Chopra. He is the creative director of the advertising agency Law Firm. He is president of entertainment for fashion designer Christian Audigier's brand-management business. And he is official 'change agent' for Nokia.

Stewart is an ideas man. He brings eclectic talents and experiences, and is more likely than most to come up with something new. He also still carries a rockstar aura. He is happy to give his wildest ideas in return for a small percentage of eventual returns, as long as he has a belief in the company that he is working with.

Stewart has become a fully fledged change agent, using his creativity to take even the most creative organizations in new directions, and has become a regular fixture at gatherings such as Cannes, Davos and TED. At Nokia his role is to connect the company with new talent and opportunities. The world's largest handset manufacturer realized that it needed to find a more engaging side to its brand to stay ahead. Having created its Ovi music and gaming platform, Nokia wanted to go beyond rivals like Apple and Samsung. Stewart got up on stage at the Consumer Electronics Show and started, 'We all know that the cell phone is an empty shell.' The Nokia executives looked concerned. '... And that content is the seed,' he continued.

Since then he has persuaded U2 to release their new album exclusively through Ovi and has 'found' a new star in Cindy Gomez, a young multilingual Canadian singer who he has moulded as the first Nokia artist in residence. Stewart has built Gomez's brand to be much more than just selling exclusive music tracks, also embracing games and community: his 'Dance Fabulous' mobile games, starring Gomez as a computer simulated avatar, have started to do things for Nokia that iTunes could only dream of.

'Companies won't succeed through technology,' he concluded in his San Diego speech. 'They will succeed through the power of ideas which inspire and engage people.'

CHAPTER 36

Market shaping ... winning in the vortex

'If you want to know your past, look at your present conditions.

If you want to know your future, look into your present actions.'

Buddhist saying

Getting an innovation to market is just the start. Making it successful is the real creative challenge.

In-market innovation is perhaps the key to value creation today – how to engage customers, change their attitudes and behaviours, shift the industry model to new designs, and disrupt the old conventions and competitors as you go. New ideas can spread in a way that was previously reserved for fads and fashions. Speed is driven by the connectivity of people through technology, the rise of non-locational communities and the constant desire of consumers to have the latest, best, coolest, smallest, fastest devices.

Whether it is the latest multidisciplinary mobile phone, a new range of Puma shoes or the latest interactive game, as soon as it enters one market, it enters all markets. In the past, movies were shown in the US up to six months before Europe. Within weeks of release in LA, it will now be bootlegged in the shops of Bangkok or available online to people anywhere.

Similarly with products: the rapid and repetitive disruption of the data storage market shows how large floppy disks were displaced by smaller disks, which were replaced by CD-ROMs, which were replaced by USB devices. The benefits of each new device were huge: scaling up storage capacity many times, shrinking in size, cheaper and more convenient. Once the new device hits the market, everybody everywhere wants it. And one click at amazon.com can deliver it within days.

Leaders and followers

There is much discussion these days about whether it is better to be first into a market or to follow others. Just like a middle distance race, it is rarely the athlete who sprints to the front of the field on the first curve who eventually emerges the winner. Conventional wisdom says that getting to the shoulder of the leader with a lap to go is the perfect position to race to victory.

A similar mindset exists in market entry strategies. First movers can grab a pioneering image, but it is the 'fast followers', as Costas Markides calls them, who learn from mistakes and eventually do better. Of course, in today's technology markets, there is not necessarily a starting point: in many ways, Apple's iPod was the first mover because other MP3 players had got stuck in the chasm and most of us hadn't even heard of digital music downloads.

First movers typically benefit through technological leadership and ownership of patents. They can also grab scarce resources first, find the best partners and scale opportunities, influence customers, and secure a pioneering image for themselves. Remember Netscape? Although Skype, eBay, Pixar and Live Nation aren't doing too badly.

Meanwhile, 'fast second' can jump on the coat tails of first movers, get a free ride by taking advantage of education, focus on improving the product, learn from the early entrants' mistakes, access cheaper resources, resolve uncertainties at lower risk, claim to be on the underdog on the customers' side, and gain government support to avoid monopoly.

The table shows markets with examples of leaders and followers – both innovators in their own ways – and showing (in bold text) how sometimes the first mover wins and in other cases it's better to follow.

Market	Leaders	Follower
Jet aircraft	De Havillland	**Boeing**
Instant camera	**Polaroid**	Kodak
Paper copier	**Xerox**	Canon
Video recorder	Sony	**Panasonic**
Web browser	Netscape	**Microsoft**

Overcoming the hype

The 'hype cycle' was developed by Gartner to reflect the evolution and adaptation of specific technologies. Since 1995, it has been used to characterize the typical over-enthusiasm or 'hype' and subsequent disappointment that typically happens with the introduction of new technologies. The real purpose of the cycle, however, is to separate the hype from the technology's more useful reality. The curves also show how and when technologies move beyond the hype, moving from abstract possibilities into relevant innovations, offering practical benefits and become much more widely accepted.

There are five phases to Gartner's hype cycle:

1   **Technology trigger:** The first phase after technological breakthrough, product launch or other events that generates significant press and interest.

2   **Peak of inflated expectations:** A frenzy of publicity typically generates over-enthusiasm and unrealistic expectations, perhaps with a few successful applications.

3   **Trough of disillusionment:** Technologies lose their shine, fail to meet expectations and quickly become unfashionable. The press usually abandon them.

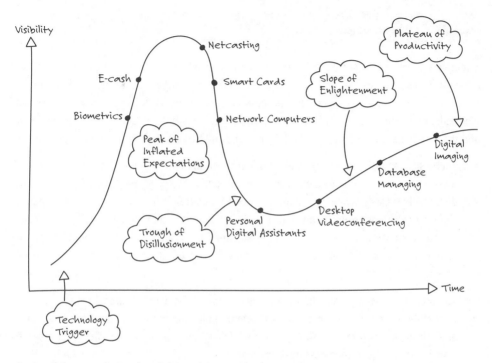

Gartner's hype cycle: turning big ideas into practical success

4   **Slope of enlightenment:** Although the hype has blown over, some businesses continue to explore the technology, understanding its benefits and practical applications.

5   **Plateau of productivity:** The technology becomes robust and accepted, evolving into second and third generations. The height of the plateau depends on whether it has broad or niche application.

Winning in the vortex

Effective market entry, particularly into emerging or newly defined markets, requires you to create a 'market vortex': establishing your position and engaging customers before others, building a momentum that keeps the process going and blows down physical and mental blocks, learning and evolving as you go. The vortex ensures that you own the space you want and that the impact is rapid. Think iPod, iTunes and the transformation of the music industry.

1   The first phase of the vortex is all about **market-making**, turning the whitespace into a viable marketspace where customers are prepared to spend money profitably. Latent demand has to be awoken: customers need education and encouragement to adopt the new solutions to problems and aspirations in a way that they have not previously encountered. It might include new language and behaviours, and letting go of others. It also requires a careful balance between positive hype and that which leads to premature death.

2   The second phase is **game-changing**, which is where the new boundaries, standards and expectations are set. Remember back to when Apple redefined the market for download-able music, or even music more generally. Whilst there were some earlier MP3 players, Apple made the whole process easy. It created iTunes' simple 99-cent downloads, a click wheel to skim through your collection and a 'shuffle' option to enjoy everything you own.

3   The third phase is **market-shaping**: the ongoing challenge of developing and evolving the market in your vision, shaping your own destiny rather than being shaped by others. It is about being a leader and staying there – not necessarily the biggest, but the most thoughtful, the best. You continue to define the standards, shape the behaviours and evolve the market model, something that Apple has become incredibly successful at. As the hype cycle reaches enlightenment, you reap the benefits.

Zaha Hadid ... a planet in her own inimitable orbit

She has been called the diva of architecture. Her personality is as big as any of her architectural visions, but her designs have long suffered from the perception of being incredible but impractical – in one critic's phrase, 'brilliant, but unbuildable'.

Her gravity-defying ideas, celebrating movement and nature without a right angle in sight, have often failed to make it off the drawing board. She was the unexpected choice to design Cardiff's new opera house before the committee lost its nerve and cancelled her commission. Only in recent years, with the help of new computer-based prototyping techniques, has she been able convince clients of the practical viability of her daring designs and win high-profile projects from Cincinnati to Singapore. Her London-based architectural design firm, Zaha Hadid Architects, has more than 250 employees.

Born in Baghdad and educated by French nuns, Hadid came to England in her twenties and studied at the Architectural Association – what some have called the 'Frankenstein Academy' for its weird and wonderful outputs. Indeed it was her tutor at the AA, the Dutch architect Rem Koolhaas, who encouraged Hadid to develop her own design language. When she graduated in 1977, Koolhaas called his prodigy 'a planet in her own inimitable orbit'.

Her graduation project, a hotel on London's Hungerford Bridge, was named Malevich's Tectonik after Kasimir Malevich, who wrote 'We can only perceive space when we break free from the earth, when the point of support disappears.' Hadid's architecture follows those principles, creating a landscape that metaphorically (and perhaps one day literally) seems to take off. For ten years Hadid survived on teaching fees, unable to find sponsors who believed in her fantasies as practical projects. Her avant-garde thinking originally confused pragmatists. However, in recent years her work has become more commercially responsive and increasingly popular across the globe.

She is finally enjoying the benefits of her patience and persistence. Her forcefulness, her and single-mindedness are her strengths and weaknesses. Her strong character can make clients run for the hills – like the directors of the Cardiff Bay Opera House, who can now be responsible for one of the world's most impressive auditoriums. However her forcefulness has eventually won through, in the most dramatic fashions.

Hadid specializes in creating 'dizzying spaces designed to lift the eyes and the heart to God' as *Wallpaper* magazine put it. She reject of the old rules of space – walls, ceilings, front and back, right angles – and recreates them as what she calls 'a new fluid, kind of spatiality' of multiple-perspective points and fragmented geometry designed to embody the chaotic fluidity of modern life.

Her first built project – the fire station at the production complex of the Vitra office furniture group at Weil-am-Rhein on the German–Swiss border – was a formal success but not a functional one. The fire service moved out and the building was converted into a chair museum.

But success started to come her way with a ski jump in Innsbruck and a tram station in Strasbourg. Her real breakthrough was the Rosenthal Center for Contemporary Art in Cincinnati, Ohio. It was a chance to try out her ideas on a large scale and conceive a stunning new take on the museum experience, imagined as 'a kit of parts' to be customized for each show. It resulted in galleries housed in rectangular tubes floating above ground level, between which ribbon-like ramps zig and zag skywards like an 'urban carpet' stretching out to the sidewalks to reach people unaware.

Speaking about her iconic design for the London Olympics, she said in an interview with *The Times*:

> 'When I was working on ideas for the 2012 Aquatic Centre, I created a shape that supports the roof of the building. From that came an idea for a table, now called the Aqua Table. It has a laminated polyurethane resin base and a tactile, non-slip silicon-gel top,

which lends stability to the uneven upper surface. Some people didn't like the feel of the silicon, so I designed a series of Perspex mats that rest on top.'

The Aqua Table was produced in a limited edition of 24. The prototype is in Hadid's London apartment, able to accommodate 16 for dinner.

The opening words of the citation when Hadid was named as the first woman to win the prestigious Pritzker Prize for architecture in 2004 were that 'her architectural career has not been traditional or easy'. Yet she has cemented her reputation as one of the world's most exciting and inspiring contemporary architects – Hadid's fantastical, futuristic ideas are certainly making the future come to life today.

CHAPTER 37

Protecting ideas ... copyright, trademarks and patents

'Nothing is more dangerous than an idea when it is the only one you have.'

Emile Chartier

Ideas are your greatest asset, so protecting them becomes crucial.

There is something of a paradox here in the evolving world of open innovation. Whilst companies are all too keen to work with customers and partners or experts and academics to generate ideas, they want to keep the best of what results to themselves. This is where tensions can rise in collaborative working and needs to be addressed clearly from the outset.

Whilst ideas can be immensely powerful, it is the innovations that result from them that have most value. This is what engages the customers and what competitors strive to imitate. Companies become obsessed with protecting their intangible assets or 'intellectual property' (IP) – discoveries and inventions, names and symbols, or phrases and designs. IP can be defined as a number of types of 'legal monopolies', and, once acknowledged in law, owners have exclusive rights to the use of their intangible assets. Common types of IP include copyrights, trademarks, patents, industrial design rights and trade secrets.

Copyright

Copyright gives the author of an original work the exclusive rights for a certain time period in relation to that work, including its publication, distribution and adaptation, after which time the work is said to enter the public domain. It applies to any expressible form of an idea or information that is substantive, discrete and fixed in a medium. It lasts for between 50 and 100 years beyond an author's death, depending on country. Occasionally countries have a formal process to determine copyright, but most recognize copyright in any completed work without formal registration. However, it does not cover ideas themselves, only the form or manner in which they are expressed – so a Mickey Mouse image and name cannot be copied, but you are free to make cartoons about other cute mice.

Trademarks

Trademarks are distinctive symbols used, mainly by organizations, to identify that the products or services with which the trademark appears originate from a unique source, and to distinguish them from others. A trademark is designated by the following symbols:

➡ ® for a trademark

➡ ™ for an unregistered trademark

➡ ℠ for an unregistered service mark.

A trademark is typically a name, word, phrase, logo, symbol, design or image, or a combination of these elements. Registered marks often need to registered separately in each region; unregistered marks offer more limited protection, often only in their originating region.

Patents

'Patents' are rights that are exclusively granted by a government to an inventor for limited periods of time in exchange for a public disclosure of an invention. The process for granting patents, the requirements placed on the holder, and the nature of protection vary widely between countries. Typically, however, a patent application must include one or more claims defining the invention that must be new, inventive and useful or industrially applicable.

In many countries, certain subject areas are excluded from patents, such as business methods and mental acts. The exclusive right primarily seeks to prevent others from making, using, selling or distributing the patented invention without permission. The WTO recommends that patents should be available in all of its member countries, providing protection for at least 20 years.

Live Nation ... redefining the music experience

The music industry was stunned.

Madonna had just signed a ground-breaking $120 million recording and touring contract over ten years with Live Nation, ending her 25-year relationship with Warner Music. She became the founding recording artist for the new music division Live Nation Artists.

Live Nation's mission is to maximize the live concert experience. Its core business is producing, marketing and selling live concerts. The Los Angeles-based company is already the largest producer of live concerts in the world, with 16,000 concerts for 1500 artists in 57 countries annually, representing more than 45 million concert tickets a year.

Artists sign up to exclusive partnerships with Live Nation in the same way that they would have signed to record labels in the past, but the company takes on the role of promoter rather than 'owner of music'. This is because, as in every creative industry, the business model has changed – there is now far more money to be made out of live events, sponsorships or merchandising than out of selling music.

The company owns, operates or has booking rights to more than 150 of the most prestigious event venues worldwide, including 39 stadiums, 58 theatres, 14 clubs, four arenas and two festival sites. It then focuses on the marketing rights of its artists, who now also include the mighty U2, the Beatles, Kiss, Jay-Z, Shakira, Nickelback and many others.

CEO Michael Rapino outlines Live Nation's strategy for reshaping the live music business in the company's annual report:

> 'Our strategy is to connect the artist to the fan. We believe that this focus will enable us to increase shareholder value by developing new ancillary revenue streams around the live music event and the artist themselves. We will continue to focus on our live music assets. We plan to expand our business through building a stronger connection with the fan through the live event and our ticketing platform. We will seek to connect corporate sponsors with this fan through the live music experience.'

Peter Gabriel, the former Genesis singer, says that record companies should reinvent themselves like Live Nation to deliver a total live and online experience for fans rather than as mere 'owners' of music. He has himself been a pioneer in distributing music legally online, co-founding We7, a website that allows users to stream and download music for free, with or without adverts.

As iTunes and other digital services fundamentally disrupt the way in which people discover, purchase and store music, the rest of the industry needs to find new roles. In a BBC interview, Gabriel said that 'there's still room for record companies but they should reinvent themselves as a service industry and not as owners. The structure of the old album and waiting for that to be finished still has some merit but you can do a lot of other things, and I think it should be a lot looser and mixed.'

CHAPTER 38

Going further ... licensing and franchising brands

'Creativity is the power to connect the seemingly unconnected.'

William Plomer, South African novelist

Once you have a powerful idea, you want to make the most of it.

'Adjacent markets' are markets that are relevant in their proximity, rather than just the closest geographically. Adjacent markets can be explored and evaluated for which offer the best opportunities to stretch out further, to apply your ideas or innovation in different surroundings.

It might seem obvious, but even when considering geographical markets, people tend to look far before they look near. Before trying to conquer the United States or China, consider entering a market nearby, with a similar culture, language or climate. Managers tend to see opportunities with blinkered vision rather looking around them to see what is nearby. Rather than investing billions in new technological developments, consider easier options such as adapting a men's product for women, or a gift version of an everyday object.

There are three primary types of adjacent markets:

➡ **Adjacent categories:** Defined by business types (e.g. drinks), product types (e.g. juices) or applications (e.g. meal times). How could you adapt your innovative product into a related category? Innocent, famous for its natural 'smoothie' drinks, extended successfully into ready meals with 'veg pots'.

➡ **Adjacent customers:** Defined by segments (e.g. teenage girls), geographies (e.g. southern Europe) or channels (e.g. supermarkets). Who else would your innovative product be relevant to? Club Med adapted its upmarket 'couples' holidays to singles, then families, then the elderly, with different propositions.

➡ **Adjacent capabilities:** Defined by capabilities (e.g. brand management), processes (e.g. retailing) or assets (e.g. distribution rights). What else could you do with the innovation that sits behind your product? Baygen, famous for wind-up radios, applied its wind-up formula to lights, computers and scooters.

Growth opportunities exist in 360-degree directions from your existing core business. Rather than working harder to sell more of the same thing, it might be easier and more effective to do other things in other ways, or in other markets.

Licensing and franchising

The power of intangible assets and ideas, and all that emerge from them, is that you can enhance the scale of their impact without having to scale up the physical infrastructure requirements too. Licensing and franchising are two of the most powerful concepts – common for hotels and convenience stores, but relatively uncommon in other sectors. Whether you are an individual entrepreneur, a small regional business or a global brand, licensing an idea, brand or formula, or franchising a more holistic format, offer great opportunities to grow without significant cost, risk or time.

Imagine you have created a wonderful spa like Haman, the contemporary brand from Turkey. How could you roll out a network of spas in the best locations worldwide? Is it better to work with one partner worldwide who has great execution or operational skills, or many local partners? Which prestige hotel or leisure brands would be interested in adding it to their facilities? Could the brand extend into a range of homewares (bath towels and clothing) or cosmetics (soaps and lotions)? Who has the skills to manufacture, package and distribute these branded items for you?

Licensing is based around a contract between the brand owner and licensee for an agreed period of time, within an agreed category or territory. Trademark licensing has a rich history in US business, largely beginning with the rise of mass entertainment such as the movies, comics and later television. Mickey Mouse's popularity in the 1930s and 1940s resulted in an explosion of toys, books and consumer products with his likeness on them, none of which were manufactured by the Walt Disney Company.

Franchising is similar but based round a more physical format and complicated business model. The franchisor grants the franchisee, usually a local operator, the right to distribute its products, techniques and trademarks for an initial fee and percentage of sales. The franchisor might continue to support the market with advertising, training and support services. Agreements typically last from 5 to 25 years. Royalty fees differ by sector and geography, but are most dependent on the strength of a brand – in the hotel business, royalty fees would vary between 2% and 12% of revenues.

The model grew rapidly in the 1950s with motel chains such as Howard Johnston along the new interstate highways. Now many hotels, such as Holiday Inn, Intercontinental and W Hotel, operate a franchise model – as do restaurants, car rental, airlines, convenience stores, designer clothing outlets and much more. McDonald's is arguably the most successful worldwide, with more partners than any other franchise network.

The table illustrates some of the typical responsibilities of the two parties involved in licensing and franchising contracts. It demonstrates the power in exploiting ideas, and also in protecting them, through a partnership of mutual contribution and significant potential reward:

Licensee/franchisee	Licensor/franchisor
Owns the trademark, product or process, and allows partner to use it for a period of time	Uses the properties in agreed ways in return for a fixed royalty fee related to sales
Specifies the terms of use of the brand and all other factors, including pricing and promotion	Complies with all terms of contract to deliver a branded product or experience locally
Continues to promote the brand, and approves all licensor marketing and packaging materials	Promotes and sells the licensed items in their agreed territories, in a relevant way locally
Provides global services relevant to the business such as international support or sales	Local partner can sell locally, but also sell internationally (e.g. airline routes, call roaming)
Manages the commercial model, and has access and can inspect local accounts	Can share best practice with and learn from other licensees in the network
Shares relevant information such as customer databases, access to loyalty schemes, etc.	Exploits the local market, delivers global schemes locally, and shares database.
Provides ongoing support in terms of marketing, training and brand updating/renewal	Pays the licensee a royalty, typically a percentage of revenues generated
Continues to support the brand through marketing and new product developments	Local partner is well positioned to also win rights to distribute other licensed products and services

The rewards can be enormous for both parties. The brand owner can scale their business without the costs or risks associated with physical growth, and branch out into sectors which they have less expertise and capability. The local partners can operate with a prestigious brand name, have a ready- made business model operating to highest standards and be part of a global network.

Christian Audigier ... the glam rock licensing machine

Christian Audigier is one of the fastest rising stars of fashion. He first made his mark in fashion with MacKeen Jeans and then worked as designer to other brands including Levi's, Diesel and American Outfitters. His style is so distinctive that he is known as the 'King of Jeans'. He became the driving force behind Von Dutch, making the brand a household name, adding trends like the 'trucker hat' that could be seen on everyone from college students to high-profile celebrities.

Learning from this experience, he began to use licensing deals to build his own fashion empire. In little more than five years he has launched nine popular brands with more than sixty licenses – including Ed Hardy, Christian Audigier, Evel Knievel, Rock Fabulous and Paco Chicano – that have then been distributed through partnerships with leading retailers.

He was granted the exclusive rights to the designs of Don Ed Hardy, seeking to create a 'life-style of street couture'. Hardy is known as 'the godfather of modern tattoo', with legendary status built up over his 40 years producing some of the most sophisticated and mesmerizing images on human bodies. He takes his ideas from his own experiences, fusing icons from US and Japanese culture, the surf, and mysticism. His broad spectrum of taste and experience, together with fascination for art history, has given his work a unique character. Celebrities such as Madonna, Britney Spears and Kanye West sought out Hardy's designs, which were then licensed across a vast array of products – from jewellery and fragrances to skateboards and stationary, chocolates and vodka, and even air fresheners.

Audigier has also branched out into the world of nightclubs, with the star-studded opening of Christian Audigier: The Nightclub at Treasure Island in Las Vegas. His glam rock style features heavily in the club, on the walls, as tableware, in the bathrooms, and even worn by waitresses. It quickly became one of the most hip destinations on the Strip.

The French designer from rural Avignon has certainly embraced the US psyche for glamour with just a hint of trash.

CHAPTER 39

Delivering results ... improving your return on ideas

'A new idea must not be judged by its immediate results.'

Nikola Tesla

High-performing companies put significantly more focus on innovation metrics than others, according to research in 2009 by McKinsey. Whilst most companies said they had useful metrics for innovation, mostly focused on product innovations, only 29% of high performers and 10% of others felt confident in assessing their innovation effectiveness.

The old adage that 'what gets measured gets done' is still true, and even more so 'what gets rewarded gets done'. Targets, metrics and rewards should therefore be a key consideration when defining the type of culture, practices and outputs you seek from innovation. Do you want people to work together or individually? Should they focus on fast deliverables or big breakthroughs? Or on product improvements or innovations that change business models and market structures?

The wrong performance indicators, an unreasonable performance target or a badly balanced 'Balanced Scorecard' (measuring people, customer, financial and improvement factors) will drive business in the wrong direction. Strategic decisions will be based on false criteria, investments will not deliver optimal returns, people will become demotivated by their inability to hit targets and investors will lose confidence.

Get the right measures, then you can make the right decisions. People and resources will be focused in the best places for high returns, and everyone can share in the rewards. Market share, for example, is increasingly meaningless, depending entirely on how you define your boundaries. You could have 100% share of one market and 0.1% share of another. As customer needs change, and market profitability varies, markets are not equal. Rarely are companies in the same market – P&G and Unilever might be big competitors in some sectors or segments, but are irrelevant to each other in others.

This gives the big picture, and unifying goal, but is less practical in enabling day-to-day decision-making. Developing a balanced scorecard with the right portfolio of metrics should be based firstly on the 'value drivers' of the business. These will differ by company, but in simple terms there are:

→ **Inputs** such as operating costs, headcount and time to market – factors that can managed directly because they relate to decisions and actions.

→ **Throughputs** such as productivity, sales growth, customer retention – factors that are direct consequences of operations and can quickly be influenced.

→ **Outputs** such as profitability, return on investment and share price – factors that are more complex to influence but are clearly driven by the previous ones.

Within most organizations, innovation-related metrics are generic and remote, often not seen as related to other tasks. Marketing people are obsessed with the customer awareness and engagement achieved through their actions. Salespeople are concerned about their reach and ability to retain the best customers. Operational people are focused on productivity or customer satisfaction. But there is little point in engaging people in great promises if they are impossible to deliver. There is little value in satisfaction if the customer doesn't come back again.

Innovation metrics

Measuring innovation typically involves a portfolio of measures structured around balanced scorecards that relate to financial performance, innovation process efficiency, employees' contribution and motivation, as well benefits for customers. Metrics typically include:

➡ New product revenue.

➡ Percentage of total revenue from new products.

➡ Spending on R&D as a proportion of total costs.

➡ Time to market.

➡ Customer and employee perception and satisfaction.

➡ Number of patents.

➡ New product launches.

The McKinsey research, *Assessing Innovation Metrics*, found that innovation metrics were rarely able to assess the effectiveness of investment or allocate resources, and few were aligned to individual or collective performance incentives. So whilst there is clearly some way to go, these are the metrics (in order of most common use) that they found most frequently used in companies:

1 Revenue growth due to new products or services.

2 Customer satisfaction with new products and services.

3 Number of ideas or concepts in the pipeline.

4 R&D spending as a percentage of sales.

5 Percentage of sales from new products/services in a given time period.

6   Number of new products or services launched.

7   Return on investment in new products or services.

8   Number of R&D projects.

9   Number of people actively devoted to innovation.

10 Profit growth due to new products and services.

Some attempts have been made to standardize innovation performance. The OECD 'Oslo Manual' proposes standard guidelines for measuring technological product and process innovation. *Business Week*, however, in seeking to find 'the world's most innovative companies', uses financial performance metrics (revenue, profitability and total shareholder return) together with perceptual rankings by business leaders.

Whirlpool ... black in white in the whirl of innovation

In 1999, Whirlpool CEO David Whitman announced that he wanted 'innovation from everyone and everywhere – we need to make innovation a core competence'. Describing his ambition in *Business Week*, he saw six challenges for innovation and that it must:

➡ Be possible from anyone.

➡ Go beyond product.

➡ Permeate our structure and culture.

➡ Create new business opportunities.

➡ Not be individual or functional.

➡ Be sustainable.

He introduced a new role, 'Global VP of Innovation', and established a dedicated team of 25 managers from across the business, who spent a year developing new creativity and innovation skills and processes. Some of these went on to become full-time innovation project leaders; others went back to become innovation coaches working within the business units.

This was innovation drive from the top, a holistic change programme that affected everyone in the business. Whirlpool created an innovation board (an online space with tools and shared knowledge), rolled out innovation training across the business, and encouraged cross-functional thinking and idea-generation. New performance metrics encouraged these new behaviours, focusing on incremental revenues from innovation, the number of new projects and IP rights, the number of people involved, and new customers. Whirlpool:

➡ Set aside seed funding for significant innovation projects, making new ideas possible and easy to start.

➡ Ruthlessly demolished real and perceived barriers across the business that seemed to hinder people.

➡ Encouraged certification in innovation and project management practices.

New incentives were introduced at individual, team and organizational levels, and there were recognition and award schemes too. Some of the benefits were emotional: exclusive parties for the best thinkers, participation in programmes with partners and rapid promotions.

Today the company's brands – including Whirlpool, Maytag and KitchenAid – have a structured process to filter ideas that continually emerge from product groups, development teams and 'i-mentors' (employees trained in innovation diffused across the organization to seek out the best ideas). Around half the ideas make it into the innovation pipeline and around 10% of those get to market. Whirlpool measures the potential sales that could emerge from the innovation pipeline every month, seeking new ideas equivalent to at least 20% of current revenues.

For an idea to be considered for development, it has to meet Whirlpool's definition of innovation. It must:

➡ Meet a consumer need in a fresh way.

➡ Have the breadth to become a platform for related products.

➡ Be able to lift earnings – incremental innovations are expected to deliver results within months, while more significant ones are given three to five years.

Research findings are written up in a document Whirlpool calls an 'opportunity brief', which is reviewed by an internal panel of innovation experts and regional managers from across the organization. This 'i-board' meets every month to review potential projects, and allocate funding.

Roughly 40% of the ideas that make it to this stage end up in the innovation pipeline. Those that don't get tripped up by the next hurdle, the 'i-box', a three-page scorecard that forces innovation teams to be very concrete about expected factors such as revenues, technical feasibility, relevance to the brand and market trends. It checks that there is a consumer need and that the concept meets it better than existing products. The i-panel then reviews the i-box, with scores determining whether the concept will get funded.

Whirlpool has around 1500 projects on the back burner, but not forgotten, at any time – maybe because of overall resources and priorities. Every year, Whirlpool sets a goal for innovation-related revenue for each product team. 'We might say we want 80% of new revenues to come from innovations to core products, 15% from innovations that leverage or expand the core, and 5% from totally new innovations,' says Moises Norena, Head of Global Innovation.

So what can we learn from Whirlpool's approach to evaluating ideas?

➡ **Clear definition:** A brief, concrete definition of innovation helps employees evaluate new concepts at the front end, screening out those that don't fit. As a concept progresses, keep returning to the definition to make sure that the idea still clears the bar.

➡ **Don't kill, just shelve:** A concept that might not be worth pursuing today – because of limited resources, for instance, or the lack of a partner – might be next year's innovation. Don't kill projects, shelve them, and annually review all concepts for possible resurrection.

➡ **Filter lightly at first:** Early in the process, Whirlpool concepts are required to meet the basic definition of innovation. As projects progress, the evaluation criteria become more rigorous. Begin with easier requirements to avoid killing off concepts before they can be developed.

➡ **Align with strategy:** A concept might be innovative but still not smart for a company to develop because it would take the company too far afield. Make sure that the people evaluating ideas do so in the context of the company's strategic goals.

Whirlpool's innovation process model links research activities with idea-generation techniques to drive the creation of new ideas. All Whirlpool employees are encouraged to participate in its innovation programme and many receive training in innovation techniques.

The results of Whitman's initiative were phenomenal. By 2005 the Whirlpool share price had hit an all-time high: profits were up to $422 million on $14.3 billion sales, and the innovation pipeline was valued at $3.3 billion (compared to $1 billion two years previously). Sixty per cent of products sold in 2006 were at least partly new, and contributed around $1 billion in sales.

CHAPTER 40

The
IMPACT
Toolkit

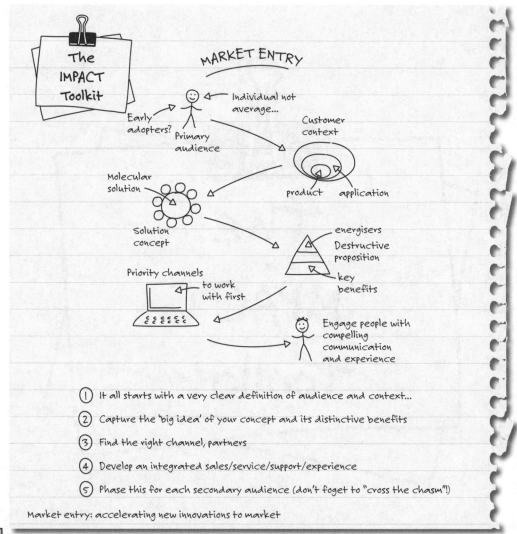

The IMPACT Toolkit

MARKET ENTRY

Early adopters?
Individual not average...

Primary audience

Customer context

Molecular solution

Solution concept

product   application

energisers
Destructive proposition

Priority channels
to work with first

key benefits

Engage people with compelling communication and experience

1. It all starts with a very clear definition of audience and context...

2. Capture the 'big idea' of your concept and its distinctive benefits

3. Find the right channel, partners

4. Develop an integrated sales/service/support/experience

5. Phase this for each secondary audience (don't foget to "cross the chasm"!)

Market entry: accelerating new innovations to market

The IMPACT Toolkit

IDEA SELLING

idea = concept, proposition, solution etc

to clients and managers internally

You walk into your client's office, and you are desperate to talk about your big idea ... but not yet! ...

1. Talk about your audience – their issues and objectives

2. Focus on a challenge — the 'oh shit' moment

3. Pose a question, a big one

4. Introduce your big idea ...

① Start by talking about your audience's issues and objectives (not yours!)

② Explain why they need to address if differently ... and why your BIG IDEA is needed!

③ Use pictures, graphics and key words

④ Add drama, and compelling facts

⑤ Don't forget to let them participate — and make it human and fun too!

Idea selling: engaging people in new ideas and innovations

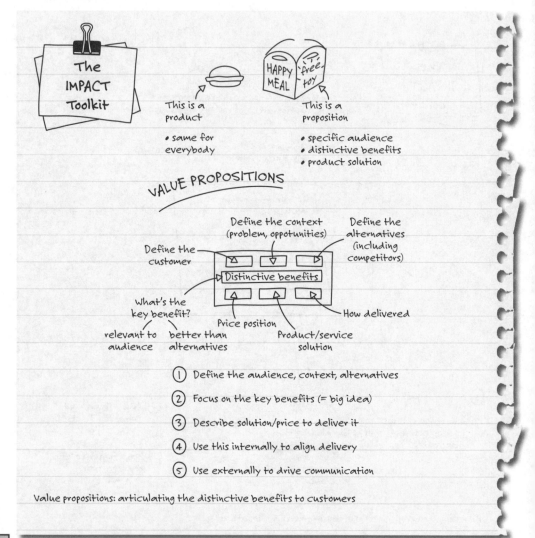

The IMPACT Toolkit

This is a product
• same for everybody

This is a proposition
• specific audience
• distinctive benefits
• product solution

VALUE PROPOSITIONS

Define the context (problem, oppotunities)

Define the alternatives (including competitors)

Define the customer

Distinctive benefits

What's the key benefit?
relevant to audience
better than alternatives

Price position

Product/service solution

How delivered

① Define the audience, context, alternatives

② Focus on the key benefits (= big idea)

③ Describe solution/price to deliver it

④ Use this internally to align delivery

⑤ Use externally to drive communication

Value propositions: articulating the distinctive benefits to customers

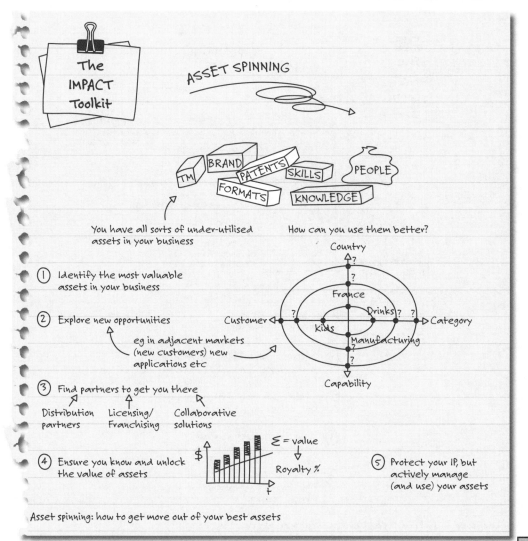

The
IMPACT
Toolkit

ASSET SPINNING

TM BRAND PATENTS SKILLS PEOPLE
FORMATS KNOWLEDGE

You have all sorts of under-utilised assets in your business

How can you use them better?

① Identify the most valuable assets in your business

② Explore new opportunities

eg in adjacent markets (new customers) new applications etc

Country
?
?
France
Customer ◀ ? Drinks ? ? ▶ Category
Kids
Manufacturing
?
?
Capability

③ Find partners to get you there

Distribution partners   Licensing/ Franchising   Collaborative solutions

④ Ensure you know and unlock the value of assets

Σ = value
Royalty %

⑤ Protect your IP, but actively manage (and use) your assets

Asset spinning: how to get more out of your best assets

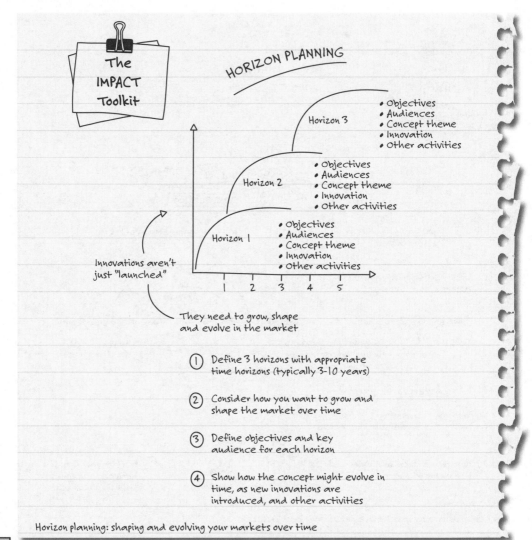

The IMPACT Toolkit

HORIZON PLANNING

Horizon 3
- Objectives
- Audiences
- Concept theme
- Innovation
- Other activities

Horizon 2
- Objectives
- Audiences
- Concept theme
- Innovation
- Other activities

Horizon 1
- Objectives
- Audiences
- Concept theme
- Innovation
- Other activities

1 2 3 4 5

Innovations aren't just "launched"

They need to grow, shape and evolve in the market

1. Define 3 horizons with appropriate time horizons (typically 3-10 years)

2. Consider how you want to grow and shape the market over time

3. Define objectives and key audience for each horizon

4. Show how the concept might evolve in time, as new innovations are introduced, and other activities

Horizon planning: shaping and evolving your markets over time

Now forward

CHAPTER 41

Creative leaders ... recreating the Medici effect

'We keep moving forward, opening new doors, and doing new things, because we are curious, and curiosity keeps leading us down new paths.'

Walt Disney

What is the DNA of extraordinarily creative leaders? What have they got, either as genetic talent or by experience and development, that makes them stand out from their peers, inspire their colleagues, and add a touch of magic?

When Steve Jobs walks across the stage at MacWorld, the huge live and online audience is brimming with expectation, waiting for the moment when Steve tells us how he has changed the world again. Yes, it's theatre, it's expectation – but there is also something about the man's character that has got him there.

Learning from Leonardo da Vinci, watching the performance of Steve Jobs, listening to Jeff Bezos speak ... we get clues as to what really creates creativity in people.

Why? Why not? What if?

When I first met Richard Branson, I was amazed by how many questions he asked. I thought I was there to learn about him, but he was more interested in learning about me and what I thought about things. Asking him what I thought his best skill was, he said, 'To ask the most provocative questions'. As chairman and conscience of the Virgin Group, his role isn't to manage the balance sheet, his people and projects, but to ask the difficult, sometimes stupid, sometimes profound questions. 'The important and difficult job is never to find the right answers, it is to find the right question,' wrote Peter Drucker almost 50 years ago.

Dell Computers emerged when Michael Dell asked himself, 'Why do computers cost five times the sum of their parts?' When he opened up a computer at the time, he found $600 of parts being sold for $3000, which made him question the whole business model.

Most managers use 'how' questions: how to make things happen, how to make things better. However, innovation is driven by more effective questioning in the more stretching forms of constructive challenge or hypothesis, asking the questions:

➡ Why?

➡ Why not?

➡ What if?

Innovators challenge conventions, assumptions and even rules (which, of course, have only been written based on the authors' existing knowledge and experiences). They like to play devil's advocate, and sometimes frustratingly (but usefully) disagree with what everyone else thinks is the right thing to do. They encourage considering alternatives, add new constraints and push for originality.

Google has a mantra that 'creativity loves constraint'. This doesn't seek to limit convention but to stretch and focus it in different ways – it often forces you out of the box rather than to stay within it. What if you gave your product away free – how would you make money? What if you didn't have your existing customers – where would new ones come from? What if you had half the budget – what would you do?

Of all the skills, questioning probably matters most, creating a better starting point from which to create. And importantly, it's not that difficult to do. Any of us, with a little practice, can get into the habit of asking why and why not, or even what if. Having set yourself on a more creative course, the other traits follow much more naturally.

The little black book

The best innovators are anthropologists, great observers of people and their behaviours. They don't rely upon the average results that emerge from conventional market research, focus groups that are conditioned by the questions asked or quantitative analysis that seeks to serve the mean or median. They look in the margins as well as the mainstream. They look for deviant or emerging behaviours: people who do things differently, perhaps as extreme users or just as free thinkers; people who have adapted products for their own needs or found completely new applications.

Look for the small, interesting, unusual things. Always carry a small notebook with plain pages and get it out when talking to frontline staff, customers or close friends: it should be full of scribbles, anecdotes, observations, maybe drawings and a treasure trove of creative ideas.

Ratan Tata, the man behind the Nano, the world's cheapest car, got his ideas from observing a family of four packed onto the kind of single motorized scooter that crowd the streets of Mumbai. They could never afford the $20,000 required to buy even a small family car and there were millions more like them. Tata set constraints based on his observation that the car needed to be small and efficient, but still quality and stylish, and, crucially must cost no more than $2500.

Medici connections

Like the Medici family of da Vinci's time, leaders encourage connections between unrelated fields, looking for the fusions and intersections to generate new ideas. The brain works by association, connecting ideas that seem related either by knowledge or experience. The more diverse our backgrounds, the more connections our brains can make. New knowledge triggers new associations, which give us the ability to have new ideas. And the more frequently we add new and different knowledge, the more naturally our brains store and connect, and the more creative we become.

Pierre Omidyar launched eBay in 1996 based on some unusual connections: a fascination for creating more efficient markets enabled by networked technologies, his girlfriend's passion for collecting obscure Pez dispensers and the inadequacy of local newspaper ads in helping her to find them. To most of us, these personal activities might seem irrelevant to our work, but might actually be our most valuable contribution.

Similarly, Steve Jobs has an eclectic range of interests – from Indian meditation to calligraphy, movie-making with Pixar to his obsession for fast cars. It would be easy to see these as the personal indulgences and toys of a billionaire. Like every one of us he is able to draw on his unique bank of personal knowledge and experiences, and often observes that 'creativity is connecting things'.

Even if you fail 10,000 times ...

Edison was famed for his experimentation, once proclaiming, 'I haven't failed. I've simply found 10,000 ways that do not work.' However, most managers and entrepreneurs work in their markets, developing prototypes and piloting new ideas. This happens in many ways, be it the continual testing of new variants by financial cards company Capital One in a relentless 'test, learn, test' sequence, or by trying out new consumer products in the Sample Labs, a unique Japanese retail chain that specializes in pilot launches with associated tracking facilities to learn from the response.

Jeff Bezos, the brains behind Amazon, began experimenting at an early age, taking apart his crib whilst still a baby. Amazon has been one long experiment in what works and doesn't, continually trying things: not content to be a mere bookstore, it was not long before he was selling everything from toys to televisions. The Kindle, Amazon's electronic reader, is another experiment: exploring whether Bezos can evolve from retail to device manufacturer or even content manager. 'I encourage all my people to go down blind alleys and experiment,' he says, just like he did himself when he walked out of his Manhattan banker's job, packed his belongings and headed west in search of Amazon.

My own experience is that the best places to experiment are in other markets – different geographies or sectors. For me this was applying the ideas of airlines to rail travel and retailing, or the US insurance model to European markets, or the French hypermarket format to Asia. Indeed, having started my career in a physics research lab, I have found that the principles and techniques of experimentation used in science can be applied very simply and usefully to any business.

P&G's A.J. Lafley spent his early adult years studying history in France and managing retail operations on military bases in Japan, an experience which he found immensely useful when returning some time later to head P&G in Asia and eventually become CEO. The diversity of his social and cultural experiences served him well in managing business as well as in driving innovation.

Creative connections

Most people network to sell themselves or their businesses to get a better job or to find new sales opportunities. However, the most powerful source of networking is idea sharing. There is nothing like a network to test ideas, and the more diverse the better. It is a source of instant feedback, illuminating discussion, and collectively improved ideas. But it can be reciprocal, too, which is why people engage – be it in something directly relevant to them, or in something more abstract.

Entrepreneurs spend enormous amounts of time networking with people from different backgrounds, alternative perspectives, and with different kinds of ideas. The more senior you are in the workplace, or lonely you are as a start-up, the more valuable an eclectic, external network can be.

'Idea' conferences, such as Davos (World Economic Forum) or TED (the Technology, Entertainment and Design gathering, held in various locations each year) are ideal platforms to extend knowledge and find new creative catalysts. Whilst most business conferences still focus on very functional, repetitive issues, TED is a smorgasbord of ideas from every field of arts, business, academia and politics. One minute you are inspired by an explorer, botanist or pianist; the next you are immersed in a fuel cell innovation think-tank, a stem cell ethics debate or a real-time open innovation lab.

The BlackBerry has its origins in such an ideas network. Michael Lazaridis was sitting in a conference audience listening to a speaker describe how wireless technology would enable a vending machine to send a signal when it needed filling, or a fridge to replenish itself when it runs low. We've all heard such stories, but the Research in Motion founder was able to relate it to his own business, and to wonder what would be possible if you connected computers with wireless technology. An idea was born.

Shanghai Tang ... a fusion of oriental glamour and contemporary fashion

'Shanghai Tang is the best of 5000 years of Chinese tradition exploding into the twenty-first century,' says David Tang Wang Cheung, the UK-educated son of a wealthy Chinese entrepreneur who launched the brand in Hong Kong in 1994.

Shanghai had the feel of exotic glamour, a spirit of limitless opportunity and a sense of danger too. The stars of the 1920s and 30s, from Charlie Chaplin to Aldous Huxley, converged on the bustling Chinese port with its cruise liners, art deco hotels, film studios and opium dens. It was a cultural melting pot, where emigrating Russians met entrepreneurial Americans and Japanese jazz was enjoyed alongside the finest French champagnes.

Almost a century later, Raphael Le Masne de Chermont, the new CEO of one of Asia's most glamorous luxury brands, is watching the launch of his new collection. A crowd had gathered to view his latest examples of Chinese elegance in a contemporary style. With spotlights on, the music turned up, the stunning Asian models make their way down the red catwalk, oozing sensuality and the distinctive Shanghai style.

Whilst the fashion label certainly represents the new China – one in which style, creativity and wealth is quickly replacing an image of much tradition, cheap production and widespread poverty – it has not been an easy ride for Tang and the brand that bears his name.

In its first year, his store attracted a million visitors, rising to 4 million within five years. The focus was on luxury, tailor-made clothing, employing some of the best Shanghai tailors, and he quickly expanded into ready-to-wear ranges targeting international visitors. The ranges were derived from traditional Chinese costumes and handicrafts: rows of vibrant *qi paos* 'Suzie Wong' dresses to velvet-lined Mao jackets for men, silver rice bowls and painted lanterns.

In 1997 he sold a majority share in the business to Richemont, the Swiss-based luxury goods company that also owns Mont Blanc, Chloe, Dunhill and Cartier. Tang wanted the investment to take his brand into the Western capitals, and most urgently to take on the designer labels of Madison Avenue. He opened his store in typically flamboyant style. But the US did not buy it. With low sales, high rents, the Asian financial crisis, SARS and demanding new owners, the founder was in trouble.

Le Masne de Chermont was brought in by Richemont in 2001 to set the business back on course. He scaled down the US ambitions, and dropped many other international plans. He

297

refocused the business back on China. Whilst the visitor market is growing rapidly – with US visitors there soon to outnumber those that visit Europe – the Chinese luxury goods market is the real opportunity.

He recruited Joanne Ooi, a brash, self-confident Asian-American from Cincinnatti, as his marketing and creative director. She immersed herself in Chinese history, culture and society. She was enthralled. She felt the existing ranges were overpriced, impractical and had little credibility with local people.

Ooi refashioned Shanghai Tang as modern and relevant. The brand needed more authenticity and depth. She dug deep into Chinese culture to find a theme for each season. She roamed art galleries, museums and antique markets, as well as pop culture, to find inspiration. The clothes had to be luxurious and prestigious, but also wearable. She ditched all the tourist trinkets. Her designs were subtle and sophisticated, yet every piece, she argued, should also be easy to wear with jeans.

From a colourful and nostalgic art deco concept store in Hong Kong, Shanghai Tang has evolved into a modern lifestyle vision of Chinese fashion. It now has a network of 39 boutiques, including Shanghai, New York, Paris, London, LA, Madrid and Tokyo. The brand is also growing rapidly in its homeland, with flagship stores in Beijing, Hangzhou and Guangzhou. The label's international designers create modern Chinese-inspired collections comprising a full range of ready-to-wear clothing and accessories using luxurious fabrics ranging from Chinese silk to the best Mongolian cashmere.

Le Masne de Chermont and his team are on a high. The Chinese economy is booming again and its people are embracing designer fashion as if there were no tomorrow. David Tang is also happy that he has created China's first significant luxury brand.

CHAPTER 42

Innovation strategy ... ideas that drive profitable growth

'Ultimately, we wanted Nike to be the world's best sports and fitness company. Once you say that, you have a focus. You don't end up making wing tips or sponsoring the next Rolling Stones world tour.'

Phil Knight in *Harvard Business Review*

Innovation is at the top of the business agenda, the most important source of competitive advantage and a driver of profitable growth. It gives an organization energy and purpose. It creates new interest and relevance for customers. It adds trust and hope to investors. And it results in a maelstrom of creative actions – some focused, others dispersed.

Yet few companies have an innovation strategy that aligns, integrates and focuses innovation efforts across the organization to deliver short- and long-term business results. Most businesses have a multitude of innovative projects going on, but most of them are within functions, categories or markets. They are dispersed, often tactical, and with limited support

Whilst everyone wants a piece of innovation, there are many different views as to what it means:

➡ New product launches and improving market share.

➡ Ways to work smarter and improve margins.

➡ Hugely technical, with tangible, patentable outputs.

➡ Creativity, generating better ideas and intellectual capital.

➡ Human progress, making people's lives better.

➡ A way of improving ROI, growth and value creation.

Innovative companies have some common factors. They see innovation as their primary source of competitive differentiation in their markets, the sustained driving force behind distinctive products and approaches. They know how to improve the return on investments and assets, doing more with them in more places, focused and prioritized as a primary component of business strategy. They focus innovation on the best market opportunities and areas of best long-term commercial return.

Intel, for example, has a relentless focus on the future that drives its business focus and cultural mindset. This strategy is based on a deep understanding of its current and future markets, customers, and non-customers. Most companies have huge amounts of research, databases and trend analysis, but few can effectively synthesize and apply it. Innovative companies put particular focus on how they interpret and exploit insights; for example, P&G's ability to 'sense and connect' was the symbolic, tangible action that shifted the consumer goods leader from being product-centric to customer-centric.

An innovation strategy would have the following components:

➡ **Alignment to business and market strategy:** A clear definition of the business purpose and direction, i.e. the reason the company exists, what it does for people and its long-term business priorities. This might also be articulated as a vision (how the world will be in the future) and a mission (what the business wants to achieve long-term). Whilst this strategy will cover three to ten years depending on industry, innovation should also recognize the business plan, with specific performance targets over one to three years – although innovation should be careful not to become too driven by this shorter-term perspective.

➡ **Optimizing the business and product portfolios:** Ensuring that there is a good balance of categories and geographies, products and services to achieve short- and long-term objectives. Whilst most businesses think through their product portfolio (for example, using the BSG growth/share matrix, identifying their dogs, cash cows, rising stars and question marks), fewer companies look more strategically (using, say, Ansoff's matrix to prioritize new and existing markets) and indeed at the broader business categories that they are in (such as Kodak missing the digital market or Microsoft being slow to see the power of the internet).

➡ **Defining the innovation priorities:** Specifying the priorities for innovation, the markets and categories where innovation is most important, and the more specific customer segment and product ranges to focus on. More strategically, it is about getting a balance between 'incremental' and 'next generation'/'game changing' projects, recognizing that a mixture of each with different levels of risk and reward is required. It might include platform strategies to optimize ranges of products developed with a similar underlying specification over time. 'Horizon planning' is particularly useful in defining the priorities in the short, medium and longer term. The strategy also defines the capabilities and resources to achieve these.

Innovation strategies are often more difficult than other strategies because they work across functions (rather like customer or sustainability strategies) so have many stakeholders and often no outright functional owner. They might be 'fixed' or 'emergent' in their nature, the former having little uncertainty and driven top-down, the latter having more flexibility, evolving bottom-up and top-down in response to new insights and opportunities. 'Emergent' strategies are more suited to a fast-changing market, like most are today.

Technology businesses are notorious for their 'product roadmaps': very definitive, fixed plans of when new technologies will be available to market. Typically driven by R&D and engineers, they encourage a 'product push' mentality in the business without much thought for whether markets actually want an endlessly higher-performance product or whether other factors matter. Philips, for example, slowly realized that this macho 'push' was one of its biggest problems, and introduced a more customer-centric approach to its business and innovation, and a 'pull' driven by a customer roadmap based on customer motivations and aspirations.

The capabilities and resources to make these innovations happen do not have to come from within. Innovative companies recognize that they can be much more successful with partners than alone, fusing capabilities and expertise to do things that others cannot, and delivering products and services that are not just components of solutions but really solve customer problems. Partners are often for unusual but related areas. An example of innovative collaborations includes H&M's celebrity partnerships with the likes of Roberto Cavalli, Kylie Minogue and Victor & Rolf.

Innovation has simple yet effective processes and systems for turning the best ideas into commercial applications, or developing and launching new solutions fast and effectively. This sounds obvious, but innovation is typically a non-functional, cross-business challenge, and sits outside business as usual and its supporting processes. Apple realizes that organizational boundaries and bureaucracies are the biggest killers of innovation.

Lego ... innovation is much more than creative play

Lego, 'toy of the century', is reinventing how it innovates through D4B (Design for Business).

In Danish, *'leg godt'* means 'play well', and that remains the inspiration for the brand. Since the creation of the timeless plastic building blocks in 1932 by Ole Kirk Kristiansen, Lego has been one of the world's most popular toys. It has come a long way from a small carpenter's workshop to become the fifth largest toy manufacturer in the world.

The Lego Group, based in Billund in Denmark and with 4500 employees, is now led by the founder's grandchild, Kjeld Kirk Kristiansen. Its purpose is 'to inspire children to explore and challenge their own creative potential'. It does this by helping children to 'learn through play' – developing their creative and structured problem-solving, curiosity and imagination, and interpersonal skills and physical motor skills.

However, in 2005, Lego started to run into trouble. It was struggling against the videogames market, the power of fashionable personalities from the likes of Disney and low-cost producers of other plastic bricks. It responded by diversifying, creating more different products – which only made things worse. After three years of headless creativity, leading to more than 14,000 branded components, the Danes realized that they needed more focus: to return to 'classic' Lego, with fewer, better products, engaging its 20 million customers more deeply.

Aligning business and innovation

Lego's new design system D4B is redefining how its whole innovation process is run. Key elements of the approach are a stronger alignment between business strategy and design strategy, more collaboration between functions, more challenge and rigour in the creativity and analysis, a more consistent approach that is easy to share, and better innovation that drives profitable growth.

There are more than 120 Lego designers, mostly based in Billund, whilst others work in satellite offices around the world, adapting ideas to local tastes and tracking new trends and technologies, particularly in Japan. The team also collaborates with many universities – especially MIT Media Lab, from which the Mindstorms system emerged. There is more stretch and stimulus, but also more rigour and evaluation. It embraces new language and tools that form an innovation 'DNA' and new computer-based simulators for rapid prototyping allow quick iterations. Time to market has also reduced, from 24 months to nine. It moved from a focus on products to customers, and how all aspects of the business and customer experience could be part of the innovation.

There are three components to D4B:

➡ **Lego innovation model:** More collaborative in the early stages, more aligned to objectives and resources, and more tested and focused on results delivery.

➡ **Lego innovation roadmap:** Clearly structured phases of development, bringing a consistency of steps and evaluation gates, and strong links between phases.

➡ **Lego foundation overview:** A simple way of visualizing the outputs through posters rather than lengthy documents, enabling more engagement, comparison and better decisions.

The process is separated into 'P' stages for prototyping and 'M' phases for manufacturing. The focus is much more on making ideas tangible quickly, thereby making more evaluation and focus possible in later stages so that all resources can be focused on the best opportunities. The stages within the phases are:

➡ **P0 (portfolio kick-off):** Defining the business objectives and focusing on key issues to be resolved across the business and portfolio.

➡ **P1 (opportunity freeze):** Exploring what opportunities would solve the issues identified, approving the business and financial case for doing the project.

➡ **P2 (concept freeze):** Making sense of the emerging concepts and how they apply to each function, from communication to customer service.

➡ **P3 (portfolio freeze):** Deciding which concepts should be turned into projects, specifying all the requirements for development and the business case.

The P cycle can take up to six months, after which it is decided whether the project enters M cycle – in which there are five more stages:

➡ **M1 (project kick-off):** Designers and product managers work together to refine the concept specification, and the plan to take it to market.

➡ **M2 (business freeze):** The business case is finalized and the product design is completed to meet the business requirements.

➡ **M3 (product freeze):** The product design evolves into packaging, marketing and communication, aligning the product concept with the overall brand proposition.

➡ **M4 (communication freeze):** The packaging and communication materials are finalized, and the supply chain is specified ready for manufacturing.

➡ **M5 (procurement freeze):** The supply chain is developed, manufacturing begins and the product is launched.

Designers were initially concerned whether such a structured process, dependent on commercial objectives, would stifle creativity. They found that they no longer needed to think about how to establish the project and gain approval: their creativity was now more focused on the design itself.

Whilst the D4B process has accelerated an improved set of innovative products to market, Lego has not lost sight of the future. Lego's 'Concept Lab' works separately from the mainstream innovation process, with a team of 15 designers focused on more stretching opportunities – more radical products that will redefine its markets. It works on a different cycle, with more intuitive evaluations of novel ideas that Lego hopes will delight our children's children one day.

CHAPTER 43

Creative culture ... working with hotspots and happiness

'People are like stained-glass windows. They sparkle and shine when the sun is out, but when the darkness sets in their true beauty is revealed only if there is light from within.'

Elizabeth Kübler-Ross, Swiss psychologist

IBM recently published *The Enterprise of the Future*, a blueprint for the next generation of business. It describes a business defined by its culture rather than structure or sector, a business that it is adaptive to unprecedented change, relentless competition and unreasonable expectations.

The future enterprise, IBM says, will be 'hungry for change', not just responding to trends, but shaping and leading them, seizing discontinuities and market shifts as opportunities to redefine the rules, and outplay the competition. It will be 'disruptive by nature' in that it will relentlessly challenge its own business model, disrupting the basis of competition, shifting the value proposition, overturning traditional approaches as opportunities arise, reinventing itself or its entire industry. And it will be 'innovative beyond customer imagination' through deep collaborative relationships that allow it to surprise customers and find innovations for mutual success.

Creative workstyles

We live in very different world from the nine-to-five corporate man who succeeded by fitting in, sitting in hour-long meeting after hour-long meeting, mostly talking about agendas and minutes rather than anything of substance. He – and it was a he – was like all the others, and that gave them comfort: a slave to the twelve-month planning cycle and the performance metrics. They didn't like diversity or change, challenge or tension. They were in the company for life, motivated more than anything else by their pension.

Is it really healthy for people to follow the rules? Do all those endless meetings help or hinder us – what if it they were 20 minutes long rather than 60? Is a pension really an aspiration that drives young people to great work? Don't we want as many different and interesting people as possible?

The table below shows some of the differences between traditional and innovative organizations.

Traditional organizations	Innovative organizations
Hierarchical	Flat
Specialist functions	Task-based project teams
Bureaucratic	Protected from bureaucracy
Operating units	Process defined
Controlled hierarchically	Project managed
Strategic planning	Flexible planning
Promotion and bonuses	Autonomy and recognition
Power and status	Shared equity
Recruited based on need	Recruited on ideas and attitude
Encourage conformity	Encourage diversity

The creative business looks and works differently, moving from hierarchy to meritocracy, from bureaucracy to autonomy. Instead of anonymous they are familiar, not clean but messy, less about experts and more about tinkerers. Professor Theresa Amabile at Harvard Business School suggests five characteristics that support creativity in the workplace:

- Encouragement – in particular through open flows of information.
- Freedom – autonomy in day-to-day tasks and a sense of personal ownership.
- Resources – the expertise, tools and materials to explore new things.
- Pressure, push and pull – in the form of both challenge and expectation.
- Impediments – the need to overcome barriers, typically organizational.

Google gave new meaning to bringing home into the workplace, the work-lifestyle. Arrive at Mountain View and you can enjoy three free meals every day in any of their gourmet restaurants. You can work on any project you like. You can take as much time off as you want. You get to busk with Sergey and Larry every so often. You get the latest cool product leases before anyone else. There are even new T-shirts twice a week.

It's not just about money – that's too rational. It's about engaging people emotionally, too. It's about being part of something, both in the sense of a sharing in a cause that will transform society and being a member of a high-energy, high-performing community.

Today people want to be happy. The pursuit of corporate happiness sounds a little too soft and cuddly for a high performance workplace. 'HAPIE' also stands for:

- Humble – leadership that is genuine, personal, inclusive, and inspirational
- Adaptive – employees are enthusiastic, creative and embrace change
- Profit – all stakeholders share in value creation for mutual benefit

➡ Invigorated – people are energized by a shared and compelling purpose

➡ Engaged – there is a genuine sense of team, citizenship and community.

At the Infosys Technologies campus in Mysore, India, the story is the same. Thousands email in their applications to share the new Indian middle-class dream. The technology leader is incredibly people-centred, big on learning, support and benefits. You might think that this is the land of the limitless, low-paid workforce; not so. Infosys's campus is dominated by a huge white dome: not the reception or executive suite, but four food courts surrounding a 96-bed-room employee hotel. A state-of-the-art gym, pool hall and bowling alley run alongside.

In Shanghai the competition for talent is even fiercer. The local managing director of Cisco, for example, maintains a huge map behind his desk with red dots reflecting each worker – not their task or performance, but where they live, so that he can schedule more shuttle busses and so make Cisco the nearest, easiest place to work.

The stories of corporate 'theme parks' are endless – gaming rooms, nap stations, media lounges, good-old bean bags and bikes on the walls – but it's not just about sociability and wellbeing.

So what really energizes an organization? Stanton Marris specializes in helping companies to build organizational energy that drives engagement and performance. They use a simple five-step approach:

➡ Being open, sharing the big strategic challenges with everyone.

➡ Opening up, seeking suggestions from all stakeholders.

➡ Letting go, giving local teams the freedom to contribute.

➡ Being supportive, showing continuous and consistent interest.

➡ Maintaining focus, monitoring progress and holding on to the big picture.

Sounds obvious? Of course it is, although not necessarily to a manager of the twentieth century. Jack Welch would be squirming in his spreadsheets. Some more of the factors that bring creative organizations to life, that create an enduring buzz inside and out, include:

➜ Personal and flexible – everything from role and benefits to working hours and location.

➜ Partners and networks – stimulating and extending ideas by tapping into the outside world.

➜ Trust and empowerment – few rules, no time sheets, asking for forgiveness not permission.

➜ Flat and accessible – decisions are not by hierarchy, anybody can talk to anybody anytime.

➜ Team and collaborative – sharing challenge and rewards, sparing and sparking with others.

➜ Resources and tools – the best tools for the job, be it computers, phones or stationary

➜ Learning and support – work and personal interests, with peer partnering and mentoring.

➜ Health and wellbeing – healthy buildings, food and fitness, lots of rest and medics on tap.

The workstyle will evolve quickly, with the best talent taking ownership of their employment and developing portfolios of work, jumping across sectors and functions – the best talent is infinitely transferable. Virtual talent networks will form to pursue their common interests and collectively negotiate the most interesting, most valuable projects.

Organizations need to rethink many of the factors that created their old glue and start working in faster, knowledge-based, connected ways.

CREATIVE CULTURE ... WORKING WITH HOTSPOTS AND HAPPINESS

Ferrari ... recreating the spirit of Enzo in Maranello

In 1919 an Italian muleskinner decided to follow his real passion for cars and became a test driver for the small Milan-based car manufacturer, Costruzioni Meccaniche Nazionali. A decade later, he was ready to start his own business founded the company that would go on to produce the world's best racing cars and most desirable sports cars. Today, Enzo Ferrari's name is synonymous with speed, glamour and performance.

From Monte Carlo to Monza, the world's Formula 1 Grand Prix circuit is defined by the red cars with the prancing horse logo that lead the snake of manufacturers around the winding circuits. They win more often than any other and are the car of choice of world champions. However, a new award sits alongside all the Formula 1 trophies and other accolades that the company has won over the last 60 years – an award that Enzo would probably be as more proud of than any Grand Prix win. This award is not based on superior technologies and engineering, but on how Ferrari manages and inspires its 3000 people.

In 2001, the company's president, Luca di Montezemolo launched '*Formula Uomo*', an internal initiative to improve the lives and work of Ferrari people. A budget of 200 million was allocated to the project, news of which had a significant impact on employee morale in itself. The project took its inspiration from the company's racing ambitions and successes. Ferrari recognized that if it wanted to keep its position at the front of the Formula 1 championship – where 1/1000th of a second can determine winners from losers, and directly affects the desirability and perceived worth of its retail vehicles – it had to be at the forefront of work practices and performance too.

'*Formula Uomo*' covers three basic areas:

➡ Workplaces and structures.

➡ Professional training and international growth.

➡ Personal and family benefits.

It is designed to put people at the heart of Ferrari's business and its future, seeking to enhance the broader 'human capabilities' of employees at all levels, and in particulate to stimulate creativity across the business. Some of the benefits relate directly to the outside world, offering participation in company events such as the '*Finali Mondiali*' and the unveilings of new cars, VIP seats at the various Grand Prix, sports groups, and discounts with many different third parties. Personal services include medical check-ups for employees and their children, specialist preventative medicine and well-being programmes. Eighty-eight per cent of all employees now participate in new ongoing training activities, all of which are voluntary, some in traditional formats, and others more informal.

Meanwhile, the Creative Club is one of the most popular initiatives, bringing together an eclectic mix of painters and sculptors, musicians and writers, and DJs and actors to introduce new skills and perspectives – encouraging people to think more radically and innovatively. Senior managers, engineers, sales people and warehouse people, all come along to learn about the world of sculpture, or talk about the big issues in life with the nightclub DJ. It breaks down the barriers, prompting curiosity, thinking differently and collaborating in new ways. There is no facilitation, no forced connections between the world of hip-hop and finely tuned engines; translating the new energy and behaviours back into a work context is natural, particularly when the subject matter of Ferrari is the stuff of normal people's dreams.

However, it is the new buildings that really symbolize the new spirit of Ferrari. With the development of *Maranello Village*, a high-specification housing complex exclusively for staff, employees can now live in the magic kingdom day and night if they want. Situated only 4 km from the factory, the two are connected, perhaps oddly for Ferrari, by a bicycle path. Each Ferrari home – there are 22 studios, 42 two-bedroom and 58 three-bedroom flats – comes fully furnished (not completely in red!). The village also has a fitness centre, restaurant and bar – and of course there is plenty of indoor and outdoor parking for those specially priced and highly prized cars.

In 2007 the transformed and high-performing world of Ferrari was voted Europe's Best Place to Work, and yet again it won the Formula 1 championship too.

CHAPTER 44

Innovative processes ... from NASA to networked innovation

'To the proverb which says a journey of a thousand miles begins with a single step, I would add the words "and a road map".'

Cecile Springer

Whilst 'new product development' (NPD) includes the word 'product', innovations can of course take many forms beyond products. However, most companies have traditionally focused on tangible objects as their focus of innovation and the process for developing ideas into commercial solutions.

It is, of course, tempting to turn NPD into a highly rigorous, controlled process, seeking to improve consistency, speed and effectiveness. Whilst it may indeed achieve this, there is a fine balance between specifying such a process in detail and giving people in the organization space to use their creative flair, look beyond the conventions and seek to create something more radical and different than before.

However, most developments are complex and significant challenges, bringing together many ideas, hundreds of people, taking years to complete – but potentially having an impact over decades (see table below).

Item	HP DeskJet 5000 printer	Volkswagen Golf car	Boeing 777 aeroplane
Number of parts	35	10,000	130,000
Development time	1.5 years	3.5 years	4.5 years
Development team	100 people	850 people	6800 people
Development costs	$50,000	$1 billion	$3 billion
Sales price	$365	$19,000	$130 million
Sales volume p.a.	1.5 million	250,000	50
Sales lifetime	3 years	6 years	30 years
Development costs as a percentage of lifetime sales	3%	3.5%	1.5%

Rocket ships

NASA has had a significant influence on the evolution of product development in business, particularly in traditional innovation leaders such as 3M. In the 1960s the US government's space agency introduced its 'phased project planning' to manage large-scale, complex projects.

NASA use four phases – analysis, definition, design and operation – and checkpoint reviews were incorporated to ensure that problems and errors could be addressed as early as possible. The NASA process, as illustrated by Peter Morris in *The Management of Projects*, is still commonly used today in a scaled-down form as the blueprint for 'stage gate' NPD processes.

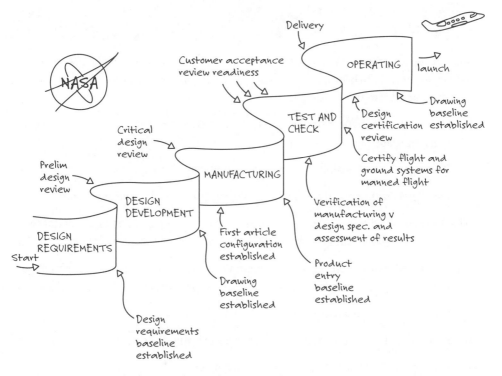

NASA innovation process for large-scale developments

Of course, business needs to ensure that its developments lead to commercial success, and Branson's development of space travel at a fraction of the cost or time shows how a more commercial approach can also lead to better technical results. Compared to NASA's approach, a business would typically start with an overall development strategy, spend more time on idea-generation and evaluation, and ensure that the solution is effectively launched and applied in the marketplace.

Stage gates

Robert Cooper, author of *Winning at New Products*, was perhaps most influential in defining the 'stage gate' idea to launch process used by most companies. He more broadly categorized the NPD process into three main phases:

1   **Pre-development:** Development of an NPD strategy, idea-generation, screening and evaluation, and business analysis.

2   **Development and testing:** Development, prototyping and adjusting.

3   **Commercialization:** Market planning, market entry, managing and improving.

What he encouraged over time was more focus on the commercialization aspects – not seeing launch as an end-point, but in many ways the starting point of solving a customer's problem.

Cooper realized that the process needed more flexibility to embrace creative thinking, and deliver something new. He added his 4Fs to the stage gate model:

➡   Fluid stages that might overlap.

➡   Fuzzy gates that might not always make black and white decisions.

➡   Focus on business priorities and best opportunities.

➡   Staying flexible.

In fact, each phase of development can require a different approach, not only in terms of process but in terms of team composition and culture. Zien and Buckler observed three 'microcultures' of innovation:

➡   **Fuzzy front end:** Experimental and chaotic, ambiguous and uncertain, lacks structure but is an excellent opportunity for individuals to establish themselves and influence the project.

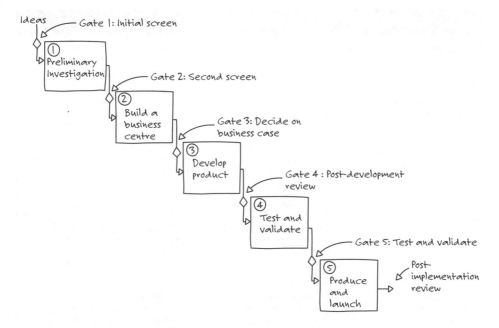

Traditional stage gate approach to innovation

➡ **Product development process:** Disciplined and focused, quantitative and controlled, underpinned by a clearly defined process delivered through teamwork.

➡ **Market operations:** Clear and commercial, the task is to effectively produce and launch the development, and make it a success in the market, requiring significant people.

Innovations of whatever size follow a similar process, although the ways in which they work through the different phases depends on the scale of innovation anticipated or demanded – as shown in the table below.

317

Phase	Incremental innovations	Breakthrough innovations
Timeframe	Short term	Longer term
	1-2 year impact	3-10 year impact
	Developed within a year	Developed in 1-3 years
Insights	Evolving	Discontinuities
	Systematic	From anywhere
	Anticipated	Unexpected
Solutions	Improvements	Significant
	Conventional	Discontinuous
	Cosmetic	Game changing
Process	Formal	Exploratory
	Certainty	Uncertainty
	Stage gates	Improvized
Team	Functional owner	High-level sponsor
	Cross-functional team	Dedicated team
	Skills to do	Skills to think and do
Resources	Functional	Partners and networks
	Conventional	Diversity of talents
	Part of 'business as usual'	Outside normal business
Business case	At start	Evolves as progress
	Defines costs and returns	Goals for value creation
	Agreed and budgeted	Funding by stages

Incremental innovations would be developed quickly with a short-term impact, largely based on existing insights with a standardized process. At the opposite end of the spectrum, breakthrough innovations would take much longer to reach market, but with a more enduring impact. The solutions would be more unique and disruptive, and so would the process for developing them, requiring much more improvization and leadership internally as well as in the market.

Innovation 2.0

Over time, NPD has become more dynamic – from linear and sequential to parallel and integrated, from a relay race to a team game with more feedback loops and connections. In addition to more focus on the front end of innovation to generate better ideas, it is now also about what happens in the market after launch – known as in-market innovation.

The progression of NPD can be summarized in five phases:

1   **Technology and product push:** A linear process with emphasis on technical-based R&D, driven by the emergence of new possibilities.

2   **Customer and market pull:** A linear process with emphasis on marketing and customer insight, driven by demand more than possibility.

3   **Push and pull:** A sequential process with feedback loops balancing push and pull, becoming a creative matching process.

4   **Open and collaborative:** Parallel processes with joint teams including partners and customers working together.

5   **Networked:** Parallel processes in open structure involving a wide range of partners, innovation exchanges, crowdsourcing and co-creation.

'Innovation 2.0', as some call it, is all about a collaborative approach to problem-solving, where the best ideas can emerge from anywhere, where ideas become the new tradable currency of business, where innovative solutions are diffused across wide networks or uniquely one-to-one, and where small companies are equal to large organizations – and sometimes at an advantage.

3M ... getting sticky at the innovation company

In 1969, Neil Armstrong took man's first steps on the moon wearing space boots with soles made of synthetic material from 3M. In 2000, Michael Johnson sprinted to an Olympic 400m title wearing shoes made from 24-carat gold 3M Scotchlite Reflective Fabric developed by 3M.

3M describes itself as 'an innovation company'. Formerly known as the Minnesota Mining and Manufacturing Company, it is now an $18 billion global leader with an unrelenting focus is on sustained profitable growth. Its 55,000 products are in areas as diverse as healthcare, safety equipment, electronics and industrial markets.

The company's 76,000 employees remain focused on creating 'practical and ingenious solutions that help customers succeed', and are encouraged to continuously seek innovation through a wide range of techniques. These include giving every employee 10% of their weekly time to 'bootleg' on crazy ideas and insisting that at least 30% of revenues come from new products.

3M has a long history of innovation, not only investing new solutions, but also transforming markets and customer behaviours too. In this way it ensures that its creations become practical and profitable too. Its innovation process consists of an integrated and parallel approach to concept, product and market innovation.

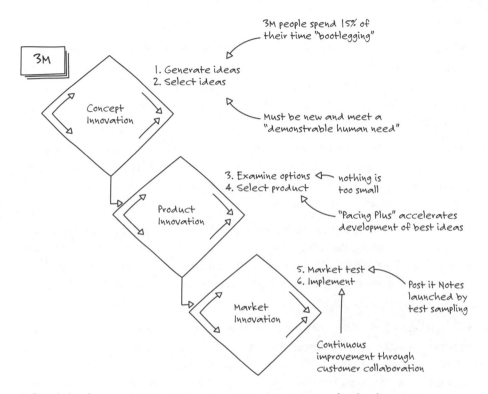

3M people spend 15% of
their time "bootlegging"

1. Generate ideas
2. Select ideas

Must be new and meet a
"demonstrable human need"

Concept
Innovation

3. Examine options ← nothing is
4. Select product   too small

"Pacing Plus" accelerates
development of best ideas

Product
Innovation

5. Market test ←
6. Implement   Post it Notes
                   launched by
                   test sampling

Market
Innovation

Continuous
improvement through
customer collaboration

3M's triple-level approach to innovation at concept, product and market levels

Perhaps most famously is the story of the choirboy who dropped his hymnbook during a church service and with it all the loose bits of paper that marked the important pages for him. The observation led to the creation of the Post-it note, now an essential part of any office desk and available in a bewildering range of colours, sizes and formats.

321

So how does 3M retain its creative streak over so many years?

1 **The whole company must be committed to innovation:** One sure way to show that is financial. In 2005, 3M spent $1.24 billion on research and development, or 6% of its $21.2 billion in revenue. Of that, a fifth went to basic research, with no immediate commercial application. 3M sees long-term investment in strategic innovation as the way to sustain organic, profitable growth.

2 **The corporate culture stays alive:** Although 3M has had a new CEO every five years on average over the past 40 years, the philosophy of William McKnight is passed on: 'Hire good people and let them do their job in their own ways. And tolerate mistakes.' New recruits are immersed in the company's history.

3 **Innovation needs a broad base of technology:** 3M claims to have leading know-how in 42 diverse technologies. That allows researchers to take an idea from one realm and apply it to another. For example, 3M scientists have used a technology behind layered plastic lenses to make more durable abrasives, more reflective highway signs and golf gloves with a tighter grip.

4 **Keep talking to each other:** Encourage formal and informal networking and collaboration amongst researchers. 3M's scientists formed their Technical Forum in 1951; the company still brings together its 9700 R&D people in an annual gathering where everyone can see what everyone else is working on. Labs also host their own conferences and webcasts and blogs.

5 **The carrot and stick:** 3M has a dual-career ladder so that experienced researchers can continue to move up without becoming managers. It also honours hundreds of employees, nominated and selected by their peers, for innovative achievements every year, and gives the top 20 'overachievers' and their spouses a four-day holiday at 3M's corporate retreat.

6 **Metrics matter:** 3M can tell instantly how much of its revenue comes from products introduced in the past four years to judge whether its R&D investments are delivering a return. Management can assess which lab is hitting its mark and which may be falling short. This provides confidence in the innovation process and sustains its momentum year after year.

7 **Stay connected to customers:** Employees spend a lot of time with customers to understand what their needs are so they can go back to the labs to come up with valuable products. By observing and listening to users one to one, researchers often learn that the bigger issues lie beyond the product, for example in terms of ordering, usage, storage or disposal.

CHAPTER 45

Creative people ... visionaries, border crossers and game-changers

'Dance like no one is watching. Sing like no one is listening. Love like you've never been hurt, and live like it's heaven on Earth.'

Mark Twain

Dr Mihaly Csikszentmihalyi explored what kinds of people are creative, saying in *Problem Finding and the Creative Process* that 'there may be certain neurological physiologies that predispose you to one or another type of creativity, but it doesn't seem to take a particular talent to be very creative'. However, he says, creativity generally requires curiosity and interest and a blend of characteristics that might seem like opposites:

➡ **Divergent and focused** – to think outside the box and then focus in.

➡ **Energy and idleness** – to drive for ideas but also to reflect on them.

➡ **Introversion and extroversion** – to understand themselves and others.

➡ **Masculine and feminine** – rational and emotional, focused and intuitive.

➡ **Passionate and detached** – loving what they do, but able to stand back.

➡ **Rebellious and traditional** – challenging the status quo whilst building on the past.

Creative people are visionary (like Jobs and da Vinci) and challenge the status quo (Banksy and Zennstrom), they are provocative (Lennon and Zuckerberg) and radical (Hadid and Rutan). They bring perspective (like Picasso and Maeda) and are expressive (Kandinsky and Stewart), they add entertainment (Bodecker and Cowell) and simplicity (Armani and Kamfrand). They are imaginative (like Disney and Yamauchi) and persistent (Edison and Dyson), they are commercial (Madonna and Tata) and extraordinary people (Einstein and Starck).

Creativity and innovation thrive in teams rather than individuals. Whilst it is hard for one person to embrace all of the attributes of Csikszentmihalyi, a team can without problem. As Richard Seymour, from design firm Seymour Powell says 'the team always wins over the lone genius'. There are therefore a number of roles that you seek in your innovation team:

→ **Dreamer** – looks for the possibilities.

→ **Handyman** – looks for the practicalities.

→ **Entrepreneur** – wants to make things happen.

→ **Designer** – thinks how to make things.

→ **Technologist** – keeps people in touch.

→ **Comic** – keeps people energized.

→ **Economist** – ensures it will make money.

→ **Everyman** – is in touch with real people.

→ **Artist** – turns ideas into great pictures.

→ **Storyteller** – turns ideas into great stories.

→ **Facilitator** – brings all the others together.

Two of the most established approaches for understanding the roles and behaviours of people are Belbin and Myers-Briggs. These can be used for all aspects of teamworking, but are particularly applicable to business. Belbin is about teams and roles within them, whereas Myers-Briggs is about individuals and their personalities. In both cases, innovation requires a good mix of people.

Team roles

Dr Meredith Belbin defines a team role as 'a tendency to behave, contribute and interrelate with others in a particular way'. She identified nine clusters of people's behaviour within teams – all important, none better or more important than another – and gave each a name. Each team role has its particular strengths and allowable weaknesses. People can often play more than one role, and so the approach does not seek to define personality types. There are nine roles, as shown in the table below.

The Belbin technique evaluates an individual's behaviours based on 360-degree feedback from observers as well as the individual's own view of their preferred behaviour, and contrasts how they see their behaviour versus how their colleagues do. Personally I have found this most helpful done in real time with a project team, where they discover and discuss the outcomes together, in relation to how they could work best to deliver a successful project.

Team role	Profile	Positives	Negatives
Chairman	Calm, confident, controlled	Focuses on goals. Encourage contributions	Average intellect and ideas
Company worker	Conservative, dutiful, predictable	Good organization, and practical, hard worker	Inflexible, unsure of new ideas
Shaper	Energetic, wants to find the solution, persuader	Challenges ideas, inertia, ineffectiveness	Gets irritated easily
Plant	Innovative, independent, unorthodox	Imagination, intellect and knowledge	In the clouds, not interested in detail
Resource Investigator	Enthusiastic, curious, communicator	Explores new things, responds to challenges, excellent networker	Loses interest quickly after initial fascination
Monitor evaluator	Prudent, detached, intelligent	Judgement and discretion, hard-headed	Not inspiring, doesn't motivate others
Team worker	Sociable, trusting, diplomatic	Responsive, encourages teamwork	Indecisive, doesn't like conflict
Co-ordinator	Confident, stable, mature, delegator	Sees the big picture, recognizes abilities in others, helps others to focus	Can be manipulative, do little themselves
Completer finisher	Orderly, conscientious, consistent, perfectionist	Follows through until the end, eye for details	Worries about small details, reluctance to stand back, unable to delegate

Personality types

The Myers-Briggs Type Indicator is based on Carl Jung's theory of psychological type, in which he proposed the existence of two pairs of cognitive functions: the 'rational' (judging) functions – thinking and feeling – and the 'irrational' (perceiving) functions – sensing and intuition. He proposed that these function are expressed in an introverted or extraverted form.

Isabel Briggs Myers, and her mother, Katharine Briggs, built on this by codifying the different types in order to identify the basic preferences of each of the four opposite pairs, implied in Jung's theory, articulated as 16 distinctive personality types. In simple terms it addresses:

➨ **Orientation:** Whether you prefer to focus on the outer world or on your own inner world, known as **extraversion** (E) or **introversion** (I). Extraverts are action-oriented and desire breadth, while introverts are thought-oriented and seek depth. Extraverts often prefer more frequent interaction, while introverts prefer more substantial interaction.

➨ **Information:** Whether you prefer to focus on the basic information you take in, or to interpret and add meaning – known as **sensing** (S) or **intuition** (N). Sensing people are more likely to trust information that is in the present, tangible, whilst intuitive people like more abstract or theoretical information, patterns and future possibilities.

➨ **Decisions:** Whether you prefer to make decisions with logic and consistency, or through people and special circumstances – known as **thinking** (T) or **feeling** (F). Thinkers tend to decide things logically from a more detached standpoint. Feelers make decisions by empathizing with the situation, considering the needs of the people involved.

➨ **Structure:** Whether you prefer clarity and absolutes, or to stay open to new informa-tion and options – known as **judging** (J) or **perceiving** (P). Judging people use decision, perceiving people use information when relating to the outside world. For extraverts, J or P indicates their dominant function, whilst for introverts they indicate a supporting function.

By considering your preference in each of the categories, usually based on a series of diagnostic questions, you codify your own personality type expressed in four letters. The most common types in business are ISTJ and ESTJ (sensing, thinking types, with slightly more introverted than extroverted), followed by ENTJ and INTJ (intuitive, thinking types, with more extroverted than introverted).

Kenneth Allinson, in his book *The Wild Card of Design*, gives examples of other professions and their typical profiles: artists are typically INFJ, designers are ENFJ, engineers are ISTJ and business leaders are ESTJ.

Creative styles

Michael Kirton's Adaption–Innovation Inventory (KAI) tool focuses on thinking styles and in particular on people's creativity, problem-solving and decision-making approaches:

➡ **Adaptors** are more conservative and will only change if they really have to.

➡ **Innovators** are more original and want to make change, and innovation, happen.

It measures style, rather than capability, on a scale from highly adaptive (low score) to highly innovative (high score). It focuses on originality, attention to detail and conformity to rules, with each component added to give a total KAI score. Within teams, the KAI score indicates the ability of members to cope with difficult problems and diversity of styles.

For team leaders, it can help get a balance in the group between adaptors and innovators. The differences between the two are shown in the table below.

Adaptor	Innovator
Accepts problems as defined	Challenges definition of problems
Does things better	Does things differently
Solving problems	Finding problems
Uses tried and tested approaches	Questions conventions and assumptions
Reduces problems by improvement	Catalyst, irreverent and step change
Effective manager in established structures	Takes control of unstructured situations
Efficient, thorough, adaptable, organized, precise, reliable	Ingenious, creative, original, independent, unconventional
See innovators as abrasive, undisciplined, insensitive, chaotic	See adaptors as compliant, timid, inflexible, confirming, stuck in a rut

Innovation can emerge from any personality type, particularly when fused together in teams. This is particularly important when remembering is about stretching ideas, being able to think from the future back, but also about implementing the ideas commercially. In particular innovation today needs some extraverted connection to the outside world, intuition to deal with new patterns and possibilities, the ability to think what nobody has thought, but a balance between focus on making something happen whilst staying open to change.

Cai Guo-Qiang ... gunpowder artist to the Olympic Games

Cai Guo-Qiang has built a career out of blowing things up.

He is most famous for creating one of the world's most spectacular firework displays of all time at the 2008 Beijing Olympics. He designed and coordinated the fireworks at both the opening and closing ceremonies, the centrepiece to what China hoped would be the turning point in its emergence in the new world order. It is a measure of his esteem and trust that he was chosen for such a task.

Cai specializes in creating such outdoor events. Even his indoor paintings often feature gunpowder and have even been exploded as part of their dynamic installation.

Worldwide, Cai's artistic gunpowder plots have proved incredibly popular. He was recently responsible for a 60-second explosion on a large flower structure attached to the façade of the Philadelphia Museum of Art. Shortly afterwards he ignited a gunpowder-sprinkled drawing on silk lying in a narrow, winding metal bed that he describes as 'like a river made of fire' inside the museum.

The explosions fanfared the opening of a real-time art creation where he and his team of weavers created 20 tapestries on old-fashioned looms. There's also a display of his enormous gunpowder drawings and another work called *99 Golden Boats*. He says it is all about the meaning of time and memory, although many people just turned up for the unique spectacle.

Cai grew up in Quanzhou, a city in the south-eastern Fujian province, on the mainland close to Taiwan. It is an area where many of China's fireworks are made, and clearly had an influence on his creativity. As an artist, he's been working with gunpowder since the 1980s, partly as a gesture to his childhood homeland, but also in response to the social oppression that he felt as he grew up, saying that it gives him a sense of freedom.

CHAPTER 46

Innovation ventures ... finding faster ways to market

'The people who get on in this world are the people who get up and look for the circumstances they want, and, if they can't find them, make them.'

George Bernard Shaw

In the US, scientific innovation has historically consisted of a loose public-private partnership. It included legendary institutions such as Bell Labs, RCA Labs, Xerox PARC alongside NASA and the Defence Advanced Research Projects Agency (DARPA). In each organization, programmes with commercial potential were developed alongside pure research.

Whilst the commercial projects delivered temporary success, it was the ongoing basic research that delivered the more significant breakthroughs. Bell Labs, for examples, delivered a long line of milestones: fax transmission, photo-voltaic solar cells, the transistor, the UNIX operating system and cellular telephony. Similarly, DARPA created the Internet in 1969 (evolving into the World Wide Web with the help of Tim Berners-Lee 20 years later), whilst Xerox PARC developed the Ethernet and the graphical interface that led to the personal computer.

However, such basic research is in decline. This is because of budgets cut and reallocated to short-term commercial projects, and a fall from grace that has coincided with a massive shift in scientific research to state-funded Asian institutions, and the subsequent emergence of their economies.

Meanwhile, companies have focused on more applied approaches to research, and its acceleration into commercial applications. Business venturing, development incubators and accelerators sprang up largely out of the dotcom boom, when a new entrepreneurial mindset infected even the most traditional of companies.

The table below summarizes the features of the different kinds of innovation.

Type	Objective	Funding	Positives	Negatives
Internal development	New or improved products or services	Functional budgets	Incremental innovation	Limited by functions and conventions
Internal venture	New products, new businesses, (maybe to spin out)	Dedicated budgets	More radical innovation	Struggle to be independent from business as usual
Joint ventures	New products developed with a partner to share	Investment from each partner	More radical innovation that taps into new areas	Need to work and compromise with partner
External incubator	New businesses, (usually to spin out)	Investment fund from existing business (and maybe others)	Radical innovation	Can be distant and risky
External venture	New businesses, (often to absorb back inside)	Investment fund from existing business	Radical innovation	Can the new venture be reintegrated into business
Mergers and acquisitions	Acquire another business to integrate into structure	Investment from existing business	Incremental or radical innovation	Integration issues tend to preoccupy management

Ventures

Many large companies set up 'business ventures' in the late 1990s on the back of the dotcom boom, although venturing has been a developing aspect of innovation, embracing entrepreneurship within the business, for much longer. Venturing inside a company allows the business to reach new markets and exploit existing assets in new ways. It is separated from the main business in order to give it space to develop in its own way, and to avoid many of the limitations and conventions that limit the business's organic growth.

There are four typical models of ventures:

➡ **New business ventures** seek to monetize ideas, patents and spare resources by selling or licensing them. Lucent New Ventures, set up in 1997, focused on commercializing IP and technology that was not immediately required or supported by core businesses.

➡ **Core business ventures** seek to improve existing business activities by using a venture-type approach. Shell's 'GameChanger' is based on the idea of spending 10% of the technical budget of Shell's exploration business in a venturing way.

➡ **Partner ventures**, where companies invest in their suppliers, customers, distributors or other partners who have complementary ideas and technologies that can help stimulate growth in the core business. Intel Capital is an example of this approach.

➡ **Private equity ventures**, where the company establishes an in-house private equity business to exploit its assets and networks. Nokia Venture Partners make proactive investments in start-ups in their respective areas of interest.

Venturing can result in a number of outcomes:

→ **Spin-outs:** When the company sells or licenses its ideas or activities – for example Egg, developed and then sold by Prudential.

→ **Spin-ups:** When a new business is created to grow profitable revenue within the organization, like Nike Considered, the sustainability venture developed by Nike.

→ **Spin-ins:** When a new business is evaluated and brought into the core business, like Geek Squad, the wacky IT support crew acquired by Best Buy.

→ **Private equity:** Where companies seek a return on their investment – PA Ventures, part of PA Consulting, would be an example.

Incubators

Business incubators are facilities or processes designed to accelerate the successful development of entrepreneurial companies through a diverse range of resources and services.

They vary in the way they deliver their services, in their organizational structure and in the types of clients they serve. Beyond the basics of business support, they might provide accounting support, loans and guarantees, links to academia and business partners, venture capital, and mentoring. Some incubators are internal; others are external and occasionally hybrid.

In their dedication to start-up and early-stage companies, incubators differ from research and technology parks, which tend to be large-scale projects that house everything from corporate, government or university labs to very small companies. Most research and technology parks do not offer business assistance services, which are the hallmark of a business incubation programme. However, many research and technology parks house incubation programmes.

Research by Stanford University in 2009 showed that incubated start-ups stay in business longer than others. In the US, incubation programmes assisted more than 27,000 companies that provided employment for more than 100,000 workers and generated annual revenues of $17 billion.

Reid Hoffman ... the most linked-in man in Silicon Valley

On graduating from Stanford, Reid Hoffman's initial plan was to become a professor. He was intrigued by the changing nature of society and the identity of people within it. Then he realized that academics typically cite writing books that no more than 50 or 60 people read, and he decided he needed a way to have more impact on the world.

After starting with Inglenook, a Napa Valley winery, he moved to Apple and then Fujitsu before co-founding his first company, socialnet.com. He also joined the start-up board of PayPal and eventually became EVP of PayPal in charge of business and corporate development. In 2007 he founded LinkedIn, the professional network, acting as CEO for the first four years before becoming Chairman and President of Products.

He has been called the 'most connected man in all of Silicon Valley', and acts as a mentor to many of the 'second-generation web entrepreneurs'. As a serial investor, he knows what he is looking for in a new business. Instead of looking for dazzling products or cash flow forecasts, he told techcrunch.com, he looks for the answers to three questions:

➡ **'How will you reach a massive audience?'** Hoffman reflects that in real estate it's all about 'location, location, location' and in consumer web-based business, it's 'distribution, distribution, distribution'. He sees the biggest challenge as rising above the noise so that people can discover you, giving examples of YouTube's use of MySpace and Facebook's 80% adoption across student campuses within 60 days.

➡ **'What is your unique value proposition?'** He looks for innovation that stands out from the pack but is not so forward-thinking as to alienate the user, and not just a repackaged or refocused version of what exists already. 'It's a dating site, but for senior citizens ...' is not an innovation to him. He looks for category-changing ideas like Digg, which lets users decide their headline, or Last.fm, which tracks music listening with an iTunes plug-in.

➡ **'Will your business be capital efficient?'** Most important commercially, he knows first-hand that a business fails without cash flow. An initial round of financing is important, but needs to be sustained at the next stage. He looks for 'intelligent scaling' like TypePad, which grew to 10 million users without second-round funding. Ideas can look great at start-up, but, he argues, it's more important to think how they will get future funding.

With these three elements in place – mass audience, unique value, stable funding – a start-up has time to discover where it can make money. The formula, he says, is to build an audience with a great product, then figure out how to make it pay.

CHAPTER 47

Creative networks ... the creativity of places and partners

Call it a clan, call it a network, call it a tribe, call it a family: whatever you call it, whoever you are, you need one.

Jane Howard, English novelist

'You always know when you are in a Hot Spot' says Lynda Gratton, author of the book *Hotspots: Why Some Teams, Workplaces, and Organizations Buzz with Energy – and Others Don't*. 'You feel energized and vibrantly alive. Your brain is buzzing with ideas, and the people around you share your joy and excitement. The energy is palpable, bright, shining. These are times when what you and others have always known becomes clearer, when adding value becomes more possible.'

Whilst Gratton focuses on the creative places where people come alive inside organizations, hot spots can also be thought of more broadly in terms of physical spaces, cities and regions where creativity can thrive. Like Venice and Milan during the Renaissance, these places get their energy from the tremendous diversity of talents who converge in the same place. In Leonardo da Vinci's time, it was the coming together of artists, craftsmen and philosophers with noblemen to support them. Today it is more likely to be the convergence of academics, technologists, engineers, designers and marketers with venture capitalists to support them.

Some of them cluster around leading universities or become part of business 'ecosystems', locating themselves in specially designed innovation parks and knowledge hubs. Some just find each other. But it also takes something more than a physical gathering; it takes a culture and environment, too. The sun and surf of the west coast of California, the ability to jump into car and surf the waves, bump into creative types in Starbucks or the Panera Bread store, or to head off to your chalet overlooking Lake Tahoe at the end of a long, creative day, are part of the mix. Creative people tend to converge in creative places.

From Lemon Orchards to Bangalore

Silicon Valley rose up out of the dusty orange orchards of northern California. The place had pioneering heritage, from the days of the gold rush, but it also emerged because of the technology leadership of Stanford University, and the laidback, aspirational lifestyle of sun and breakers. Towns like Mountain View and Sunnyvale had a scattering of wooden houses occupied by farmers or free-spirited youth. Its name emerged because of the area's large number of silicon chip innovators and manufacturers that gathered in the region, followed by the technology companies that used the chips, and then by anybody who wanted a bit of inspiration and venture capital. Whilst most chip-making has largely moved on, the Valley continues to be the leading high-tech hub because of its large number of entrepreneurs, engineers and venture capitalists.

Bangalore is called the Silicon Valley of India because of its own large concentration of technology companies that together contribute 33% of India's $150 billion technology exports. The city's technology industry is divided into three clusters: Software Technology Parks of India (STPI), International Tech Park, Bangalore (ITPB) and Electronics City. Companies such as Infosys and Wipro, India's second- and third-largest software companies based here, as is the huge United Breweries. Biotech is also very strong, with more than 50% of India's companies. However, the new growth has presented the city with unique challenges: ideological clashes sometimes occur between the city's technology geeks, who demand an improvement in the city's infrastructure, and the state government, who are elected primarily by the people in rural Karnataka.

In Finland, Otaniemi is famous largely thanks to Nokia, but it also contains a host of other cutting-edge technology clusters, including mobility-based software and webware, as well as nanotechnology and microelectronics. Companies, institutes and universities do world-class research in a close-knit community that encourages collaborative R&D and commercial collaboration. In Japan, Kansai Science City sits between Kyoto and Osaka, specifically constructed to help the advancement of creative arts, sciences, and research, as well as to spur the creation of new industries and cultures.

These high energy hubs attract the best talent, the richest investors, and the most advanced businesses. Ideas are usually conceived, partnerships formed and deals done on the jogging trails or in the coffee shops. But as well as creative culture, these hubs also have structure. They work in the ecosystems of the biggest players and sometimes vice versa. Ecosystems emerged out of the realization that companies didn't need to do everything themselves, and could often find other companies who could do many of their activities cheaper, faster and better. They included researchers, technologists, suppliers, designers, manufacturers, packagers, distributors, advertisers, lawyers and accountants.

Cisco Systems was one of the first companies to really exploit the ecosystem model. It formed partnerships for all business functions except for developing its core patented products and business strategy, thriving on the motto 'Do what you do best and leave the rest for others to do'. The flexibility enabled it to evolve with the industry and to scale without excessive cost or risk. Cisco's 'locally global' business model became the most respected in the technology industry and has been widely replicated.

Innovative nations

Whilst creative hubs are more about specific regions and a concentration of related talents, whole nations can also be seen as fertile grounds for innovation. The 'Global Innovation Index', supported by the Boston Consulting Group, measures the level of innovation of a country (see table below). To rank the countries, the study measures both:

➡ Innovation inputs, including government and fiscal policy, education policy, and the innovation environment.

Rank	Country	Overall	Innovation inputs	Innovation outputs
1	South Korea	2.26	1.75	2.55
2	USA	1.80	1.28	2.16
3	Japan	1.79	1.16	2.25
4	Sweden	1.64	1.25	1.88
5	The Netherlands	1.55	1.40	1.55
6	Canada	1.42	1.39	1.32
7	UK	1.42	1.33	1.37
8	Germany	1.12	1.05	1.09
9	France	1.12	1.17	0.96
10	Australia	1.02	0.89	1.05
11	Spain	0.93	0.83	0.95
12	Belgium	0.86	0.85	0.79
13	China	0.73	0.07	1.32
14	Italy	0.21	0.16	0.24
15	India	0.06	0.14	-0.02
16	Russia	-0.09	-0.02	-0.16
17	Mexico	-.16	0.11	-0.42
18	Turkey	-0.21	0.15	-0.55
19	Indonesia	-0.57	-0.63	-0.46
20	Brazil	-0.59	-0.62	-0.51

Source: Boston Consulting Group

➡ Innovation output, including patents, technology transfer and other R&D results, business performance such as labour productivity and total shareholder returns, and the impact of innovation on business migration and economic growth.

IBM ... InnovationJams for a smarter planet

'Just over a year ago, we began a global conversation about how the planet is becoming smarter ... intelligence is being infused into the systems and processes that make the world work - into things no one would recognize as computers: cars, appliances, roadways, power grids, clothes, even natural systems such as agriculture and waterways.

'Trillions of digital devices, connected through the Internet, are producing a vast ocean of data. And all this information - from the flow of markets to the pulse of societies - can be turned into knowledge because we now have the computational power and advanced analytics to make sense of it. With this knowledge we can reduce costs, cut waste and improve the efficiency, productivity and quality of everything from companies to cities ...'

That is IBM's vision for a 'Smarter Planet', as stated on its website. This is not just words, but also what IBM is doing, by itself and for clients. IBM registers more patents than any other company on the planet - more than 3125 in 2009, which works out at 60 patents per week. Thomas Edison would be staggered.

Of course, IBM has come a long way since deciding to move away from consumer electronics, redefining itself as an ideas company with experts in every industry and perhaps the most diverse, and prolific, innovation business. Recent breakthroughs include a self-assembly nanotechnology process in computer chip manufacturing that creates vacuums between wires, allowing signals to travel faster while consuming less energy. Add to this a tool to predict how an emerging infectious disease such as bird flu will mutate, helping drug-makers whip up an effective vaccine. Then there is a system that analyses data from thousands of sensors along New York's Hudson River to gauge its health and forecast changes.

Equally impressive is IBM's relentless search for new ideas. Behind this is a process called the 'InnovationJam', a truly big thinking event. Back in 2003, CEO Sam Palmisano wanted to find a way to bring together the organization's creativity, so he invited more than 300,000 employees, as well as tens of thousands of partners and clients, to participate. It resulted in one of the largest online events in business history. Palmisano pledged to invest $100 million in the most promising proposals. More than 150,000 IBM people, and many more partners from over 100 countries, logged onto the two 72-hour sessions.

The discussions were analysed by sophisticated text analysis software known as eClassifier to mine online comments for themes. The first session produced 37,000 ideas; the second, a few weeks later, focused in on improving the top 50 best ideas, and from this, ten new projects emerged to secure the jackpot funding. The projects focused on challenges like how to integrate an entire region's transport system, and creating a one-avatar-fits-all platform for any 3-D virtual world in a way that could fuel real-world revenue.

Subsequent annual InnovationJams have gone further. The next brought together 52,000 employees exchanging new practices non-stop for 72 hours. They focused on finding action-able ideas to support implementation of the values previously identified. A new JamRatings event, after the main sessions, was developed to allow participants to select key ideas.

Palmisano says that the benefits are huge, describing how leaders from across the globe were able to engage ideas that could lead to profound change in their companies and industries. They learnt about new opportunities, best practices and breakthrough business models. They shared ideas about key issues they face from managing global talent to serving new generations of customers, to developing essential new skills. And they now recognize IBM as a business and technology leader that uses innovation to create a smarter planet.

InnovationJam demonstrated that IBM was willing to experiment in a way that few companies its size dare to attempt. It gambled on several emerging businesses without the usual rigorous filters, letting each team set its intuitive direction. The jam also inspired similar events at other companies, often with the licensed processes and support of IBM, making 'Big Blue' a leader in facilitating collaborative innovation across businesses and their partner networks.

Palmisano believes that participants will come away enlightened, inspired and, as we have said, armed with specific, practicable ideas for moving their companies from where they are today to where they need to be to flourish in the years ahead.

CHAPTER 48

Managing innovation ... managing people, projects and portfolios

'Change is one thing, progress is another. Change is scientific, progress is ethical. Change is indubitable, whereas progress is a matter of controversy.'

Bertrand Russell

Starwood Hotels has a Chief Creative Officer to drive creativity and innovation across every part of its business, including the funky W Hotels and every aspect of its customer experience. Meanwhile, ad agency Saatchi & Saatchi, which calls itself 'The Ideas Company', has a Chief Ideas Officer, recognizing that its ideas are what clients value most. And at Shell there a Chief Innovation Officer, to drive its scenario planning and long-term research and drilling programmes, potentially over 50 years.

Managing innovation can be a functional or cross-functional challenge, a specific project responsibility or part of everyday work. Some organizations have designated innovation leaders, whilst in others there is nobody with the specific responsibility and innovation is embraced with everyone's role, like at Google.

Managing innovation needs to work at different levels:

➡ **Managing products and portfolio:** Managing the 'lifecycle' of products (and equally, services), from introduction through growth to maturity and then decline. Products need different marketing strategies in their different phases in order to maximize their profitability. A product in decline can be revitalized through innovation, or maybe sold or licensed to a third party who can do better. A balanced portfolio of products should ensure that a replacement product is well on the way to maturity when an older one reaches decline, to ensure continuity of supply to customers and presence of the brand.

➡ **Managing process and practices:** Managing the capability within the company to drive creativity and innovation, ensuring that processes are well defined and developed in each part of the organization, and modified if appropriate to different needs. Practices are supported through consistent planning templates, whilst good practices are encouraged by sharing examples of work across the business and replicating tools and techniques between areas, often facilitated by intranet-based workflow software. Culturally it is also encouraged through workplace design, environments and role models.

➡ **Managing pipeline and performance:** Managing the progress of innovation in the business through a structured approach to reporting, reviewing, performance targets and rewards. Managing the pipeline is about managing the portfolio of innovation projects, ensuring their investment and resources are allocated appropriately and looking for synergies in projects, or ways to avoid replication and accelerate time to market. Innovation, and greater commitment from the business, can be driven by:

➡ Output metrics such as the percentage of revenues from new products.

➡ Throughput measures such as the number of new proposals.

➡ A weighted estimate of likely future cash flows due to the innovations under development.

➡ **Managing people and projects:** Managing projects and the people working on them requires a more hands-on team leadership (see below) and project management role. This would follow the classic phases of set-up, planning, executing, reviewing and closing as a frequently iterated cycle. Of course, it is easy to think of an innovation project as focusing on product development. But it is equally and often more importantly the parts before and after – the idea-generation and creative design processes upfront, plus the market diffusion and adoption processes later. Innovation in distribution channels, retail merchandising, communication media, sales techniques pricing structures and ongoing service and support can often influence customers more than the product itself.

Innovation teams

The structure of an innovation team depends on the level of complexity anticipated in the innovation – complex in the sense of technical difficulty, organizational politics and market ambition. However, a number of key roles emerge: somebody to champion or sponsor the programme at a board level, somebody who is the hands-on leader, somebody to bring innovation expertise, and people to add insights and ideas. The table below summarizes these roles.

Team role	Responsibility	Capabilities
Innovation champion	Making innovation matter Defining innovation strategy Influencing business strategy Managing innovation portfolio Initiating major initiatives	CEO or director level Visionary communicator Respect and acceptance Protects and nurtures ideas
Programme leader	Leader of major initiatives Managing start to finish Developing partnerships Influencing cross-functionally Ensuring market delivery	Experience across business Programme management Understands processes Influencer, communicator
Innovation coach	Supports project teams Adds specialist expertise Encourages better practice Connects insights and ideas Training and development	Innovation expert Training and facilitation Collates best practices Change agent
Creative catalyst	Introduces new perspectives Adds new insights and ideas Challenges the status quo Adds radical creativity Symbolizes innovativeness	Imaginative and creative Networker and organizer Confident and assured Ensures its fun too
Future scout	Searches for new opportunity Tracks technologies Builds futures scenarios Links outside to inside Helps people think ahead	Curious and exploratory Comfortable with ambiguity Makes sense of complexity Networker inside and outside

Aligning the teams to the degrees of innovation discussed earlier, we can explore the different roles required in teams, the specific capabilities and knowledge styles and personalities, and whether they need to be dedicated full-time or come together part-time whilst retaining their functional roles.

➡ **Teams for incremental innovation** would be largely achieved within existing organization functions, with teams brought together part-time with a focus on action. Key requirements are technical expertise and deep knowledge of existing product and services, resources on top, focus on processes and standardization, and without the need for political power.

➡ **Teams for next-generation innovation** need to be cross-functional to open up more ideas, address the whole customer experience and have the ability to innovate in different areas. Again, part-time it would have more organizational strength, with strong leadership and control. However, a cross-functional team inevitably has mixed loyalties and priorities,

➡ **Teams for breakthrough innovation** require dedicated teams, drawn from across the business but working full-time on the innovation. They need autonomy, potentially separated from the normal demands and incentives of the core business. The team needs focus and integration. However, people can become detached from the organization over time.

The best innovation project teams have breakthrough-like characteristics. They are typically of not more than ten people in total, made up of volunteers from across the business. They're in the project full-time from start to finish and report only to the innovation leader. They typically bring diverse and interesting backgrounds, and together represent all the key functions – marketing, operations, technical and finance. They work closely together, with shared goals and rewards, effective communication, and regular team sessions for review, ideas and debate. There is a clear sponsor and mandate within the business, and the team ensures that it engages all key stakeholders throughout the project.

Google ... creativity lives at the Googleplex

'Googol' is the mathematical term for a 1 followed by 100 zeros. It perhaps symbolizes the magnitude of Google's ambition and increasing impact on the whole dynamic of markets and marketing.

Google has a simple but daunting mission 'to organize the world's information and to make it universally accessible and useful'. As co-founder Larry Page puts it, 'the perfect question and answer machine – one that understands exactly what you mean and gives you back exactly what you want'. With more than 10 million users, searching through 10 billion webpages, Google is well established as the world's leading search engine.

The best place to work

Maybe that doesn't surprise you, particularly when you learn that the company only has a 2% turnover within its 5000 workforce each year and receives almost 500,000 applications for that handful of vacancies. More significantly, when the people from 'Best Company to Work For' arrived to evaluate Google's Mountain View headquarters, they decided it really was the best workplace.

Sitting in one of Google's eleven gourmet restaurants within the campus, you might reflect on what makes this such as extraordinary place. Maybe it's the long list of unique benefits that enable people to learn, grow, travel and have a truly fantastic day. Maybe the free breakfasts, lunches and dinners, or the unlimited sick leave, gym and 27 days paid leave each year. Or the more conventional aspects, such as the free WiFi-enabled bus to work, the on-site medical and dental care, the car and bike repair shop, and the lunchtime language classes. As the culture audit states:

> 'There is no hard data that can ever prove that a free lunch and a multicultural,
> campus-like environment contribute to the organization's success and profit. What can

be proven is that Google is growing at an immense pace – retention of employees is high, attrition is low and revenues are strong. People are eager to work at Google and applications to our job openings are exceedingly high (approximately 1300 resumes a day).'

Yet this is also an organization that works and grows at breakneck speed. It is constantly developing new products, entering new markets, extending its portfolio. As one Googler commented:

'Google is a great company and I am very proud to be a part of it. The perks are extraordinary and this is the most unique working environment I have ever been in. The products, ideas, creative minds that we have continue to amaze and inspire me.'

Don't be evil ...

When Sergey Brin and Larry Page founded the company in 1998, they believed in a better way of doing business – certainly better than their Stanford University bedroom, which doubled as their global headquarters at the time. They established their motto 'Don't be evil' and always believed that a creative business needs to treat people with respect and support if they are to unlock their talents.

Since the early days, the two founders recognized that the success of their business fundamentally lay in being able to attract and retain the world's best technologists, and indeed the business people too. CEO Eric Schmidt is given this as a primary responsibility, in the belief that if they get this right, then operational and financial success will follow. He seeks out 'brainy, creative, entrepreneurial people' – rounded people, not narrow-minded technology geeks – then puts much effort into supporting their personal development and performance. He also works hard to ensure that they have a lot of fun to relieve stress, improve collaboration and drive creative solutions.

So what else would you experience working in Google world?

→ TGIF is the weekly company-wide get-together, often with the founders. It is a time to welcome new recruits, update on key activities and, most importantly, hold a no-limits question and answer session that is webcast around the world.

→ Google Ideas is a website where Googlers add, connect and discuss their ideas. Anything is possible; colleagues rate ideas from 0 (dangerous) to 5 (do it now).

→ Professional development is also provided in the form of $8000 budgets for each employee to find what they believe is right for them, from anywhere in the world, be it technical training or a one-year MBA.

→ The '20% projects' are what all Googlers are encouraged to spend 20% of their time working on – things outside their responsibilities, wacky ideas they believe in, or getting involved in the developments going on in completely unrelated areas.

→ The Founders Award is incredibly prestigious within the company. It goes to the team that has created enormous value for Google and is rewarded with shares in the business – last year $45 million worth was divided between 11 project teams.

→ Community activities matter greatly to Google. Encouraging females and minorities to embrace technologies at school or home is a key diversity initiative, whilst $90 million was donated through google.org to projects that utilized Google skills charitably,

→ 'Googleyness' is the special quality that Google seeks in its people: those can work well in small teams and fast-changing environments, well rounded but with unique interests and talents, and enthusiasm for Google and in making the world a better place.

'To organize the world's information' doesn't sound like the most exciting job in the world, but Google is a truly amazing, inspirational place to work.

CHAPTER 49

Game changing ... creative revolutions and X Prizes

'The more that you read, the more things you will know. The more that you learn, the more places you'll go.'

Dr Seuss

Nobel laureate James Watson, who discovered the DNA double helix, and genomics pioneer J. Craig Venter, were recently awarded Double Helix Awards from Cold Spring Harbour Laboratory for being the founding fathers of human genome sequencing. They are the also first two human beings to have their complete genetic information decoded.

During his acceptance speech, Watson said that he didn't think governments should try to control how people handle information about their genetic make-up, and that it should be left to individuals and innovative market forces to see how our genetic-coded lifestyle emerges.

Meanwhile, Venter is on the brink of creating the first artificial life form on Earth. He has already announced transplanting the information from one genome into another; he believes that such development, when structured in safe and ethical ways, will change everything.

Many breakthrough innovations have had a transforming effect on our lives and the world around us: the printing press, electricity, penicillin and antibiotics, email, space travel ... these are 'game changing' innovations that are ways to make life better. Whilst that might seem an idealistic goal for innovation, it is what I believe innovation is ultimately about.

It is about improving our own lives – our personal lifestyles and wellbeing, our abilities and achievements – either by making money from the innovations or by what they enable people to do. It is also about improving the lives of others, reducing poverty, improving education and health, supporting local communities and those in distant lands, improving the environment for the nine billion people who will share the planet with us, and our future generations.

The new game-changers

So how do you drive game changing innovations? How do you make a spaceship or non-polluting car? How do you design animal-friendly meat or land a lunar robot? The answer, based on recent successes, seems to be to offer prizes. Other people will do the rest for you.

An X Prize is a $10 million-plus award given to the first team to achieve a specific goal set by the X Prize Foundation and its sponsors, with the overall goal of stimulating innovation that has the potential to benefit humanity. Rather than awarding money to honour past achievements or directly funding research, an X Prize taps into our competitive and entrepreneurial spirit.

The Automotive X Prize, sponsored by Progressive, the insurance company owned by Warren Buffett, has a $10 million incentive and is drawing innovators from around the world who believe they can create a viable ultra-high-mileage, low-emission vehicle to combat the challenges of global warming and soaring oil prices.

The teams have a year to prepare for the first-round heats, in which they will have to prove their vehicles can exceed 75mpg. The following year, the competitors will battle it out in a ten-stage showdown in cities across the US, with spectators able to watch on a live Web link. In the finals, the cars will have to achieve at least 100mpg consistently – less than a third of the 32mpg average fuel consumption of today's average car.

The company competing for the main prize must provide an affordable, safe, four-seat family car with the potential to appeal to ordinary buyers and a business plan to produce 10,000 a year. The team that meets the criteria and clocks up the best time across all ten races will win the prize.

'We don't want science projects, laboratory experiments or exclusive high-end products that most of us can't buy,' says Don Foley, executive director of the competition in an interview with *The Times*. 'We don't want vehicles that just look nice on the covers of magazines. We want super-efficient cars that people will want to go out and buy, right now.'

The power of prizes

The X Prize Foundation was founded in 1996 by Dr Peter Diamandis, an expert in commercial space travel, with the mission to stimulate 'revolution through competition'. It was inspired by the amateur aviation competitions of the 1920s, which captured the public imagination and encouraged the development of commercial air travel.

The first prize, the Ansari X Prize, was awarded in 2004 to Burt Rutan, the aerospace engineer who created the spaceship now adopted by Virgin Galactic in an original projected financed by Paul Allen, the co-founder of Microsoft. Together they became the first team to build and launch twice in two weeks a spacecraft capable of carrying three people more than 60 miles above the Earth's surface.

There are X Prizes under way in the fields of lunar exploration and genomics. The Google X Prize, worth $30 million, is now being offered for the first private-sector robot on the moon. A $10 million X Prize from Warren Buffett's insurance company Progressive is seeking to stimulate a super-efficient car, and $10 million from Archon for getting an instant readout of your DNA.

Many other organizations have embraced the power of incentive-driven innovation too. Scientist Andrzej Bartke recently made a laboratory mouse live 1819 days and won the Mprize, run by the Methuselah Foundation, which aims to find ways of extending human life. PETA (People for the Ethical Treatment of Animals) is offering a $1 million prize to anybody who can make meat in a laboratory and sell it by June 2012.

X Prizes are proactive, stretching and capture the imagination. They benefit technological development whilst releasing innovation from either government bureaucracy or private sector anxiety. They encourage people think differently, and to make their best ideas happen. They open people's eyes to what they thought was not possible, and when commercialized, they are game-changing innovations.

They are like the famous prizes of the past, like the £1000 that Louis Blériot won for the first flight across the Channel. They bring an aura of heroism to innovation, an aura lost in the age of big government and multinationals.

Niklas Zennström ... the relentless entrepreneur and game-changer

Niklas Zennström is the smooth-talking, technology-thinking Swedish entrepreneur who likes to break rules. In the 1990s he helped build Europe's leading low-cost phone company, Sweden-based Tele2, which managed to attract more than 30 million customers from established competitors in 24 countries across the continent.

After a number of more conventional business development roles, including launching and being responsible for the ISP Get2Net and as CEO of the everyday.com portal, he got together with Danish business partner Janus Friis to launch Kazaa, a free peer-to-peer music download service that, in those pre-iTunes days, created quite a stir in the music business. After selling Kazaa for a small fortune, Zennström founded his next venture, Joltid, a software

company that developed and marketed peer-to-peer solutions and optimzed the performance of similar networking companies. Next in his rapid stream of businesses came Altnet,
the world's first secure peer-to-peer network that integrated promotion, distribution and
payment of digital content for branded partners.

However Zennström and Friis's most successful venture so far has been Skype, the internet
phone company – a 'voice over Internet protocol' business, to give it its full name – that is
sustained by peer-to-peer networks. Skype used the technologies developed in Kazaa to
offers free audio and video calls from one computer to another over the Internet. By down-
loading a small piece of free software onto your PC and clicking on the name of another
Skype user you want to reach, users can talk as long as they want to anyone else registered
as a user, anywhere in the world. Young people and small businesses across the planet rapidly
adopted the service. It really was game-changing. Whilst the quality was initially poor, and
put some people off, it has now improved to a level as good as landline phones, and often
better than reception-dependent mobile calls.

In 2005, Skype was acquired by eBay for $2.6 billion, plus the potential to earn further
performance-based bonuses that could double the sum. By the end of that year, Skype had
75 million registered users, which had grown to 525 million by the end of 2009. Of this latter
number, around 5% are online at any one time, clocking up more than 100 billion minutes
of talktime between users. Calls from Skype to other networks are charged at a minimal fee.
These accounted for a further 12 billion minutes in 2009, generating around $750 million in
revenue. Skype is also now available on more than 50 million mobile phones, an alternative
to conventional networks, at flick of a button.

After Skype came Joost, an online video distribution service that is now competing in a
crowded download and streaming market. Zennström and Friis now run Atomico Ventures,
a venture capital fund based in London, through which they have funded more than 15 new
start-ups, including the music business Last.fm and Fon, which makes wireless routers.

The relentless Swedish game-changer wasn't born a revolutionary. He describes himself as 'a well-behaved child' who studied hard while growing up in Stockholm and Uppsala. Degrees in business and computer science turned him on to technology. He is also one of the Young Global Leaders, part of the World Economic Forum, and has also founded Zennström Philanthropies, a charity that addresses issues including climate change and human rights, and supports social entrepreneurs.

CHAPTER 50

Now forward ... finding your edge

'For tomorrow belongs to the people who prepare for it today.'

African proverb

Jeff Bezos wants to 'make history'; Steve Jobs seeks to 'put a ding in the universe'; Niklas Zennstrom believes in 'being disruptive, but in order to make the world a better place'. Innovators want to change things, challenge the status quo, take risks and make change happen. They are talented, creative thinkers, with the courage to drive practical action too.

Creative people are happy and positive, looking for possibilities and the best in people. They look at what is and what can be instead of what is not. They interpret their own world and don't rely upon the interpretation of others. They enjoy searching for newness, solving problems and making life better. Ask yourself:

➡ Did van Gogh ever think that because nobody bought his paintings he had no talent?

➡ Did Edison give up on his idea, despite failing 5000 times?

➡ Did Einstein fear he would look stupid writing a theory of relativity as a patent clerk?

➡ Did Disney give up on his dreams after being fired from his first job as a newspaper editor?

➡ Did Ford give up on his ideas for the motor car because others said it would never work?

➡ Did Picasso live the life of a monk and hope that nobody would ever notice him?

➡ Did Yunus turn his back on the farmers of Bangladesh because they had little money?

➡ Did Madonna give up on her talents, choosing to grow old gracefully?

No!

Some of the ideas, approaches and challenges in this book will seem obvious, whilst others will feel much more difficult to achieve in your business. Yet many businesses are embracing exactly these principles today, innovating from the 'future back' and making it happen 'now forward':

➡ O_2 has a trend-scouting team who look for external trends and then how they could fit in a business or consumer context for mobile communications. Once a year the group meets with the executive board to explore and select ideas.

➡ BASF, using scenario planning, has chosen to focus on 'aging population' as a starting point, working with people from other companies to discuss what life will be like for the aged in 2020, and then considering the potential impacts with internal colleagues.

➡ BMW has created a virtual innovation agency, an online forum where existing and potential suppliers can contribute new ideas, either focused on product or process, creating more openness and competition between its partners.

➡ Coloplast, the medical devices business, uses panels of doctors and nurses to gain much deeper insights than through traditional research surveys in order to shape more radical product and service developments.

➡ Bang and Olufsen created an innovation hub that focuses on articulating and turning new ideas into prototypes as early as possible. It then works with consumers to evolve the prototypes, improving the solution, rather than just generating ideas.

➡ IDEO, the design and innovation consulting firm, hires people from diverse backgrounds – artists, scientists, musicians and doctors – to create a team able to think differently, work differently and generate radically different solutions.

Stay crazy

Extraordinary results rarely come out of a formula. As with Einstein and Picasso, Jobs and Buffett, there is typically something unusual that drives them. Perhaps some of the 'quirks' of the best performing companies will inspire you to dare to deliver:

➡ **Graffiti walls:** Let the walls become the voices and minds of your people, to express their views and ideas (3M).

➡ **Silver networks:** Keep in touch with retired staff, tapping into their capabilities, contacts, time and experience – give them a laptop rather gold watch when they go (Intel).

➡ **Catalyst kit:** All the materials, gadgets and tools you need to stimulate new ideas and articulate innovative solutions anytime, anywhere (IDEO).

➡ **Corporate fool:** The devil's advocate of your best ideas, ready to challenge every decision and action, and recognizing it as a positive activity (Google).

➡ **Extreme measures:** Obsessively measuring yourself against the very best comparison in each thing that you do, not just direct competitors (Ford).

➡ **Beat the plan:** If frontline teams can do their jobs cheaper or faster than planned, then share the gain with them – a bonus in their pay packet or going home early (Whole Foods).

➡ **Action meetings:** Don't let review meetings become nice rubber stamping exercises – make them no-holds-barred debates and innovation sessions (P&G).

➡ **Team bonuses:** Encourage collaboration rather trying to measure each hour and every action of individual people, and bonuses based only on collective results (Egon Zehnder).

➡ **Peer pressure:** Who knows who would make the best team leader? Well, the team, of course – so let peers rather than superiors decide who should be boss (Pret A Manger).

➡ **Value sharing:** Earning a stake in the business through high performance, encouraging equity rather than profit share and building ownership by your best people (Microsoft).

But the edge is really about you.

Whilst we have focused largely on the business attributes of a marketing genius, performance ultimately comes from people, and an inspired individual in business derives that energy from all aspects of their life and wellbeing.

The one

Paula Radcliffe, the world record holder for the marathon, uses the analogy of five balls to reflect on her unbelievable success in obliterating the competition in her first three marathons, knocking almost four minutes off the previous record time. She pushed the boundaries to the limit, training 150 miles per week, lifting weights well beyond her own and jumping into an ice-cold bath after each run to help stimulate her blood flow. Yet all this seemed wasted when she failed to finish the 2004 Olympic Marathon in Athens.

In trying to rationalize her excellence, but misfortune, she mused that life is about juggling five balls in the air: health, family, friends, integrity and career. The career ball is made of rubber but the others are more fragile.

You can take more risks with the rubber ball, throwing it higher and higher. You may try to throw it through higher and higher hoops because if you do drop it, it will eventually bounce back. Normally, this ball does not suffer long-term damage. The other four balls need to be looked after more carefully because if you drop one, it will be damaged and may even shatter.

In sport, just like in business, athletes constantly take risks with that career ball, throwing it higher and higher, pushing themselves into the unknown to get an edge on their competitors, to strive for excellence, to realize their potential. Radcliffe, for one, has used the story of the five balls in good times and bad: to maintain a sense of balance and humility whilst the world went crazy about her stunning world record-breaking performances, and to put failure into perspective and to pick herself up again, in her case by rebuilding her reputation only months later by winning the New York City Marathon and the next year becoming world champion.

Record-breaking athletes, just like innovators, push themselves beyond normal limits to discover what is possible, what others said was not possible and to achieve their destiny.

The ones

The legendary ad man Lee Chow once wrote the words of perhaps the most famous ad from Apple, a tribute to all those people who have the vision and courage to see the future, and to make their big ideas happen in wonderful ways that made the world a better place:

'Here's to the crazy ones.
The misfits. The rebels. The troublemakers.
The round pegs in the square holes.
The ones who see things differently.
They're not fond of rules. And they have no respect
for the status quo.
You can praise them, disagree with them, quote them,
disbelieve them, glorify or vilify them.
About the only thing you can't do is ignore them.
Because they change things.
They invent. They imagine. They heal.
They explore. They create. They inspire.
They push the human race forward.
Maybe they have to be crazy.
How else can you stare at an empty canvas and see a work of art?
Or sit in silence and hear a song that's never been written?
Or gaze at a red planet and see a laboratory on wheels?
While some see them as the crazy ones, we see genius.
Because the people who are crazy enough
to think they can change the world,
are the ones who do.'

Creative resources

Books

The Art of Creative Thinking by John Adair

Rethink: How to Think Differently by Nigel Barlow

Glimmer by Warren Berger

Innovation and Entrepreneurship by John Bessant and Joe Tidd

Creative Strategy by Chris Bilton and Stephen Cummings

Change by Design by Tim Brown

The Innovator's Dilemma by Clayton Christensen

The Medici Effect by Chuck Frey

Hotspots by Lynda Gratton

The Ten Faces of Innovation by Tom Kelley

Anything but Ordinary by Anja Foester and Peter Kreuz

Mavericks at Work by William Taylor and Polly Labarre

Breakthrough Zone by Roy Langmaid and Mac Andrews

Everything We Know is Wrong by Magnus Lindkvist

Simplicity by John Maeda

The Design of Business by Roger Martin

Tinkertoys by Michael Michalko

The Creative Edge by William Miller

Return on Ideas by David Nichols

Smart World by Richard Ogle

The Age of the Unthinkable by Joshua Ramo

Innovation X by Adam Richardson

You Can Find Inspiration in Everything by Paul Smith

Future Files: A Brief History of the Next 50 Years by Richard Watson

Microtrends by Mark Penn and Kinney Zalesne

Websites

bigthink.com

canvas8.com

contagiousmagazine.com

coolhunting.com

creativeroots.org

creativity-online.com

designcouncil.org.uk

edge.org

entrepreneur.com

fastcompany.com

fastleader.com

futureagenda.org

futureexploration.net

iftf.org

innocentive.com

innovationtools.com

manyworlds.com

nowandnext.com

psfk.com

shapingtomorrow.com

springwise.com

ted.com

trendhunting.com

trendwatching.com

wfs.org

About the book

Peter Fisk ... about the author

Peter Fisk is a best-selling author and inspirational speaker, an advisor to leading companies around the world, and an experienced business leader.

He grew up in the remote farming community of Northumberland in the north-east of England, and after exploring the world of nuclear physics entered the world of business, seeking to combine his entrepreneurial skills with a passion for how businesses should do more for people and make the world a better place.

Peter went on to work with some of the world's most innovative companies: creating flat beds out of yacht designs at British Airways, translating credit cards into digital experiences at American Express, adding more rigour to creativity at Microsoft, embracing sustainability as a creative force at The Cooperative, and more substance at Vodafone, whilst inspiring Coca-Cola to think bigger, reinventing food with Marks & Spencer, redefining brands for Tata, and bringing them to life with Visa.

He was also the transforming CEO of the Chartered Institute of Marketing, the world's largest marketing organization, MD of Brand Finance, Partner of The Foundation, and leader of PA Consulting Group's marketing consulting team. He is a non-executive director of a number of entrepreneurial ventures.

Peter now leads the Genius Works, an 'accelerated innovation' firm that works with business leaders to develop more inspired strategies and programmes, embracing the best ideas within the business, and engaging people to think how can they make them happen in more effective and remarkable ways. *InnoLab* is a facilitated process for rapidly addressing problems through deeper insights and more creative thinking, *Zoom Ventures* brings together business investors and social entrepreneurs, and *The Fast Track* is a range of executive coaching and personal development programme.

He was recently described by *Business Strategy Review* as 'one of the best new business thinkers' and is in demand around the world as an expert advisor and energizing speaker.

To find out more, read his blog and visit www.theGeniusWorks.com, or contact him directly at peterfisk@peterfisk.com.

Contributors ... the people who inspired me

The stimulus for exploring the worlds of creativity, design and innovation comes from an eclectic mix of places, and many people have given me fantastic encouragement and support in writing this book. However, my biggest inspiration comes from close to home – from Alison, Anna and Clara for keeping me real, and smiling – and my parents, who encouraged me as I grew up to explore different worlds and not to jump into a box.

Also thanks to the great publishing team at Wiley Capstone – Holly Bennion, Jenny Ng and Iain Campbell – and Simon Benham at Mayer Benham. And to the many others around the world who have inspired this book in different ways, including Brendan Barns, Peter Barrett, Simon Brown, Tim Brown, Ross Dawson, Reinier Evers, Linda Grattan, Jonathon Hogg, Tom Kelley, Prof. Harry Kroto, Roy Langmaid, Magnus Lindkvist, Martin Lindstrom, Alina Lisina, Prof. Costas Markides, Ed McCabe, Chris Meyer, Endrik Randoja, Jonas Ridderstale, Kevin Roberts, Carl Sharples, Mark Thomas, Alper Utku, John Vincent, Richard Watson, Will Whitehorn, Jane Young and Laurie Young.

And to you for reading the book ... thank you and good luck!

Genius Works ... helping to make your ideas happen

It's not easy to stretch your mind, think in new ways or challenge your conventions from the inside. You need the right environment, processes and support to do it. We bring together a wide range of tools, methods and experiences to help you to address business issues and opportunities in more powerful ways, and find stretching and original solutions. The Genius Works includes:

InnoLab – accelerating innovation

A single or series of workshops that inspires your people to think creatively – to challenge and shape their ideas, design and shape new concepts, and deliver innovative strategies and propositions ready for implementation. The lab creates a high energy environment where people work fast and collaboratively to stretch for the future, then add focus and practicality to make it happen today.

Fast Track – accelerating development

Explore the very latest ideas and best emerging practices in the areas of strategy and leadership, customers and innovation – a series of one- or two-day development workshops that combine inspirational thinking with practical application. From Apple to Zappos, it gives you the inspiration and practical tools to make your best ideas happen.

Zoom Ventures – accelerating business

Working in partnership with leading brands, investors and entrepreneurs to make the best new ideas happen, with a particular focus on 'social entrepreneurship' – encouraging new ideas that also do good. We uniquely bring a customer-centric approach to venturing, the allocation of funds, development of concepts, and accelerated development of ideas into practical, commercial implementation.

More information at thegeniusworks.com.

Genius Books ... more ideas to inspire you

You can explore more 'genius' ideas and insights in three other books from Peter Fisk. Each book brings together a more intelligent and imaginative approach to specific aspects of business, exploring the emerging ideas and very best practices from every corner of the world.

Customer Genius – doing business from the 'outside in'

'Hello, I am your customer. Do you see the world like I do? It's simple, really. Start with me and everything else follows. Together we can do extraordinary things ... Are you ready?'

Customers are now in control of our markets, demanding that we do business on their terms. Their expectations are high, and loyalty is rare. They are individual and emotional, well-informed and highly organized. They know what they want, and only accept the best. The ten-step customer-centric blueprint brings together the tools to develop better customer insights, strategies, propositions, solutions, experiences and relationships – inspired by the likes of Air Asia and Amazon, Zipcars and Zopa.

Find out more about the book at customergeniuslive.com.

Marketing Genius – the 'left and right-brain' of competitive advantage

Marketing injects the customer insight and creative thinking that gives business its edge. However, it must combine this with the analytical and commercial rigour that drives strategy, innovation and profitable growth. Digital media and social networks have transformed the way in which people engage with brands, and what they expect from them. Genius marketers, like Einstein and Picasso, apply intelligence in more imaginative ways. They use their left and right brains to seize the best opportunities, to stand out from the crowd and to lead the business. From Apple to Coke, Jones Soda to Virgin, we explore how to shape new markets in your vision and build brands and customer solutions that deliver extraordinary results.

Find out more about the book at marketinggeniuslive.com.

Business Genius – a more inspired approach to strategy and leadership

How do you lead a business in turbulent times, when change is essential but the destination is uncertain? What kind of strategy provides focus and agility, to create extraordinary value to all stakeholders in the long term, whilst still succeeding in the short term? In the past we focused on core capabilities; today we are driven by opportunities which we address through partnerships across markets. How can you combine the entrepreneurial passion of start-ups with the commercial rigour of large enterprises? With insights from the likes of Richard Branson and Renzo Rosso, Jeff Immelt and Warren Buffett, the book explains how.

Find out more about the book at businessgeniuslive.com.

All books are available from Amazon and bookshops, and also from the Genius Store at wiley.com/go/genius, where you will find special offers and a range of new articles and book extracts to download.

Index